THE TRIAL OF

LOUIS RIEL

JUSTICE AND MERCY DENIED

A CRITICAL LEGAL AND POLITICAL ANALYSIS

GEORGE R. D. GOULET,
B.A., LLB. (U. Manitoba), LLM. (U. Toronto)

Member (rtd.) of the Canadian Bar Association,
the Bar of Alberta and the Bar of British Columbia

TELLWELL PUBLISHING
CALGARY, ALBERTA, 1999.

Published by
TELLWELL PUBLISHING
#269, 4037 – 42nd Street N.W.,
Calgary, Alberta, T3A 2M9

The publisher hereby acknowledges the following permissions that have been granted to the author:

The Province of Manitoba, Department of Culture permission to print the photograph (owned by the publisher) of the Louis Riel sculpture located on the legislative grounds.

The University of Toronto Press permission to reprint the quotations from *The Queen v. Louis Riel* [Trial transcript], Desmond Morton, introduction (1974).

"Copyright 1998 *Canadian Lawyer*. Reproduction by permission" for the quotations from "Louis Riel and the Crown Letters" by R. L. Olesky; "An Apology for Louis Riel Too?" by Michael Fitz-James; and the Table of Contents (February 1998).

Professor J. M. Bumsted permission to reprint the quotation from "Riel trial complicated by citizenship", *Winnipeg Real Estate News* (Friday, January 16, 1998).

Canadian Cataloguing in Publication Data

Goulet, George R. D. (George Richard Donald), 1933-
    The trial of Louis Riel: justice and mercy denied : a
critical legal and political analysis

Includes bibliographical references and index.
ISBN 0-9685489-0-3

1. Riel, Louis, 1844-1885—Trials, litigation, etc. 2. Trials
(Treason)—Canada. I. Title

KE228.R54G68 1999   345.71'0231   C99-900938-9

Consultant Tag Goulet, B.A.,M.A.
Printed by Friesens Corporation, Altona, Manitoba, Canada

But, if there is justice, as I still hope, oh, dear,
it seems to me I have become insane to hope still.

Louis Riel
The Queen v. Louis Riel

The quality of mercy is not strain'd ... it is twice
bless'd; It blesseth him that gives and him that takes.

William Shakespeare
The Merchant of Venice
Act IV, Scene 1

He [Riel] shall hang, though every
dog in Quebec bark in his favour

John A. Macdonald
Prime Minister of Canada

but you have overlooked the weightier demands
of the law – justice, mercy, and good faith.

Holy Bible
Matthew Ch. 23 verse 23

ACKNOWLEDGEMENTS

I wish to express my appreciation to various people and institutions who in one way or another assisted me in this project. My wife, Terry, gave me the benefit of her extensive hands-on experience in editorial work with an international legal publishing firm, and her research talents honed as a librarian at the University of Manitoba. As well Terry excelled in searching out ancient and obscure statutes, cases and legal texts, in negotiations with printers and distributors, in her drafting and transcription skills, and in her insightful criticism and ideas. The book would not have come to publication without her gifted contributions.

My brother Lionel E. Goulet of Toronto, a McGill University graduate in law, devoted many hours of research finding correspondence and other data related to Louis Riel. My former law partner B. Vincent Reed, Q. C. kindly reviewed and commented on the manuscript. My brother L. Joseph Goulet, a doctoral student at the University of Manitoba, helped with translation of certain documents. Any errors herein are the responsibility of the author.

Thanks are due to various staff members of the following archives, institutions and libraries:

> the National Archives of Canada; the Archives of Manitoba, Saskatchewan and British Columbia; the National Archives of England (Public Record Office); the Glenbow Alberta Institute in Calgary; the Gabriel Dumont Institute in Saskatoon; the St. Boniface Historical Society (particularly archivist Bill Benoit); the Hudson's Bay Company Archives in Winnipeg; the Calgary Public Library; the University of Calgary MacKimmie Library; the University of Calgary Law Library; the Law Society of England Library in London; the University of London's Sterling Library and Library at the Institute of Advanced Legal Studies; and the Judicial Committee of the Privy Council in London.

My daughter Tag, a communications instructor at the University of Calgary and an author and entrepreneur, provided invaluable consulting and other services. I also wish to thank my other children for their support and encouragement during the writing of this book.

This book is dedicated to my wife Terry and to Kitty, Manthe, Amor, Mitchums, Lambers, and Dev.

Calgary, Alberta
July, 1999.

TABLE OF CONTENTS

Acknowledgement 2
Table of Contents 3
Acronyms and Abbreviations 6

Section A The Trial

I   Introduction 9
II   Louis Riel, Founding Father of Manitoba 15
        1.   Birth, Upbringing, Education 15
        2.   The Red River Resistance 19
        3.   Riel's Elections to Parliament and Exile 25
III   Canadian Expansionist Movement and Unrest in the North-West 33
IV   Surrender, Trial Site, Charges, and The Magistrate 43
        1.   The Surrender of Riel 43
        2.   The Trial Site 44
        3.   The Charges 48
        4.   The Trial Magistrate 56
V   The Jury and its Selection 63
VI   Riel: British Subject or American Citizen 67
VII   Jurisdiction and Venue of the Magistrate's Court 73
VIII   The Lawyers 82
        1.   Crown Counsel 83
             (a)   Christopher Robinson 83
             (b)   Britton Bath Osler 84
             (c)   George Wheelock Burbidge 86
             (d)   Thomas Chase Casgrain 88
             (e)   David Lynch Scott 89
        2.   Defence Counsel 90
             (a)   Charles Fitzpatrick 90
             (b)   François-Xavier Lemieux 92
             (c)   James Naismith Greenshields 94
             (d)   Thomas Cooke Johnstone 95
        3.   Other Lawyers Involved in Riel's Appeal 96
             (a)   James Albert Manning Aikins 96
             (b)   John Skirving Ewart 97
IX   Application for Adjournment of the Trial 99
X   Crown Witnesses and Evidence 105
XI   Open Court Dissension Between Riel and His Counsel 117
XII   Witnesses for the Defence and Rebuttal Witnesses 125
        1.   The Defence Witnesses 127
        2.   The Crown's Rebuttal Witnesses 141

XIII   **Addresses to the Jury** 148
     1. Fitzpatrick's Address to the Jury 148
     2. Riel's Address to the Jury, the Magistrate and the Justice of the Peace 155
     3. Crown Counsel Robinson's Address to the Jury 159
XIV   **Magistrate's Charge to the Jury and the Verdict** 163
     1. Magistrate Richardson's Charge to the Jury 163
     2. The Jury's Verdict 167
XV   **Riel's Closing Statement and the Sentence** 169
     1. Riel's Last Hurrah 169
     2. The Sentence 171

Section B Legal, Judicial and Political Injustices

XVI   **Riel's Unlawful Conviction and Execution** 175
     1. Charges Laid under the English *1351 Statute of Treasons* 175
     2. Scope of the Charges Against Riel 177
     3. Meaning of "Realm" in the *1351 Statute of Treasons* 178
        (a) Joint Legal Opinion of England's Attorney General
            and Solicitor General 178
        (b) Definition of "Within the Realm" 180
        (c) Sir Matthew Hale's Interpretation of the "Realm" 181
        (d) *Statute of 36 George III*, Chapter VII (1795) 181
        (e) *Statute of 57 George III*, Chapter VI (1817) 183
        (f) British *Statute of 11 & 12 Victoria*, Chapter XII (1848) 184
        (g) Canadian *Statute of 31 Victoria*, Chapter LXIX (1868) 187
     4. Arguments as to Applicability of *1351 Statute of Treasons* 189
        (a) The William Smith O'Brien Case 190
        (b) Section 1 of the 1868 Canadian Treason-Felony Statute 192
        (c) Applicability of Pre-Colonial English Statutes in Canada 193
     5. Strict Interpretation of Penal Laws 195
        (a) Strict Construction of *1351 Statute of Treasons* 196
        (b) Examples of Strict Construction of Penal Statutes 198
        (c) Review of Riel Case With Respect to Strict Construction 198
     6. Summary 201
XVII   **Appeal Court Judges** 203
     1. Chief Justice Lewis Wallbridge 203
     2. Thomas Wardlaw Taylor 205
     3. Albert Clements Killam 206
XVIII **Riel's Appeal of his Conviction** 207
     1. Riel's Application to Appear at the Appeal Hearing 207
     2. Riel's Appeal of His Conviction 207
XIX   **Riel's Application to the Privy Council in England** 217
XX   **Improprieties of Chief Justice Wallbridge and**
     Justice Minister Campbell 220

XXI   Mercy Denied 227
XXII   Shortcomings of Riel's Lawyers 242
    1.   Doomed Strategy 243
        (a)   Insanity Plea 243
        (b)   Challenge to Jurisdiction of the Court 246
        (c)   Lack of Justification Plea 248
    2.   Defence Counsel's Mistreatment and Defiance of Riel 255
    3.   Fitzpatrick's Conflict of Interest 258
    4.   Errors and Omissions 260
        (a)   The Trial 260
        (b)   Appeal to the Court of Queen's Bench 262
        (c)   Application to the Privy Council 262
XXIII Conclusion 264
        (a)   Magistrate's Bias and Lack of Independence and Acumen 264
        (b)   Judicial and Political Improprieties 266
        (c)   Deprivation of Riel's Right to Full Answer and Defence 267
        (d)   Unauthorized and Deficient Legal Representation 269
        (e)   Inapplicability of the *1351 Statute of Treasons* to the Riel Charges ... 270

Bibliography 273
Table of Cases 278
Index 279

ACRONYMS AND ABBREVIATIONS

Acronyms and abbreviations used in the text include the following:

bk. — book
Ch. — Chapter
C.O. — Colonial Office
CPR — Canadian Pacific Railway
CSP — Canada Sessional Papers
ed. — edition and/or editor
E.R. — English Reports
HBC — Hudson's Bay Company
Man. — Manitoba
NAC — National Archives of Canada
No. — Number
NWMP — Northwest Mounted Police
p. — page
Q.B. — Queen's Bench
Q.B.R. . — Queen's Bench Reports
Q.C. — Queen's Counsel
s. — section
Sask. — Saskatchewan
SCR — Supreme Court Reports
U — University
v. — versus
Vol. — Volume

SECTION A

The Trial

From left to right: Charles Nolin; interpreter (standing); prosecutor Christopher Robinson (in robes); Magistrate Richardson and Justice of the Peace Lejeune (on bench); Louis Riel; prosecutor B.B. Osler (in robes); NWMP Superintendent Burton Deane (seated at right)

Louis Riel, a prisoner, outside the guard tent

The members of the jury, from left: Francis Cosgrove (foreman), Walter Merryfield (standing), Edwin J. Brooks, Peel Deane, Henry J. Painter (standing), Edward Eratt

Chapter I

INTRODUCTION

Louis Riel – the very name conjures up visions in stark contrast to one another: martyred hero – murderous renegade; rational leader – mindless lunatic; cultured gentleman – irate rabble-rouser; selfless advocate – grasping self-seeker; inspired leader – faithless heretic; unjust victim – guilty traitor.

No one who is familiar with the Riel saga is indifferent to the man. He is either revered or reviled, often on the basis of raw emotion rather than bare facts. A French Catholic Quebecer would likely have a more benign interpretation of Riel's conduct and motives in the last year and a half of his life than a militant Protestant Orangeman from Ontario. Regardless of one's feelings or perspective, Louis Riel was a remarkable personality whose life profoundly influenced Canadian society, politics, the founding of Manitoba and the rights of Western Canadians. His impact continues to this day and will continue into the next millennium.

Riel was a wunderkind, a *rara avis*, a natural-born charismatic leader, highly intelligent, handsome and educated. He was elected to the Parliament of Canada on three separate occasions, while he was still in his twenties, but due to politics was never able to take his seat. His fascinating life combined the acme of success and the nadir of defeat, the sacred and the profane. To some he conjoined fame and infamy; to others he was an iconoclast who became an icon. To Riel himself he had a prophetic mission – to lead and champion his people, the Metis, in having their grievances remedied, their rights obtained, and their lives uplifted.

Riel may have seen himself as a prophet in some respects. He was brought up in a highly religious Roman Catholic atmosphere imbued with saints, sacraments, prayers and priests. He was undoubtedly familiar, from his Montreal studies, with the great Biblical prophets. These prophets pervaded the Old Testament with sagas of fiery passion, humility and even ecstatic eccentricity. Stories of their lives have prevailed down the centuries, influencing the faith of the believers. Many acted in an unconventional manner. Isaiah walked naked and barefoot; Ezekiel ate a scroll of the words of God. Although many prophets were from humble beginnings they often confronted those in authority and criticized them for injustices done.

9

Although he did not see himself in the mould of a Biblical prophet, Riel during the trial stated that half-breeds acknowledged him as a prophet. He said "I can see something into the future" adding "we all see into the future more or less" and "the half-breeds as hunters can foretell many things." Although Riel may not have been the prophet of the New World, to many of his followers he was a messianic leader, one who would help his oppressed people.

Riel has also been called the first prairie populist politician. Some consider him to be the precursor of Thomas Crerar of the Progressive Party in the 1920s; of William Aberhart of the Social Credit Party in the 1930s and 40s; of Peter Lougheed of the Alberta Conservative Party in the 1970s and 80s; and of Preston Manning of the Reform Party in the 1990s. Riel is a symbol of the alienation that Western Canadians frequently feel as a result of the disregard or meddlesome policies towards the West of the Eastern-dominated federal government.

There have been numerous biographies written about Riel. A postage stamp bearing his likeness was issued a generation ago, when Canadian stamps sold for six cents each. Harry Somers, a leading Canadian composer who died in 1999, wrote an opera entitled *Louis Riel.* It was his masterpiece and was premiered by the Canadian Opera Company in 1967. It was also the first Canadian opera to be performed at the Kennedy Centre in Washington, D.C. Riel's life has been the subject of stage, radio, film and television productions, as well as historical fiction. The city of Saskatoon celebrates *Louis Riel Days* every summer. There is even a CD-ROM on Riel and the North-West Uprising. The home of the Riel family in St. Vital (a suburb of Winnipeg, Manitoba) has been designated a National Historic Park by Parks Canada. Statues of Riel have been erected on the legislative grounds of Winnipeg and Regina, the capital cities of Manitoba and Saskatchewan where the Red River Resistance and the North-West Uprising respectively occurred. The statue of Riel in Regina has recently been removed because of its controversial depiction of Riel, a fate similar to that which befell an earlier sculpture of Riel in Winnipeg.

The monumental statue of Louis Riel in Winnipeg stands between the banks of the Red River and the magnificent Manitoba legislative buildings. The accompanying plaque briefly recites highlights of his life and concludes with the statement:

In 1992, the Parliament of Canada and the Legislative
Assembly of Manitoba formally recognized Riel's
contribution to the development of the Canadian
Confederation and his role, and that of the Metis, as
founders of Manitoba.

In March 1998 the government of Canada issued a Statement of
Reconciliation relating to past treatment of the aboriginal peoples of
Canada. The Statement referred to "the sad events culminating in the
death of the Metis leader Louis Riel." It added that it would look for
ways of "reflecting Louis Riel's proper place in Canada's history."

On Canada Day in 1998, *Maclean's* (Canada's Weekly Newsmaga-
zine) published its list of "The 100 Most Important Canadians in
History". Louis Riel was one of the select few and appeared under the
category of "Activists". The writer of the Riel profile in *Maclean's*
ventured the view (repudiated by many including the author of this text)
that Riel was likely insane at the time of the North-West Uprising.

In June 1998 Bill C-417 entitled *An Act respecting Louis Riel* received
first reading in the Canadian House of Commons. A member from
each political party is sponsoring the Bill. It recites that the purpose of
the Act is to reverse the conviction of Louis Riel for high treason and to
commemorate his role in the advancement of Canadian Confederation
and the rights and interests of the Metis people and the people of
Western Canada. Section 6 of Bill C-417 reads:

Louis Riel is hereby recognized as a Father of Confederation
and the Founder of the Province of Manitoba.

Riel himself in his address to the jury at his trial stated:

I know that through the grace of God I am the founder of
Manitoba.

The Bill will likely generate heated debate when it comes up for
consideration. Much of the argument against the Bill will be based on
the assertion that Riel was legally, fairly and justly tried, convicted and
sentenced to death for high treason and deserved to be executed. One
may expect a number of historians, many from Ontario, to decry the
"revisionism" which they see in the Bill. They will not accept it as a re-
assessment of the facts, or that many points of view (espoused by some
historians) related to Riel's trial, conviction and execution call out for
revision to correct errors of the past.

The purpose of this treatise is to provide a critical legal and political
analysis of the trial for high treason of Louis Riel (under the *1351 English*

Statute of Treasons), the appeal, Riel's execution and the surrounding circumstances. After giving background information and the events leading up to the 1885 trial in Regina, there is a review of trial procedures, testimony of witnesses, performances of Crown and defence counsel and of the presiding stipendiary magistrate. Profiles of the lawyers and magistrate are given. Process of selection of the trial site and the jury, legal arguments, addresses of counsel to the jury, the magistrate's charge to the jury, and the direct political involvement in the trial and appeal of the highest judicial and political officers are dealt with. The 534 year-old English Statute under which Riel was convicted and executed, as well as other statutes, are analyzed in detail.

Riel's mistreatment at the hands of his own counsel, the serious deficiencies exhibited by these same counsel, and Riel's address to the jury and subsequently to the magistrate, are examined and commented upon. Correspondence from Justice Minister Alexander Campbell to Prime Minister John A. Macdonald is reviewed. It discloses judicial and political meddling in the Riel trial of an improper nature.

The manner in which the unanimous recommendation of the jury for mercy was handled by Prime Minister John A. Macdonald and rejected is investigated. The appointment of a medical commission to examine Riel prior to his execution and Macdonald's blatant attempts to manipulate the commission's reports and his government's gross political deception and mendacity concerning the reports are looked at.

Although short monographs or chapters have been published relating specifically to Riel's trial,[1] no historians or biographers have done an in-depth study of the trial, likely due to their lack of legal training. This treatise is intended to fill that void, and in so doing it arrives at some unique and startling conclusions not made by historians.

In a marvelously entertaining book, which incidentally is scathing of many prominent historians, Professor David H. Fischer wrote that "all historians ... must and should make value judgments ..." He added some amusing comments such as "whether or not history repeats itself, historians repeat each other"; and much "humbug has been pro-claimed to the world as the objective truth of history, ...". He quotes Nietzsche:

---

[1]   See e.g. Lewis H. Thomas "A Judicial Murder – The Trial of Louis Riel" Howard Palmer ed., *The Settlement of the West*, p. 37-59; Thomas Flanagan, *Riel and the Rebellion*, Ch. Six p. 116-34; Desmond Morton intro., *The Queen v. Louis Riel*, p. vii *et seq.*

"Historians begin by looking backward. They often end by thinking backward."[2]

Hopefully, the analyses in this dissertation will not attract similar droll comments for, as Disraeli stated, it is easier to be critical than correct. In this critique the author will be making judgments and giving opinions based on his research and assessment of relevant documentation. The better part of these judgments and opinions is reflected in the sub-title of this volume. A polemical tone as to the absence of justice and mercy in relation to the trial, conviction and execution of Riel may be noted.

One frequently hears laments from historians and others with respect to the sorry state of the study of history in our schools. These are often accompanied by complaints bemoaning the fact that Canadian heroes are not being recognized. One well-known Ontario historian recently labeled Riel a "bastardized hero".[3] He added that Riel lacked credentials as a hero to all Canadians and that his life should not be taught in schools as if he was such a hero. Using that credentials test, no one in Canada or in the world would qualify as a hero. Others have a different view of Riel. Another historian, Professor Gerald Friesen, doesn't apply this insurmountable test. In Professor Friesen's view, Louis Riel is "paramount" among "multicultural heroes".[4] Professor J. M. Bumsted has called Riel "one of our few mythic heroes".[5] The prominent Canadian journalist and author Peter C. Newman pithily stated that Riel "was one of our genuine frontier heroes."[6] On June 30, 1999, the results of a national survey to nominate Canada's top 10 "heroes" were published in the *National Post* newspaper. The Dominion Institute and the Council for Canadian Unity conducted the survey.

---

2   David H. Fischer, *Historians' Fallacies – Toward a Logic of Historical Thought*, p. 79; 25; 41; 131.
3   J. L. Granatstein, *Who Killed Canadian History?*, p. x . This book was reviewed in a critical manner by Robert Fulford in "Is it possible to be too patriotic about Canadian history?" *Globe and Mail Newspaper*, May 22, 1999, p. D9.
4   Gerald Friesen, *The Canadian Prairies: A History*, p. 73.
5   J. M. Bumsted, "The 'Mahdi' of Western Canada? Louis Riel and His Papers", *The Beaver*, August/September 1987, p. 47.
6   Peter C. Newman, "Rewriting history: Louis Riel as a hero", *Maclean's Magazine*, April 12, 1999, p. 48.

Louis Riel was among the top ten heroes selected.[7] Professor George F. G. Stanley, an eminent historian (and incidentally the designer of the Canadian flag in the 1960s) referred to Riel as "A Canadian legend" and "our Hamlet, the personification of the great themes of our human history."[8]

In addressing the jury at his trial, Louis Riel stated:

> I will perhaps be one day acknowledged as more than a leader of the half-breeds, and if I am I will have an opportunity of being acknowledged as a leader of good in this great country.

---

[7]   James Cudmore, "Canadian Heroes", *National Post*, June 30, 1999, p. A8. John A. Macdonald was also among the ten listed.

[8]   George F. Stanley, "The Last Word on Louis Riel – The Man of Several Faces", Hartwell Bowsfield ed., *Louis Riel, Selected Readings* p. 42, @ 56.

Chapter II

LOUIS RIEL, FOUNDING FATHER OF MANITOBA

1. BIRTH, UPBRINGING, EDUCATION

Louis Riel was born in the Red River Settlement, Rupert's Land on October 22, 1844. His parents were Jean Louis Riel and Julie Lagimodière, both born in what is now Western Canada.

Jean Baptiste Lagimodière and Marie-Anne Gaboury, both born in Lower Canada (Quebec), were the maternal grandparents of Louis Riel. Marie-Anne was the first white woman to live in Western Canada, travelling there with her husband in 1806.

On his paternal side Louis Riel's grandfather was Jean Baptiste Riel, a Quebec French Canadian. In 1812 Jean Baptiste married Marguerite Boucher, a Metis, at Ile-à-la-Crosse in what is now Northern Saskatchewan(Marguerite Boucher's mother was a Chipewyan, and it is through her that Louis Riel inherited his only source of Indian blood.)

As a child Louis was brought up on his parents' farm in the parish of St. Vital. The farmhouse was on the banks of the Seine River. A settlement, the Red River Settlement, had grown up in the area centered around the forks of the Red and Assiniboine Rivers. These forks are today the background setting for an up-scale shopping complex (called "The Forks") with trendy boutiques, restaurants and shops in the heart of Winnipeg, the capital of Manitoba, which has a current population in excess of 600,000 people. In the 1840s the Red River Settlement area consisted of a mixed population of perhaps 10,000 people. There were several distinct groups living in the settlement primarily the French Metis, the English and Scotch mixed bloods (called "half-breeds"), and the offspring of the Selkirk settlers.

The Selkirk settlers came to the Red River in 1812 at the instigation of Lord Selkirk. Selkirk, who came from an aristocratic family in Scotland, received a grant of a huge tract of land from the Hudson's Bay Company ("HBC") and wished to colonize part of it with poor immigrants from Scotland and Ireland. Many of these Celtic immigrants brought their wives and children.

The Scotch and English half-breeds were the progeny of Hudson's Bay Company employees and their Indian wives. They spoke English and, while some were Roman Catholics, most of them were Protestants.

The Metis were the descendants of the French Canadian fur traders, coureurs de bois, voyageurs and adventurers, and their female Indian mates. These mixed-blood descendants had common bonds in their French Canadian-Indian lineage and their birth in the West. Over time, they developed a sense of belonging and distinctiveness, a Metis identity, a "New Nation", based on their shared background and experiences, such as the fur trade and the buffalo hunt. Many of the Metis were voyageurs for the North West Company, formed in Montreal in the latter part of the 18th century to trade in furs. The North West Company and the HBC were unfriendly competitors in the fur trade. Officials of the North West Company encouraged the Metis to see themselves as a New Nation. They wanted the Metis to believe that the coming of the Selkirk Settlers and the practices of the HBC were a threat to the Metis. Animosity and competition between the two fur-trading companies led to their merger in 1821 under the continuing name of the Hudson's Bay Company.

The Metis buffalo hunt, besides being an essential food-gathering expedition, provided an opportunity for a convivial get-together. An almost festive atmosphere prevailed in the prairie encampment, which was set up immediately prior to the hunt, for the many hunters, women and children. The rollicking fellowship and merry-making in the camp enhanced the sense of camaraderie among the Metis. The hunt was a grand socio-economic affair and was carried out in a highly democratic manner. These democratic principles were later used as a model in the formation of the provisional government during the Red River Resistance. By the 1820s the Metis had materialized as a distinct group. The "Metis" have been written about by a number of authors including Gerald Friesen and John Foster.[9] Many of the Metis lived in the Red River Settlement.

By the time Louis Riel was born in 1844, there was a distinctive self-conscious Metis group who were a western people united by racial, religious, social and cultural ties. At the time of Louis Riel's birth the

---

[9]   Gerald Friesen, p. 91-128; John Foster, "The Metis: The People and the Term", A. S. Lussier ed., *Louis Riel and the Metis*, p. 77-86.

HBC effectively controlled the political system of the Red River Settlement. It did so through the Council of Assiniboia, the governing body whose members were appointed by the HBC governors.

The HBC was created on May 2, 1670 by the issue of a royal charter granted by King Charles II of England to "Our Deare and entirely Beloved cousin Prince Rupert" and his associates. The charter embraced all the sea and lands of Hudson Bay and its entire drainage system. This gigantic grant of land, called Rupert's Land, embraced over 35% of the Canada of today including most of the Prairie Provinces. The HBC was granted a monopoly over all the trade and commerce in this vast tract of land and the right to build forts. Its powers over the inhabitants were truly awesome. It was empowered to make and administer laws, and to

> lawfully impose, ordeyne, limitt and provide such paines,
> penaltyes and punishments upon all Offenders

as it deemed necessary for the observance of these laws. It also received the right to raise an army and navy.

In 1811 the HBC granted Lord Selkirk 16,000 square miles in the Red River Valley (known as Assiniboia) to establish an agricultural colony. The Selkirk settlers arrived in the Red River Settlement in 1812. Lord Selkirk's nominees controlled the undemocratic government, but in the 1830s the HBC repurchased Assiniboia from the Selkirk estate.

In the 1840s many of the inhabitants of the Red River Settlement were fed up with the HBC and its monopoly over fur-trading, and the manner in which they were governed. For example, to enforce its monopoly the HBC searched trains of Red River carts travelling to and from Pembina and St. Paul, and settlers' homes for contraband furs and even checked the mails. The Company penalized those who breached its monopoly but, because of unduly low prices which it paid compared with those paid at St. Paul and Pembina, smuggling and illicit trading occurred. Matters came to a head with the trial of Pierre Guillaume Sayer in 1849. Sayer and three other Metis were charged with illegally trading in furs. Jean Louis Riel (Louis' father) organized a courthouse demonstration and at the trial in the Red River Settlement hundreds of armed Metis showed up at the courthouse. Judge Thom was told that if Sayer was jailed they would forcibly free him. The court found Sayer guilty but did not impose any punishment. Outside the courtroom a Metis shouted "Le commerce est libre. Vive la liberté." (Commerce is free. Long live liberty.)   This outcome effectively ended the HBC monopoly.   The leading role which his father played in the Sayer trial must have been recounted from time to time and doubtlessly made a deep impression on the young Louis Riel as he matured.

Louis Riel received his pre-adolescent education from Roman Catholic priests and nuns in the Red River Settlement. His intellectual talents and religious devotion attracted the attention of Bishop Alexandre Taché of St. Boniface who in 1858 selected Riel to receive a scholarship from Sophie Masson, a wealthy Quebec chatelaine, to attend a prestigious college in Montreal run by the Sulpician Order of Roman Catholic priests. Bishop Taché's intent was that Louis would study for the priesthood and return home to minister to the faithful in Red River.

On his arrival in Montreal, Louis was a strapping 14 year-old, soon to grow to about five feet ten inches tall, handsome with piercing brown eyes and dark brown naturally wavy hair. At the Sulpician College, in a hieratic atmosphere, Riel was educated in the classics, as well as in science, French, English, history, philosophy, mathematics and oratory. He was a fine student, but often somber and reserved, although he became less so as his studies progressed. He could also be headstrong and short-tempered in discussions and debates. He had a consuming interest in politics, and was kept up-to-date on matters in the Red River Settlement by letters from his father. Young Louis also took to writing poetry. The following is a 1920s translation by Philippe Boyer de la Giroday of a poem written by Louis after his father's death which first appeared in William McCartney Davidson's biography of Riel:

In the midst of the crowd
which ebbs and flows,
When the mob sees a man
with a pensive look,
And an air of sadness,
they throw him a
Glance of suspicion.
They whisper:
"Brother, who is that one?"
This attention which he arouses
is a cause for his worries.
He goes on aloof,
Sadness in his heart;
He suffers
In the depth of his heart

18

So full of sighs,
Alone with his sorrows,
An exile from pleasures.
In sorrow he consumes his life,
His days are full of sadness. [10]

During a part of each summer, Louis stayed at Terrebonne, the home of his patron Sophie Masson. There he became familiar with the life style of a prominent and wealthy family and their conservative politics, and grew in self-confidence. He also witnessed how the rights of the French-Canadian minority were protected by constitutional guarantees, an observation that would play a part in his future actions.

In February 1864 Riel's father, Jean Louis, died at Red River. Louis, 19 years old, and thousands of miles from home, was grief stricken. His father had been his hero. Louis soon lost interest in his education and in a priestly vocation. Although he was only a few months short of obtaining a degree, in March 1865 Louis left the college. He had received an intensive education over a seven-year period in Montreal and was a highly intelligent, intellectual and erudite young man, much better schooled than most of his contemporaries. He wrote and spoke English well and French fluently, was learned in Greek and Latin, and was a poet.

After leaving college, Louis worked as a law clerk in a Montreal law office for a brief time, but soon he decided to leave Montreal. This decision, while influenced in part by the untimely death of his father the previous year, was undoubtedly precipitated by his being rebuffed by the parents of Marie Julie Guernon, a young lady of whom he had become enamored and wished to wed. Her parents did not countenance the marriage and their daughter abided by their wishes.

2.   THE RED RIVER RESISTANCE

Although Louis Riel wished to return home, he worked in St. Paul, Minnesota as a clerk in a general store. This was in 1867. Here he met Red River Metis transporters, friends and relatives who came to St. Paul and who told him of the growing apprehension back home. A group of

---

[10]   William McCartney Davidson, *Louis Riel 1844-1885*, p. 20. The translator, Phillipe Boyer de la Giroday (now deceased), was the father-in-law of the author of this book.

newcomers from Ontario, primarily Anglo-Saxon Protestants, had arrived in the Red River area after young Riel's departure for Montreal. They styled themselves the "Canadian Party" and wanted Rupert's Land to be annexed to Canada. They also detested the HBC's control of government.

Louis determined that it was time to return home. After an absence of 10 years, the 23 year old Riel arrived at Red River in the summer of 1868, little realizing that he would shortly become a *deus ex machina*, an intervener who was to unexpectedly change the course of events in the Red River Settlement.

In 1867 John Christian Schultz, an Ontarian by birth (who had forsaken the medical profession), acquired ownership of the *Nor'Wester*, a newspaper in the Red River Settlement. This organ was used by Schultz to push for Canadian annexation of the North West. Schultz also opposed the dominant influence of the HBC, and was hostile to the half-breeds. In 1868 a Canada First movement was founded, led by the recently arrived Ontarian Charles Mair who soon married Schultz's niece. This movement espoused Anglo-Saxon imperialistic views, pushed for extensive immigration from Ontario, and looked down on the French Catholic Metis with whom they would have no truck nor trade. There was unrest in the Settlement in large part due to the opposing views of the annexationists and those, not keen on annexation by Canada, who did not know what the future held.

Although the Red River Settlement and the North West were not part of Canada, in the summer of 1869 the Canadian Minister of the Interior commissioned a party to survey the Settlement. The leader of the survey was Colonel John Stoughton Dennis, whom the notorious Schultz befriended. The Metis and others were apprehensive about the survey, fearful that the long narrow river-front lots they lived on and worked (with a common hay privilege at the back) would be adversely affected. The long narrow river-front lots were the same type of land holdings that had prevailed in the Province of Quebec. Most had occupied the land for years but had no title to it. Matters came to a head when on October 1, 1869 André Nault (a Metis) objected to the surveyors being on the hay privilege lands. Since Nault could not speak English to tell them to stop trespassing he summoned Louis Riel for this purpose. Over a dozen Metis arrived with Riel. After a verbal altercation, the surveyors left the land. This was the commencement of the Red River Resistance.

Only a couple of weeks earlier, settlers in the Red River had learned through the public press that the HBC intended to transfer Rupert's Land to Canada on December 1, 1869, and that the undiplomatic Minister of the Interior (William McDougall) would be appointed Lieutenant Governor. Neither John A. Macdonald nor the HBC consulted, or discussed terms of takeover with, the local inhabitants. Macdonald's drive for Canadian ownership of Rupert's Land was accompanied by his disregard for humanitarian concerns of the people resident there, a neglect he was to repeat in relationship to settlers' grievances in Saskatchewan prior to the 1885 North-West Uprising.

Several days after the André Nault incident, the Metis formed a National Committee with the soon-to-be twenty-five year old Riel as secretary. The Committee was opposed to the unilateral infliction on the community of a Lieutenant Governor with almost despotic powers. Riel made clear that access to the Settlement by McDougall would be prevented unless Canada conferred with the representatives of the Settlement on the terms of the takeover. On November 2, 1869, true to their word, the Metis on ascertaining that McDougall had crossed the United States border forced him to re-cross the border back into the United States. On the same day a number of Metis under Riel's leadership took control of Fort Garry. This was the Hudson's Bay Company's fort in the heart of the Red River Settlement at the junction of the Red and the Assiniboine Rivers. No blood was shed.

Several meetings of English and French speaking inhabitants were held in November. At one meeting Riel told the delegates that a provisional government should be formed "for our protection and to treat with Canada" on terms of union, but that was not done at this meeting. On December 1 (the day that Rupert's Land was originally to be taken over by Canada) Riel tabled before a meeting of English and Metis delegates a List of Rights. The List set forth terms which Riel and other delegates wanted Canada to accept. These terms called for a local legislature and elections, free homesteads, public lands for schools, use of French and English in the legislature and the courts, Indian treaties, Parliamentary representation, etc.

On that very same day, December 1, 1869 (the day that Canada was originally supposed to annex Rupert's Land), Lieutenant Governor designate William McDougall was waiting impatiently in Pembina across the United States Border. Without having received official documents confirming the takeover and not knowing that Macdonald had postponed it, McDougall took it upon himself to draft and issue a proclamation to which he forged the Queen's name. This falsified document proclaimed that the North-West was now part of Canada and that he was officially the Lieutenant Governor. He stepped across the border and, in bone-chilling cold and snowy weather, he read the fake proclamation to the inhuman elements after which he hied himself back across the border to Pembina. However besides being asinine and comical, McDougall's acts were illegal. They had a most significant effect as well. The Prime Minister, John A. Macdonald, had written a letter dated November 27, 1869 to McDougall reading in part:

> An assumption of the Government by you, of course, puts an end to that of the Hudson's Bay Company's authorities, and Governor McTavish [sic] and his Council would be deprived even of the semblance of legal right to interfere. There would then be, if you were not admitted into the Country, no legal government existing and anarchy must follow. In such a case, no matter how the anarchy was produced, it is quite open by the Law of Nations for the inhabitants to form a Government *ex necessitate*, for the protection of life & property, and such a Government has certain sovereign rights by the *jus gentium* [i.e. the law of nations]...[11]

Professor Stanley quotes a minute of a Report of the Privy Council dated December 16, 1869 written by Macdonald to the effect that a proclamation would put an end to the Government of the HBC, but not substitute the Government of Canada. The minute added that a state of anarchy and confusion would ensue, which might result in legal status to a *de facto* Government formed for the protection of their lives and property by the inhabitants.[12]

McDougall did not receive Macdonald's letter before his droll escapade. The result, which Macdonald warned him about in his letter, came to pass. On November 24, 1869 the HBC had executed the transfer papers to transfer Rupert's Land to Canada to take effect on an

---

[11]   National Archives of England Public Record Office, CO (Colonial Office) 42/678, Macdonald to McDougall, November 27, 1869, p. 29-31.
[12]   George F. Stanley, *The Birth of Western Canada*, p. 85.

agreed date, originally to have been only seven days later. Because of the pending transfer, the HBC and its Council of Assiniboia had effectively given up government. Consequently when McDougall made his illegitimate proclamation it was open to the inhabitants of the Settlement by the law of nations (as Prime Minister Macdonald had advised McDougall) to form a government for the protection of the life and property of the inhabitants.

Riel found out some days later that McDougall's proclamation was a fraud. Colonel Stoughton Dennis, who with Schultz and others was opposing Riel's initiatives, made a call to arms at McDougall's request. Riel's men captured Schultz and a number of Canadians who intended to attack Upper Fort Garry and had them imprisoned. In keeping with his earlier suggestion that a provisional government be formed "for our protection and to treat with Canada", Riel and other inhabitants constituted a provisional government exactly one week after McDougall purported to usurp authority. Riel became president of the provisional government two days after Christmas.

This provisional government formed *"ex necessitate,* for the protection of life and property" had, at the very least and consistent with Macdonald's advice to McDougall, a colour of right and legitimacy.

Macdonald sent Donald A. Smith (the future Lord Strathcona who was then the chief HBC official in Canada) as a secret commissioner to the Red River Settlement and Smith bribed some of the Metis to desert Riel. Riel found out about Smith's commission and assented to Smith addressing a large assembly on January 18, 1870 and on the following day, where Smith made promises on behalf of Canada to the crowd relating to representation and title to land.

Riel in turn proposed that a Convention of Forty, one-half French and one-half English, be convened to discuss Smith's proposals. The Convention met some days later. It struck a committee of six to draft a List of Rights. A couple of Riel's proposals, including provincial status, were voted down by the English members and by several Metis influenced by his cousin Charles Nolin. This led to acrimony between Nolin and Riel, which was to have repercussions in Saskatchewan fifteen years later.

Smith now stated that a delegation should be sent to Ottawa to meet with government officials to discuss the territory's entry into Confederation. This offer was received with alacrity. Riel then proposed formation of a provisional government, composed of both French and English speaking settlers, to administer the colony until matters were settled. The Council of Assiniboia had ceased functioning, thanks to the proclamation of the hapless McDougall. It was agreed to put the matter of formation of a provisional government to the Governor of Assiniboia William Mactavish. The ailing Mactavish said he was dying and would not delegate his authority, then said to them

> Form a Government, for God's sake, and restore peace and
> order in the Settlement.[13]

The provisional government and a legislative council were formed on February 10, 1870, the latter to consist of 12 French and 12 English-speaking members. Louis Riel was elected President.

In the background were Schultz, Mair and an odious, bigoted and violent Orangeman Thomas Scott. Scott had previously been in trouble with the law. While working as a labourer on construction of the Dawson Road to Fort Garry being built by the federal government, he attacked and tried to drown his boss John A. Snow in a row with Snow about wages. Scott was convicted of robbery and assault with violence. In January 1870 Schultz, Mair and Scott had escaped from imprisonment by the Metis and were trying to get Canadian and English-speaking settlers to take up arms presumably to release other prisoners but in reality to overthrow the Provisional Government. On February 17 an armed group from Portage la Prairie, led by Captain Charles Boulton, headed for Fort Garry but were arrested by the Metis and imprisoned, including Boulton and Scott.

Scott showed his contempt for the Metis guards by obscenely vilifying them and shouting that when he was released he would have them hanged. He and another prisoner attempted to overpower a guard but they were subdued. Riel went to talk to Scott but Scott swore at him. The Metis guards would no longer tolerate Scott's abuse and threats. Riel as President of the Provisional Government ordered the court-martial of Scott. Riel was not a member of the court-martial. After presentation of evidence on March 3 the court-martial by a vote of four to three voted for the death penalty. The next day Scott was executed by a firing squad. Although Riel had suggested mercy he did not intervene to stop the execution. Perhaps Riel believed it was

---

[13]   This quotation appears in a number of biographies of Louis Riel. See e.g. George F. G. Stanley, *Louis Riel*, p. 97.

necessary to demonstrate to the enemies of the Provisional Government that they had better beware of attacks on the Settlement, and also to illustrate to Canada that the Provisional Government was for real.

However, news of the death of Thomas Scott soon reached Orange Ontario. A mighty furore, fueled in speeches in Toronto and elsewhere in Ontario by Schultz and Mair vilifying Riel and praising Scott, erupted over what they saw as the murder of one of their own. Scott's execution was to have serious repercussions on Riel's life both soon after and fifteen years later in Saskatchewan.

The "cabinet" of the new Provisional Government prepared a new "List of Rights" on March 22, 1870 for its delegates to take to Ottawa. It included many of the provisions in the previous List of Rights and several additional items including, at Riel's insistence, status as a Province. A provision for separate schools among religious denominations was added.

Father Noel Joseph Ritchot of St. Norbert led the delegates to Ottawa. Riel was not a delegate. The end result of the Ottawa discussions was the entry of Manitoba into confederation as a province, a grant of 1,400,000 acres of land to be allotted to the Metis, bilingualism in the legislature and courts and other important provisions, all embodied in the *Manitoba Act*. Manitoba joined Confederation as a province on July 15, 1870. As the driving force behind the creation of Manitoba as a Province, many people consider Louis Riel a "Father of Confederation". The amnesty which Ritchot, Archbishop Taché and Riel had been assured was forthcoming never materialized. Failure to obtain the promised amnesty later proved calamitous to Riel.

3.   RIEL'S ELECTIONS TO PARLIAMENT AND EXILE

While events were going on in Ottawa, Riel busied himself administering the Settlement.

In May 1870 Colonel Garnet Wolseley with an army of soldiers and volunteers from Ontario had set off for the Red River to set up a "peaceful" presence. In fact Macdonald's real reason for sending Colonel Wolseley's expeditionary forces to the Red River Settlement was because he mistrusted Riel. According to George Parkin in a biography of Macdonald, Macdonald stated in a letter to his friend and former finance minister, John Rose, that he feared that:

> the longer he [Riel] remains in power, the more unwilling will
> he be to resign it. ... Under these circumstances the prepara-
> tions for the expeditionary force may not be delayed.[14]

In this letter Macdonald acknowledged that Riel was in power in the Red River Settlement.

On receipt of the news of the execution of Thomas Scott these preparations for an expeditionary force were hurried on. As well, the *Manitoba Act* was introduced by Macdonald "and hurriedly passed through the House." Parkin further states that the long strain on Macdonald had been too great and he became deathly ill and unfit for work for four months.

There is no doubt that the strains and vexations Riel caused Macdonald in Manitoba generated an intense dislike by Macdonald for the Metis leader. Macdonald called Riel "a gone coon"[15] and sometime before the events in Saskatchewan in 1885 he also stated that Riel had:

> committed a cold-blooded murder in 1870 which will never
> be forgotten by the whites, either in Manitoba or Ontario. [16]

This was obviously a reference to the execution of Thomas Scott. After Riel's conviction for high treason in 1885 and notwithstanding the jury's unanimous recommendation for mercy, Macdonald would treat Riel with a vengeance.

Many of the Wolseley troops sent out by Macdonald to the Red River, ostensibly for peaceful purposes, were Orangemen determined to do Riel and the Metis serious harm. When the troops were almost at Fort Garry in August, the civilian lieutenant governor (Adams George Archibald) to whom they would be subject, had not arrived. Riel received word that Colonel Wolseley's men were going to kill him. He fled a few hours before their arrival on August 24. It was a prudent move on his part.

The thirst for blood of Wolseley's extremist troops led directly to the assassination of Elzéar Goulet (a prominent, intelligent, educated and respected Metis). A photograph of Goulet in W. McCartney Davidson's biography of Riel shows a well-groomed, handsome young

---

14   George R. Parkin, *Sir John A. Macdonald,* p. 160-61.
15   Joseph Pope, *Correspondence of Sir John Macdonald,* p. 127-28; February 23, 1870, Macdonald to Sir John Rose.
16   Pope, Macdonald to Governor-General Lord Lansdowne on August 12, 1884, p. 317-19.

man in shirt, tie and jacket. Goulet was a direct descendent of Louis Hebert, the first permanent colonial settler in Canada, who had arrived in Quebec City with Samuel de Champlain in 1617. Goulet had been a member of the court martial, which sentenced Thomas Scott to death. When Goulet was seen in Winnipeg, he was pursued by a number of men, among them Ontario soldiers of Colonel Wolseley. Goulet ran to the Red River and was swimming to the other side when his pursuers threw rocks and stones at him. The result was that he was drowned, stoned to death. Although this happened in daylight, his body was not recovered until the next day; the malefactors simply returned to their activities rather than attempting to retrieve the body. The culprits were never prosecuted. The historian Alexander Begg wrote that "a large number took part in the disturbance."

It is said that when the body was recovered Goulet's widow had her children kneel before the body of their dead father and pray not only for their father's soul but also for the souls of his murderers.[17] A number of biographers of Riel, including George F. G. Stanley, cite the killing of Elzéar Goulet as the first of many reprisals against the settlers (in retaliation for Scott's execution) which occurred subsequent to the arrival of Wolseley's troops.[18]

The Prime Minister's son, Hugh John Macdonald, was involved in both the Red River Resistance and the uprising in the North-West Territories. Hugh John was a member of Colonel Wolseley's troops that arrived in Red River after the Provisional Government of Riel was disbanded. In a newspaper interview many years after the incident, Hugh John Macdonald recalled the killing of Elzéar Goulet. He was a witness to "a crowd of our men running … towards the river." He later referred to Goulet doing a "record run" pursued by "a large party of soldiers." He added that Goulet could not swim sufficiently well and drowned "while the infuriated soldiers were struggling to rescue him that he might be brought to justice."[19] Hugh John made no mention of

---

[17]   Davidson, p. 95. Other sources dealing with Goulet's death are: Stanley, *Louis Riel,* p. 160-61 and note 16; Judge L. A. Prud'homme, "La Famille Goulet", in *Memoires de la Société Royale du Canada,* (1935) Vol. 29, 3rd series, p. 30-32. The author is a grand-nephew of Elzéar Goulet.

[18]   Stanley, *Louis Riel,* p. 161.

[19]   *Winnipeg Telegram,* July 18, 1911 (Interview with Hugh John Macdonald).

Goulet being stoned by Hugh John's fellow soldiers, or of Goulet's body being left in the river overnight.

Lieutenant-Governor Adams G. Archibald ordered an investigation into this murder.[20]   No one was ever charged although it was believed within the community that Goulet's murder had been carried out by the soldiers of Colonel Wolseley's regiment.   The Lieutenant Governor sent the report of the investigator dated September 27, 1870 to the federal Secretary of State for the Provinces.   The report recommended that arrest warrants be issued against three parties, two for feloniously causing Goulet's death.   However, after receiving the report the Lieutenant Governor had Judge Johnson look at the papers.   Johnson advised him that the evidence was "not sufficiently strong" to issue warrants and none were issued.

In an August 2, 1911 open letter published in the *Winnipeg Free Press*, the son of Elzéar Goulet (Roger Goulet) replied in detail to the Hugh John Macdonald interview of July 18, 1911.   In this letter Roger Goulet (who was then the Provincial Inspector of French Public Schools in Manitoba) stated:

> After reading your statement, sir, I am convinced that you
> could not make it without having been one of the "crowd"
> that pursued my father in that race to death.[21]

Hugh John Macdonald replied in a letter of August 3, 1911 in the *Winnipeg Free Press* that he had no hand or part in Goulet's death.

Most sources believe that Elzéar Goulet's participation in the court martial of Thomas Scott was probably the cause of Goulet's murder.   It should be noted that Goulet was a close friend of Riel and although Riel was not in Winnipeg when Goulet was murdered, he was well aware of the circumstances.   It should also be noted that the death of Elzéar Goulet was not the only penalty inflicted on the Metis in the Red River Settlement for their support of the Provisional Government. There were a number of retaliatory incidents, against members of the Settlement, with respect to the execution of Thomas Scott after Wolseley's troops arrived at Red River.

After he fled the Red River area in August 1870 to escape violence at the hands of Colonel Wolseley's troops, Riel spent most of the next nine months in Dakota Territory in the United States, primarily at St.

---

20   *Canada Sessional Papers* (1871) 34 Victoria (No. 20), p. 15; 52-54.
21   *Winnipeg Free Press*, August 2, 1911, Letter from Roger Goulet.

Joseph. He lived in constant fear that Schultz's cohorts would attempt to assassinate him. He returned to St. Vital in May 1871 but laid low publicly.

In October 1871 there was a Fenian scare in Manitoba. The Fenians were members of the Irish Republican Brotherhood, a militant nationalist organization founded by the Irish in the United States. The term "Fenian" is most likely derived from fiann, warriors reputed to have fought for the defence of Ireland in the time of Finn and other legendary Irish kings. The Fenians were responsible for isolated revolutionary acts against the British and were abhorred by the Orangemen. William B. O'Donoghue (who had been in Riel's provisional government but had subsequently had a falling out with Riel) wanted to have the United States involved in Manitoba. O'Donoghue had assembled a group of Fenians in Dakota Territory and on October 5, 1871 they crossed into Manitoba and occupied a trading post of the HBC not far from the border. Lieutenant Governor Archibald had issued a proclamation the day before calling upon all loyal men "to rally around the flag of our country." Riel and the Metis did so. O'Donoghue was arrested and this small Fenian uprising dissipated.

Archibald's approval of Metis participation backed by Riel did not go down well in Ontario. There was Orange outrage. After winning the election of 1872, the Premier of Ontario Edward Blake offered a $5,000 reward for the capture and conviction of the "murderers" of Thomas Scott, notwithstanding that Ontario had no jurisdiction in the matter.

To avoid hostility between Quebec and Ontario in the 1872 federal election, John A. Macdonald offered what amounted to a bribe on his part of $1,000 (through Taché) to have Riel leave the country for a period of time. Donald Smith contributed £600. Riel, realizing his life was in danger, accepted the money and left for St. Paul. However, his friend in St. Boniface Joseph Dubuc talked Riel into running in the constituency of Provencher in the September 1872 federal election. Riel had the nomination all but locked-up when word came that Macdonald's Quebec lieutenant George Étienne Cartier had lost his seat. Riel agreed to step aside so that Cartier could win the safe Provencher seat. Riel stated that his only condition would be the pledge by Cartier to fulfil the promise of the land grant to the Metis. Riel was willing to trust Cartier's conscience as to the question of his amnesty.[22] However, Cartier died in May 1873. Riel decided to run in the by-election and won Provencher in October 1873, but afraid for his life he did not take his seat. In any event the corruption in John A. Macdonald's government, known as the Pacific Scandal, caused it to resign. In the general election of February 1874 the Liberal Party under Alexander Mackenzie won, as did Riel for a second time in Provencher.

Riel went east and with the aid of his old Montreal school chum Romuald Fiset (the member from Rimouski) crossed the river to Ottawa where, without naming Riel, Fiset asked the Clerk of the House to administer the oath to Riel who then signed the members role and scurried out. Riel did not appear at the opening of Parliament. Mackenzie Bowell (who was to become the Conservative Prime Minister in 1894), a high officer of the Orange Order, moved that Riel appear in the House on April 9, 1874 or be expelled. Riel did not appear and was expelled from the House of Commons. He was in Keesville, New York near the Canadian border, staying with Father Fabien Barnabé in his parish rectory. However Riel ran in the by-election in Provencher created by his expulsion and was elected for a third time in September 1874 when he was not yet thirty years old.

When Parliament convened in February 1875 Prime Minister Alexander Mackenzie proposed a resolution granting a full amnesty to Riel and Ambrose Lépine with respect to all acts committed by them during

> the North West troubles ... conditional on five years
> banishment from Her Majesty's Dominions.

Lépine chose to serve a two-year prison term rather than accept exile.

Riel went into exile in the United States, a political refugee. His adversities, constant fear of assassination, forced exclusion from his family and friends in the Red River Settlement, and no future prospects led to an emotional breakdown. He spent some time in the eastern United States. While there his emotional distress and vulnerability led him to believe he had a mission to lead the Metis to greater things. His thought that Divine Providence was with him was bolstered by a letter of June 14, 1875 from Bishop Ignace Bourget of Montreal (replying to Riel's letter) telling Riel that God "has given you a mission which you must fulfill in all respects."

---

[22]   Dr. Peter Charlebois, *The Life of Louis Riel*, p. 98.

Riel spent some time in Washington D.C. in the fall of 1875 with Edmond Mallet, an expatriate Quebecer, and even had a meeting with President Ulysses S. Grant. While at Mass in Washington in December 1875, Riel suddenly became ecstatic and wept uncontrollably for a short time. Mallet then made plans to send Riel to Father Primeau in Worcester, Massachusetts. Father Primeau tried to help but felt Riel was not normal. Father Richer at Suncook fared no better. Father Barnabé came back into the picture but at his rectory Riel was agitated, frequently weeping and bellowing like a bull. Barnabé arranged for John Lee, Riel's uncle in Montreal, to come for him because he felt Riel was not in his right mind. After a number of days at his home, Lee had Riel placed in an asylum in Longue-Pointe, Quebec on March 6, 1876 under an assumed name. Dr. Henry Howard, the supervising doctor, was uncertain whether Riel was acting. When Riel was addressed by his pseudonym, he showed a nun his prayer book in which his beloved sister Sara had written his name. The nun immediately tore out the page and Riel justifiably became berserk. In May 1876, fearful that Riel's presence at Longue-Pointe would be discovered, the nuns wanted him out. He was transferred to Beauport Asylum near Quebec City where he stayed until January 1878. The Superintendent of Beauport was Dr. François Roy who would later testify at Riel's 1885 trial for high treason.

On his release from Beauport Riel returned to Father Barnabé's rectory at Keeseville in New York where he and Father Barnabé's sister, Evelina, soon fell in love. Towards the end of 1878 Riel decided to go to St. Paul, Minnesota. He met many Metis who could not accept that he had ever been deranged. Riel told some that he had feigned mental sickness. Over the next few years Riel moved a couple of times in the mid-western United States; he was an interpreter, woodchopper, supplies purchaser, and trader. In 1881 while working in the Carroll, Montana area he met and married a young Métisse, Marguerite Monet *dit* Bellehumeur. It was a common-law wedding since there were no priests in the area. A priest solemnized the marriage in March 1882. Riel then had the delicate task of writing Evelina Barnabé in Keeseville to let her know she had been jilted. She was not amused.

Riel became involved in Montana politics on behalf of the Republican Party, and he denounced the whisky trade with Indians and Metis. In the Congressional elections of 1882, Riel helped get out the

Metis vote. In 1883 he was charged with urging Metis who were not United States citizens to vote, but the charge was dismissed.

Louis Riel's banishment from Canada, imposed by the Alexander Mackenzie administration, had expired while Riel was in the western United States. However, Riel had decided to apply for American citizenship, which was granted to him on March 16, 1883 at Fort Benton, Montana. Shortly after, he accepted a position as a schoolteacher at St. Peter's Mission, Montana. He and his wife had had a son in May 1882 and their daughter Marie was to be born in September 1883. His life as a schoolteacher was pedestrian and unemotional, but secure.

This secure, placid life was soon to be displaced by one much more hectic. While at Sunday Mass on June 4, 1884 Riel found out that a delegation of French and English half-breeds from the North-West (Saskatchewan), over eleven hundred kilometres distant, had arrived on horseback at St. Peter's Mission to see him. The four men (Gabriel Dumont, James Isbister, Michel Dumas and Moïse Ouellette) had come at the behest of the North-West Settlers. They came to plead with Riel to come to the North-West and help them to obtain their rights and to seek remedy for their grievances against the Canadian government which was completely ignoring their petitions and complaints and treating them as second class citizens. They knew from past experience in Manitoba that immigration from the east would threaten their way of life and their land. The settlers had no right of election to or representatives in the Canadian Parliament and needed an effective voice to speak for them and to get their message through to Ottawa.

Riel told the delegation he would think on it overnight but there was no doubt in his mind that he would agree to go with them. In a sense he thought it was a Heaven-sent opportunity to help his Metis people. He would, in a sense, be their prophetic messiah. The next day Riel accepted their invitation, putting his acceptance in writing, adding at the same time that the Canadian government owed him his Manitoba land grant and "something else" not specified. He stated he would return from the North-West to Montana in September. Several days later Riel, his wife and children left with the delegation on the long journey to the South Saskatchewan; a fateful journey that would cost Louis Riel his life in less than eighteen months and revolutionize Canadian politics for generations.

Chapter III

CANADIAN EXPANSIONIST MOVEMENT AND UNREST IN THE NORTH-WEST

In the mid-1850s a movement developed in the Toronto and Ottawa Valley areas to annex Rupert's Land to Canada. King Charles II in 1670 had originally granted Rupert's Land to the Hudson's Bay Company, which was led by the King's cousin, Prince Rupert. The land grant roughly encompassed the modern day Prairie Provinces (Manitoba, Saskatchewan and Alberta), Yukon Territory and the Southern Northwest Territories. Rupert's Land is sometimes referred to herein as the North-West (indicative of the whole grant of land under the Hudson's Bay Company Charter). In 1870 a new province emerged out of Rupert's Land when Manitoba joined Confederation under the terms of the *Manitoba Act*. This creation was a direct result of the efforts of the Provisional Government in the Red River Settlement under the leadership of Louis Riel. At the time of the formation of Manitoba, the remaining area of Rupert's Land was designated as the North-West Territories. It was within the North-West Territories that the Saskatchewan Uprising occurred in 1885.

The instigators of the movement in the 1850s to annex Rupert's Land to Canada were primarily English-speaking Anglo-Saxon Protestants many of whom were Orangemen. At the time, the remaining undeveloped arable land in Upper Canada was minimal, due to the Canadian Shield. The expansionists in Canada saw Rupert's Land, with the North-West, as a *lebensraum*, as a golden opportunity to enlarge their hinterland and extend their commercial frontiers. They were inspired by a sense of being a part of the British Empire, of an imperial community. They wished to populate the West with agricultural settlers who adhered to the same British values and British traditions that they themselves observed. The expansionist movement to annex Rupert's Land to Canada was fueled principally by Toronto and Upper Canada, not by the inhabitants of the West.

Initially the Ontario-based expansionists wished the West to be a pathway to the Pacific Ocean and, from there, a gateway to the riches of the Orient. However this aspiration would require a transcontinental railway and immigrants to the North-West to build the infrastructure for the railroad and to settle there. To attract settlers it was essential that the prevailing image in Upper Canada of the North-West as that of a cold, sub-arctic wilderness, suitable only for the fur trade, be transformed. It had to be mentally metamorphosed into that of a fertile land capable of producing abundant crops in climatic conditions which, while on the brisk side in winter, were generally salubrious and refreshing. It was necessary to create the notion of an agricultural "fertile belt" in the West. This would have the added advantage in the expansionists' minds of developing a settlement base for further movement west to the Pacific Ocean. Another necessary step was to attack the Hudson's Bay Company's monopoly on government and trade in Rupert's Land. The expansionists campaigned on all fronts:

(i)   to change the perception of the North-West from a barren harsh wilderness into a plenteous land suitable for farming and settlement in a healthy climate;

(ii)   to lobby the federal government for a transcontinental railway to the Pacific;

(iii)   to portray the HBC as a monopolistic oligarchy whose interest was protection of its fur trade monopoly even at the expense of thwarting expansion of the British Empire into the West, with its attendant beneficial humanitarian and civilizing influences on the aboriginal peoples in the name of imperial progress;

(iv)   to push for annexation of Rupert's Land by Canada.

Proponents of annexation equated it with nationalism and imperialism. They saw the West for what it could do for them and for Canada in the future and they saw the Red River Settlement as the home base for spreading westward. They gave little consideration to the way of life of the Metis or the Indians. The xenophobic William McDougall, the Lieutenant Governor designate of Manitoba, in a letter to Prime Minister Macdonald of November 13, 1869 branded the Metis as "semi-savages and serfs of yesterday."[23] In December 1869 Macdonald referred to the Metis as "miserable half-breeds" and a few weeks later he referred to them as "wild people".[24]. The annexationists cared little about the Metis, the Indians or the North-West, or the heritage, culture and lifestyle of the Metis and residents of the prairie plains particularly

---

[23]   Douglas Owram, *Promise of Eden, the Canadian Expansionist Movement and the Idea of the West 1856-1900*, p. 85.
[24]   Pope, p. 113 & 119.

in the Red River Settlement. One of their main thoughts was about the grand future that would result from the civilizing and other benefits their western intrusion would bring. A cultural kismet of Ontario and British values would descend on Rupert's Land when it became part of Canada.

The Canadian mercantile interests also witnessed the prosperity that had accrued in the United States as a result of its western frontier expansion and settlement. Completion of the railway and large-scale immigration increased Minnesota's population by 30 times in the 1850s. Canada also perceived that with construction of a railway to the west accompanied by an abundance of immigrants who would settle in and cultivate the western lands, the North-West would not only create additional markets for Canadian products, but would protect the West from appropriation by the United States. Wheat would become the chief commodity in place of furs and buffalo. This scheme would require settlement and an agricultural plan and, in due course, private land ownership in the West.

The creation of Canada in 1867, pursuant to the *British North America Act* of that year,[25] united the Provinces of Canada (which became Ontario and Quebec), Nova Scotia and New Brunswick into a Confederation which established a federal government of which John A. Macdonald was prime minister. With Confederation, more voices were added to the push for western expansion. Doug Owram, in pointing out that by the late 1860s nationalism and expansionism had become intertwined, quoted a comment on a speech by an ardent Canadian nationalist, Thomas D'Arcy McGee, in 1868 that "the future of the Dominion depends on our early occupation of the rich prairie land."[26] This sentiment was not uncommon in Canada. Some months after Confederation the infamous William McDougall, a leading proselytizer of national expansion, tabled resolutions in the House of Commons, which led to the request to Britain to transfer the HBC lands to Canada. Shortly after, the Canadian Government entered into serious negotiations with the British Colonial office concerning acquisition of Rupert's Land from the HBC.

---

[25]   (30 & 31) Victoria, c. 3 (U.K.).
[26]   Owram, p. 77.

In July of 1868, the British Parliament passed the *Rupert's Land Act* to authorize the surrender of the HBC lands and privileges and to transfer them to Canada. After much negotiation in England involving Canadian delegates, including William McDougall, terms of transfer were settled in April 1869. There included a payment to the HBC of £300,000, extensive land grants to the HBC and other matters. The official transfer was to occur on December 1, 1869. However no one, especially McDougall, had thought to discuss the terms of transfer with the inhabitants of the West. Lands which many of these inhabitants had previously purchased from the HBC, and which the HBC no longer had a right to, were included in the lands being sold by the HBC to Canada. Soon after, and without consultation with or warning to the inhabitants, a Canadian survey party appeared in the Red River area in August 1869, at a time when Canada had no legal right to make surveys there. Under John Stoughton Dennis, the survey followed the American system of dividing the lands into rectangular townships. This system, as indicated previously, was contrary to the narrow river-front lots occupied by the Metis, who also enjoyed water rights and land stretching back several miles from the river, the back part of which was for hay privileges for livestock. In October, a Canadian crew ran the survey lines across André Nault's hay privilege. Nault, who could not speak English, contacted the fluently bilingual Riel who, with a group of Metis, peacefully but firmly made the surveyors desist and withdraw.

This was the start of the Red River Resistance (also known as a Rebellion or Uprising). The Metis seized Fort Garry (the heart of the Red River Settlement) from the HBC on November 2, 1869. No blood was shed. On the same day, the Metis expelled William McDougall (lieutenant governor-designate of Manitoba who then had no official or legal status in Rupert's Land) from the area. This subsequently led to:

(i)   establishment of a Provisional Government by Riel and others;

(ii)   the execution of Thomas Scott;

(iii)   negotiations leading to the *1870 Manitoba Act* pursuant to which Manitoba entered the Canadian Confederation as a full Province; and

(iv)   the departure of Riel in advance of the arrival of Colonel Wolseley's troops, his election to Parliament three times, his five year government imposed exile and so on (as discussed in the preceding Chapter) until in 1884 a delegation of French and Metis half-breeds enticed him to the North-West to lead them in dealing with the federal government.

After Manitoba became a province the expansionist movement saw many more Ontarians move west. The *Manitoba Act* had set aside a total of 1,400,000 acres to be distributed among the half-breeds. Many Metis found that, on their return home after hunting buffalo, easterners had usurped their land. The author Douglas Hill cites one instance of this. Hill wrote that Governor Archibald talked the Metis out of the use of force to reclaim their lands located near a stream. Colonel Wolseley's soldiers were still present. As a result many of the Metis picked up and moved their homes into the less populated areas further west. The "Ontario land-grabbers", many of them Orangemen, then insultingly renamed the little stream "the Boyne".[27] The Boyne was a river in Ireland where in 1690 the Protestant army of William of Orange (William III) defeated the Catholic army of the recently deposed James II. The confrontation is known as the Battle of the Boyne. Many other Metis who had received scrip certificates, entitling them to land grants in Manitoba out of the 1,400,000 acres, sold the certificates to land speculators for a fraction of their worth. Others were defrauded out of their entitlements. As well, the buffalo (a principal source of food and clothing for the Metis) were vanishing from the eastern plains. A Metis exodus to what is now Saskatchewan ensued. Many Metis emigrated to the South Branch of the Saskatchewan River, south of Prince Albert. A number of them settled in the St. Laurent area, a mission established by Father Alexis André. André was an Oblate priest who was later a witness at Louis Riel's trial.

With the passage of time the South Branch Metis wanted government assurance of their rights to their land, as well as land grants (similar to those in Manitoba) and river-lot surveys. The white and half-breed settlers in the Prince Albert area wanted the same. The settlers in the area sent petitions to the government. The government did send a survey crew in the late 1870s and, in the first year, river-lot surveys were started. For some reason in 1879, this method was reversed and the square-lot principle was followed. The government ignored the settlers' complaints in this respect as well as those relating to their inability to

---

27   Douglas Hill, *The Opening of the Canadian West*, p. 85.

obtain title to their land. A number of petitions were sent over the years to the government outlining the grievances but nothing was done. By 1884 the whites, the half-breeds and the Metis in the North-West were fed-up. They had no right to elect members of Parliament and had no representatives in Ottawa to speak for them and to press their case. This was another of their grievances. They decided to send a delegation to Montana to invite Louis Riel, the hero of the acquisition of rights in Manitoba, to represent them in dealings with the government.

When Riel arrived in Saskatchewan, he addressed a number of meetings of Metis, English half-breeds and whites. His speeches at the outset were moderate, and the agitation was peaceful and constitutional. However, the priests were not supportive of him. During his tenure in the North-West Riel advocated for responsible government; parliamentary representation; land grants for Metis, half-breed and white settlers; income from land sales for hospitals, schools and farm equipment; better provision for the Indians; the establishment of Alberta and Saskatchewan as provinces; and other matters. The December 16, 1884 Petition to the federal government requested the organization of the District of Saskatchewan as a province, among other items. Section 3 of the Bill of Rights of March 8, 1885 called for the provinces of Alberta and Saskatchewan to be forthwith organized with their own legislatures. Most of these policies were achieved after Riel's death. The North-West Territories achieved parliamentary representation in 1886 and responsible government in 1897. Saskatchewan and Alberta were granted provincial status in 1905.

The unrest in Saskatchewan and disregard of settlers' petitions by the federal government in the first half of the 1880s led to a rebellion in the North-West Territories. At the Gabriel Dumont Institute in Saskatoon, one of the research historians told the author of this text "We use the term 'resistance'; 'rebellion' is an English term." In this text the author has generally used the term "Resistance" with respect to the troubles in the Red River area and the term "Uprising" with respect to the troubles in the North-West Territories. One may note that on August 28, 1885 after Riel had been convicted, Prime Minister John A. Macdonald, for political reasons, downplayed the North-West outbreak as a "mere domestic trouble ... not to be elevated to the rank of a rebellion."[28]

During the 1870s the Eastern Canadian expansionists continued their push for populating the West with Anglo-Saxon Protestants. They were disappointed with the meager numbers who were immigrating to the prairies. They blamed the absence of a railway into the area. The railway would foster economic activity and a demand for the goods and products of eastern manufacturers; its rails would bind the nation together; and its settlers from Ontario would plant British traditions and values in the West.

These views coincided with those of Prime Minister John A. Macdonald. In the early 1870s manufacturers in the east lobbied Macdonald for tariff protection, and since many were supporters of the Conservative Party, Macdonald was in favour of granting protection. He came up with an inspired euphemism for high tariffs for Eastern manufacturers – the "National Policy". He pushed for this Policy in the 1872 election as well as for construction of a railway to the Pacific. Macdonald won the election but shortly after corruption in Macdonald's government reared its ugly head. Sir Hugh Allan, whose company had been granted the charter to build the railway by the Macdonald administration, had made campaign contributions of sizeable amounts specifically, among others, to Macdonald and his Quebec lieutenant Cartier. One of these contributions to Macdonald was made pursuant to a telegram from Prime Minister Macdonald to Sir Hugh Allan marked "Immediate, Private". Macdonald telegraphed

> I must have another ten thousand; will be the last time of
> calling; do not fail me; answer today.

When the corruption became public in 1873, Macdonald's government resigned in disgrace. Professor W. G. Hardy wrote "John A. went on a prolonged drunk."[29] Other historians have noted the bibulous Macdonald's intemperate drinking habits.[30]

Alexander Mackenzie became Prime Minister of Canada in 1873 but because of a depression, construction of the railway to the west did not proceed during his tenure. Allan's company lost its charter to build

---

28   Pope, p. 355.
29   W. G. Hardy, *From Sea Unto Sea, The Road to Nationhood 1850-1910*, p. 261.
30   Michael Bliss, *Right Honourable Men: The Descent of Canadian Politics from Macdonald to Mulroney*, p. 4; 21 & 27.

the railway. In the 1878 election campaign, John A. Macdonald resurrected his so-called "National Policy". Macdonald's Conservative Party won the election; however he lost his own Kingston seat and was parachuted into a seat in Victoria, British Columbia, which he won. With victory, Macdonald was now able to renew his pursuit of nation building. The National Policy developed beyond tariff protection for eastern manufacturers to embrace greater development policies; western immigration; construction of the railway to the west; etc. This Policy of the Government of John A. Macdonald (who as recently as 1883 had referred to the West as a "Crown Colony") ignored the West's history and way of life. This way of life of the Metis and the Indians was fading away with the disappearance of the buffalo and implementation of the Indian treaties to settle the Indians on reserves. The development of Western Canada was to be determined by the interests of eastern Canadian manufacturers and expansionist imperialists (the British Empire and its influence in Ontario were then in its heyday). Hence the federal policies of high tariffs; massive western immigration; movement of Indians to reserves, sometimes involving starvation; and a taxpayer bailout of the near-bankrupt Canadian Pacific Railway ("CPR"). Federal authorities had continuously disregarded the numerous plaints and petitions by the inhabitants of the North-West relating to land rights; surveys; corrupt officials; lack of representation in Parliament; etc. Ottawa's deaf ear to Western grievances, coupled with its eastern-based policies, set the stage for the uprising that ensued.

With respect to the railway, a charter was granted for construction of the CPR to a syndicate in which Donald A. Smith (well known in Manitoba in 1870) of the Hudson's Bay Company, and George Stephen of the Bank of Montreal were prominent. The CPR received huge money and land grants, tax exemptions and other benefits from the government. Times were prosperous and by 1882 railway construction was well advanced. However, in that year the economic boom was dying. By 1883 the CPR was in financial difficulty. Stephen went to Macdonald and cadged a government loan for the CPR. He pleaded for and received a further government loan of $22,500,000 in 1884. On March 18, 1885 the canny Scottish-born capitalists and financiers, Stephen and Smith (who were cousins) unashamedly decided to beg John A. Macdonald (also Scottish-born) for a further CPR bailout. These free-enterprisers brazenly came with outstretched hands to clamour for a further $5,000,000 loan from the government. The members of the Cabinet had had enough. They rejected the CPR's loan application. The CPR was on the verge of bankruptcy, its principals on the verge of ruin. There was no hope or so George Stephen, Donald A. Smith and Cornelius Van Horne (the CPR triumvirate) thought. Pierre Berton has written an absorbing account of events relating to the CPR during this period. [31]

Fortune smiled on Stephen, Smith, Van Horne and the CPR from the most improbable of sources – Louis Riel. Only eight days after the federal cabinet had rejected their loan request, and Stephen, Smith and Van Horne had sunk into the "slough of despond", the battle at Duck Lake in the North-West Territories erupted between the Metis and the troops of Major Crozier of the North West Mounted Police. Blood was shed initiated by Major Crozier's assistant Joseph McKay, who shot dead on the spot Isadore Dumont and Assywin, the Metis and Indian representatives, who had come to parley with Crozier in an open field. The slayings of Dumont and Assywin resulted in an outbreak of shooting between Major Crozier's forces and the Metis. There were a number of fatalities on each side before Crozier's forces retreated in defeat. The North-West Uprising had commenced. Van Horne seized the opportunity. He told the government that he could get the troops from Ontario to the North-West in ten days. It seemed to be a wild pledge. There was close to 90 miles (almost one hundred and fifty kilometers) of track that had not been laid in Northern Ontario. This incomplete mileage was made up of four gaps of icy, barren hinterland. Macdonald saw a golden opportunity to resurrect his National Dream and coincidentally the CPR. He talked the cabinet into approving Van Horne's promise. Van Horne responded immediately. The CPR mobilized for the immense mission of transporting troops, matériel, weapons and animals across the country to the North-West. The gaps in the track north of Lake Superior were bridged by horse-drawn sleighs which carried the troops and supplies to the next point to which track had been laid. It was a remarkable performance. The first detachments made it to Winnipeg within ten days. The CPR had survived due to an unlikely saviour, Louis Riel. Under other circumstances the CPR might have erected a statue to him to match the magnificent statue of William

---

[31]   Pierre Berton, *The Last Spike: The Great Railway 1881-1885*.

Van Horne in the centre of the roundabout at the stately Banff Springs Hotel in Banff, Alberta.

With the arrival of the overwhelming forces from the East, the crushing of the Metis and the death knell of Riel were nigh. The actions of Riel had indirectly saved the CPR. The actions of the CPR indirectly, and of Macdonald directly, condemned Riel.

Chapter IV

SURRENDER, TRIAL SITE, CHARGES, AND THE MAGISTRATE

Some four weeks after the fighting at Duck Lake, there were hostilities at Fish Creek, and both General Frederick Middleton's soldiers and the Metis suffered casualties. Another battle occurred at Batoche in May and on May 12, 1885 General Middleton's troops vanquished the Metis. The North-West Uprising was over.

1.   THE SURRENDER OF RIEL

On May 11, 1885, the day before the Metis were routed at Batoche, Middleton prepared a letter to Riel stating:

> I am ready to receive you ... to protect you until your case
> has been decided upon by the Dominion Government.[32]

Riel replied on May 15

> Would I go to Batoche, who is going to receive me?   I
> will go to fulfill God's will.[33]

Louis Riel voluntarily surrendered to Major General Frederick Middleton's scouts on May 15, 1885 three days after the defeat of the Metis at Batoche. Shortly after the battle of Batoche, Captain Hugh John Macdonald (Prime Minister John A. Macdonald's son) wrote to his second wife Gertrude:

> ... had our fellows taken [Riel], he'd have been brought
> in in a coffin, and there'd be no thoughts of a trial.[34]

If Riel had so chosen, he could have escaped to the United States with Gabriel Dumont and Michel Dumas. On arriving in the United States, Dumont and Dumas were initially arrested but U.S. President Grover Cleveland ordered them freed soon after, probably because he considered them political refugees.[35] They were never brought to trial. In deliberately giving himself up, Riel likely thought that his trial could

---

[32]   Desmond Morton and Reginald H. Roy, *Telegrams of the North-West Campaign* 1885, p. 278.

[33]   *The Queen v. Louis Riel,* p. 381 (Exhibit No. 19).

[34]   "Sore Feet, No Whiskey", *Winnipeg Tribune,* August 26, 1958. Letter read posthumously at the Manitoba Historical Society.

[35]   Charlebois, p. 204.

be used as a showcase for exposing the grievances of the Metis and of himself. These would include the manner in which the Metis had been ignored by the federal government and federal officials. The trial would also be a forum whereby Riel could justify his actions. This is indicated by his speeches to the court, one before and one after the guilty verdict. In the first speech he referred to some of the tribulations suffered by the Metis and in the second one he stated that he wished "to have a trial that will cover the space of 15 years" and "... I wish my career should be tried; not the last part of it." In the result, as will be seen, these objectives were not realized.

After his surrender, a forlorn and dishevelled Riel was turned over to General Middleton. Middleton (a paunchy, rotund, 59 year-old, mustachioed, British career soldier) was the commander of Canada's home militia force and was the head of the Canadian forces in the North-West, specifically appointed to deal with the North-West Uprising. Middleton testified at the Riel trial that he had conversations with Riel and that Riel

> was a man of rather acute intellect ... able to hold his own
> upon any argument or topic we happened to touch on.[36]

2.   THE TRIAL SITE

Middleton's original instructions from Minister of Militia Caron in Ottawa were to send Riel to Winnipeg.[37] He was to be escorted there by Captain George H. Young of the Winnipeg Field Battery. In his evidence at the trial, Young stated that he was Brigade Major of the Infantry Brigade of General Middleton's forces. Also along on the trip from Gariepy's Crossing to Regina was Rev. Charles B. Pitblado, a Winnipeg clergyman. Reverend Pitblado was later called as a Crown rebuttal witness with respect to Riel's sanity. Young later testified that as he had known Riel "in the rebellion of '69 and 70", General Middleton had him identify the prisoner as Riel. He also stated about Riel that

> I found that I had a mind against my own, and fully equal to
> it; better educated and much more clever than myself.[38]

---

[36]   *The Queen v. Louis Riel,* p. 281.
[37]   Morton and Roy, p. 288.
[38]   *The Queen v. Louis Riel* , p. 277-78.

By a remarkable coincidence, Young was the son of Rev. George Young who had been Thomas Scott's pastor in 1870 at the time of Scott's execution by Riel's provisional government.

However, while Riel was en route to Winnipeg, Ottawa feverishly telegraphed to Middleton to take Riel to Regina instead of Winnipeg. The legal and political explanation for this sudden switch, never publicly declared, is discussed hereafter. However Militia Minister Caron said in his telegram to General Middleton

> Minister of Justice for judicial reasons wishes prisoners sent
> to Regina and not to Winnipeg.[39]

In his letter of May 21, 1885 to Prime Minister Macdonald, the Minister of Justice Alexander Campbell stated that if Riel and the others were "tried in Manitoba, there will be a miscarriage of justice."[40]

The entourage escorting Riel departed from Batoche on Monday, May 18th and arrived in Regina on Saturday May 23rd. There he was turned over to Inspector R. Burton Deane of the North West Mounted Police ("NWMP"). Riel was incarcerated in a small cell in the NWMP barracks and a 20 pound ball and chain were fastened to his leg.

The relaxed and friendly atmosphere he experienced at the hands of General Middleton and Captain Young was not to be replicated under the imperious Inspector Deane. Deane, somewhat of a martinet, resolved that Riel would be allowed no visitors without the Prime Minister's approval (and subsequently that of the Chief Crown Prosecutor) nor permitted to read newspapers or anything related to the uprising. Deane subsequently recorded that "I religiously held to this regulation of my own making, and it saved me a great deal of trouble."[41] Riel was held incommunicado and was unable to obtain relevant information until he was able to retain lawyers in mid-June, primarily through the efforts of B. Romuald Fiset, a Quebec physician and Riel's former Montreal classmate. Riel was held in custody for 66 days prior to the first day of his trial in Regina on July 20th. The courtroom was on the main floor of a two-story office building owned by the Canada

---

[39]   Morton, and Roy, p. 308.
[40]   "Macdonald Papers", National Archives of Canada ("NAC") MG26A, Vol. 197, p. 82819-24.
[41]   Captain R. B. Deane *Mounted Police Life in Canada; A Record of Thirty-One Years Service*, p. 185.

North West Land Company, which was ironically a subsidiary of the Canadian Pacific Railway.

The reason why the Minister of Militia redirected Riel from Winnipeg to Regina was that if Riel's trial were to take place in Winnipeg he would have legal rights unavailable to him in Regina where the less advanced laws of the North-West Territories prevailed. With these additional rights noted below, a Winnipeg conviction was most unlikely. Without these rights, the prospects of a conviction in Regina were much stronger.

Prime Minister John A. Macdonald and Minister of Justice Alexander Campbell, who were intimately involved in various decisions relating to Riel's trial, were thoroughly aware of the more expansive legal rights which Riel would enjoy in Winnipeg. To prevent Riel from having these additional legal rights they made a conscious decision to have Riel tried in Regina. In fact as noted above Campbell wrote to Macdonald stating in effect that if Riel was sent to Winnipeg Campbell would be fearful of "a miscarriage of justice".[42] A trial in Regina as opposed to a trial in Winnipeg would be a major beneficial contributor to the aim of the Prime Minister, the Minister of Justice and other persons determined to see Riel hang. A Regina trial would be an ominous portent for Riel and those who wished to see him avoid the gallows.

The following were the principal disparities between the laws applicable in Winnipeg and the laws applicable in Regina as they related to the Riel trial. In Winnipeg, Riel would have been entitled to: a jury of 12 men; a mixed jury of one-half French-speaking and one-half English-speaking jurors; and an independent superior court judge with security of tenure. None of these would be available to him in a trial at Regina. In Regina the jury would consist of only 6 men; Riel would have no right to insist on having French-speaking jurors; a stipendiary magistrate (holding office at the pleasure of the federal government)[43] and an even more inferior justice of the peace would preside at the trial.

As noted below in Chapter V "The Jury and its Selection", the jury in Regina consisted of white English-speaking, Anglo-Saxon Protestants.

---

42   "Macdonald Papers", NAC MG26A, Vol. 197, p. 82819-24.
43   Tenure was effectively at the discretion of the Cabinet lead by John A. Macdonald in which Alexander Campbell was Minister of Justice. A stipendiary magistrate could be peremptorily discharged at any time.

It was obvious that the likelihood of obtaining a unanimous verdict in Regina with jurors of that make-up would be more attainable than one on which a half-dozen French speaking Metis would be members.

Macdonald and Campbell were cognizant of the different legal procedures that would prevail in Regina over those applicable in Winnipeg and elsewhere in Canada. Because of the politically sensitive nature of a treason charge, Campbell was obviously concerned about the highest criminal charge in the land being tried before the lowest judicial official in the land. He requested a legal opinion from his hand picked Crown prosecutors, Britton B. Osler and Christopher Robinson of Toronto, with respect to a treason trial being held before a stipendiary magistrate. Osler and Robinson replied that it would be "anomalous and inappropriate" to have a stipendiary magistrate preside over such a trial based on an ordinary information without an indictment.[44] The problem was that the applicable law in the North-West Territories made no provision for a grand jury. Osler and Robinson posed a couple of legislative alternatives to a trial before a humble magistrate, i.e. a special commission to carry on the trial, or a law empowering the government to have the accused tried anywhere in Canada. These suggestions were politically unpalatable to Macdonald and Campbell, as they would give the Opposition a parliamentary opportunity to publicly upbraid the Government over its handling, or mishandling, of affairs in the North-West Territories. Osler and Robinson clearly anticipated the unacceptability of their advice in this respect and added a comment that in that event their opinion was to use the procedure under the *North-West Territories Act* of 1880 giving Riel the benefit of any other law not clearly inconsistent with it. The Government naturally elected to proceed under the 1880 Act, which related to the make-up of the court and trial procedure. However the charge itself was laid under the *English Statute of Treasons* of 1351.

The change of location was another telltale sign which made manifest the political nature of the impending trial and the determination of the Prime Minister to ensure that no stone was left unturned which would assist in the conviction and hanging of the prairie rebel. A further indication was the selection by Macdonald and Campbell of Osler and Robinson, two highly experienced senior lawyers

---

44   "Macdonald Papers", NAC RG 13 A2, Vol. 62, File 596, June 16, 1885.

from Toronto, to act as Crown prosecutors. These legal heavyweights were to be assisted by the Deputy Minister of Justice, by a Quebec lawyer and by a fifth lawyer from Regina. Brief biographies of the Crown prosecutors and the defense counsel appear in Chapter VIII. This majestic array of legal talent for Her Majesty was intended to make good Justice Minister Campbell's assurance to the Prime Minister that great care would be taken "to satisfy the Country that the prosecution is well done" and that there would be no unpardonable want of thoroughness.[45]

3. THE CHARGES

Other demonstrations of the unwavering resolve of Macdonald and Campbell (the two former law partners from Kingston, Ontario) to see Riel's neck broken on the gibbet was the fact that of the 72 persons charged with treason only Riel was charged with "high treason". They had Riel charged under an ancient statute of the British Parliament (not Canada) enacted over 530 years previously. The other 71 prisoners were charged with the lesser offense of treason-felony under an *1868 Statute of Canada*. There was a life and death difference between "high treason" and "treason-felony". A conviction for high treason under the archaic British statute called for a mandatory death penalty, while a finding of guilt for treason-felony, the made in Canada law, carried a maximum punishment of life imprisonment. When the *1351 Statute of Treasons* became law in England, a high treason convict after being hanged was disembowelled, decapitated and dismembered, his four limbs being cut or ripped asunder from his body. An aristocrat usually paid an executioner between £7 to £10 for being beheaded.[46]

An example of a macabre sentence of drawing and quartering is that imposed on Sir Thomas More who was convicted of treason with respect to King Henry VIII. The sentence was as follows:

> Sir Thomas More, you are to be drawn on a hurdle through the City of London to Tyburn, there to be hanged until you be half dead, after that cut down yet alive, your bowels to be taken out of your body and burned before you, your privy parts cut off, your head cut off, your body to be divided in

---

45   "Macdonald Papers" NAC Vol. 197, p. 82813-15, letter of May 18, 1885.
46   Ivor H. Evans, ed., *Brewer's Dictionary of Phrase & Fable*, p. 528.

four parts, and your head and body to be set at such places
as the King shall assign.

King Henry VIII mercifully commuted the sentence to beheading and impaling of More's head upon a pole above London Bridge.

However, fortunately for Riel, this savage mutilation under English law had ceased by the time of the Riel trial. There was no doubt that the Prime Minister, John A. Macdonald, wanted Riel (a bane in his life during and after the Red River Resistance), executed. There was no doubt that charges carrying a mandatory death penalty would be laid. In addition to his longstanding enmity for Riel there were other factors which undoubtedly influenced Macdonald. There was a clamorous anti-Riel cacophony emanating from many supporters in Macdonald's main political constituency, Ontario, who were vitriolically shrieking for the revenge of the 1870 death of Thomas Scott, and of others during the most recent insurrection. There was also Macdonald's firm resolve to show the West that his government was in charge and that the ringleader of the resort to force to remedy "perceived" grievances against his administration would be faced with the harshest penalty of the law.

Macdonald knew that treason was a political crime. He also knew that if Riel was acquitted the verdict would be a slap in the face to Macdonald and to his government for their negligent handling of the affairs of the North-West Territories. As well it would be an implicit recognition that their maladministration was a *"sine qua non"*, leading inevitably to the North-West Uprising.

Macdonald could have had Riel tried for treason-felony, as 71 others were. However as noted, this would have meant, at the most, a sentence of life imprisonment on conviction, not Riel's dispatch to "the undiscovered country from whose bourn no traveler returns."[47]

On July 6, 1885, Riel was charged with six counts of high treason. Three of the charges, relating separately to activities at Duck Lake, Fish Creek and Batoche, were based on the principle of law known as the doctrine of natural allegiance. The other three charges, while almost identical to the first three, were slightly varied to encompass the doctrine of local allegiance. Natural allegiance was the legal obedience, which a subject owed to his or her sovereign at all times, and in all places, so long as the relation of subject and sovereign subsisted. The term

---

[47]   William Shakespeare, *Hamlet*, Act III scene 1.

49

"subject" is generally used to refer to a person born in a state which has a monarch or other sovereign and also one naturalized therein. The term "citizen" refers to a member of a state or nation, such as one with a non-monarchial form of government, who owes his allegiance and is entitled to full civil rights either by birth or naturalization. Local allegiance was the allegiance owed by an alien while he or she was resident or continued within the dominions and the protection of the English Crown. English common law had established, between sovereign and resident alien, the reciprocal duties of allegiance and protection.

In 1945 the British House of Lords went so far as to hold that the duty of local allegiance extended to an American citizen living in Germany who, while living in Germany and holding a British passport, broadcast German propaganda. This was in the famous high-treason trial of "Lord Haw-Haw", William Joyce. This case is a leading English case dealing with the doctrine of allegiance in relation to treason and provides an historical analysis of the doctrine of allegiance.[48]

In the Riel case, the first three charges were founded on a breach of the duty of natural allegiance owed to the Queen, the other three on a breach of the duty of local allegiance owed to the Queen. The reason for the duplication lay in the fact that several years after the expiry of Riel's government-ordered five-year exile in 1875, he became an American citizen. British law had been that if one was born a British subject one died a British subject regardless of whether that person later became a naturalized citizen of another country.

This British stand on natural allegiance was contrary to that of the United States. To forestall potential antagonism by the American government to Riel, a United States citizen, being charged only as a British subject, government officials prudently added the charges based on the doctrine of local allegiance, a doctrine also observed in the United States. It was fortunate that they did so since the doctrine of natural allegiance under British law was wiped out by the *Naturalization Act, 1870 of the United Kingdom* which came into force on May 12, 1870, three days before Rupert's Land became part of Canada. Section 6 of

---

[48]   *Joyce v. Director of Public Prosecutions* [1946] 1 All E.R. 186 (House of Lords). Lord Coke in *Calvin's Case* (1608), 7 Co. Rep Ia; 77 E.R. 377; Foster's, *Crown Law,* and William Blackstone, *Commentaries on the Laws of England, 1795* all dealt with allegiance.

this Act provided that a person ceased to be a British subject by voluntarily becoming a naturalized citizen of a foreign state. Section 9 of the *Naturalization Act, Canada, 1881* was virtually identical to the English Act, but it was not clear whether it, as well as the English Act, were in force in the North-West Territories in 1885. In light of the foregoing, as well as the fact that no testimony whatsoever was adduced at Riel's trial proving that he was a British subject, the first three charges against Riel, founded on natural allegiance, were invalid.

Riel had been charged both as a British subject and as an alien. The six charges were couched in a fusty, musty early Edwardian legal argot which, aside from the gravity of the charges, would in some respects now be considered rather droll and eccentric. Each charge stated that Riel was "moved and seduced by the instigation of the devil as a false traitor." In every instance it was "our Lady the Queen" from whom he withdrew his allegiance, to whom he was not faithful, whom he endeavoured "to depose ..." etc. The charges stated somewhat pleonastically that Riel "most wickedly, maliciously and traitorously did levy and make war against our said Lady the Queen ...". All charges also stated that he attempted and endeavoured "by force and arms to subvert and destroy the constitution and government of this realm ...", including depriving and deposing "our said Lady the Queen of and from the style, honor and **kingly** name of the Imperial Crown." [Emphasis added.] Nowhere was there any mention of Riel being an American citizen. Three of the charges referred to his "being a subject of our Lady the Queen" (to cover natural allegiance) and the other three (to cover local allegiance) to his

> then living within the Dominion of Canada and under the protection of our Sovereign Lady the Queen.

Because of the apparent omission of some words in the first charge relating to Duck Lake in the printed copies of the transcript of the trial such as the *Canada Sessional Papers*, and *The Queen v. Louis Riel*, the author endeavoured to obtain a copy of the original indictment of July 6, 1885 actually signed by Alexander David Stewart and Magistrate Hugh Richardson. However none of the National Archives, the Saskatchewan or Manitoba Archives, or the Privy Council Office in London were able to locate the originally signed and sworn indictment. The original Riel indictment appears to be lost. The omission of certain words from the first charge in the printed copies is due to a stenographic error that occurs from time to time. Errors happen when, in transcribing a document, a stenographer skips a line and the error goes unnoticed. This same problem of skipping a line occurs in printing and publishing.

Five of the six charges printed in the *Canada Sessional Papers*, included the phrase:

> ... gathered together against our said Lady the Queen, **most wickedly, maliciously and traitorously did levy and make war against our said Lady the Queen,** at the locality of ... [Emphasis added.]

However, the first charge (re natural allegiance and Duck Lake) did not contain the emphasized words. The transcriber mistakenly jumped from the first "Lady the Queen" to the second "Lady the Queen" inadvertently leaving out the emphasized words in the first charge.

The author obtained from the National Archives of Canada ("NAC") a photocopy of a signed copy of a Notice to Louis Riel dated July 8, 1885 ("Records relating to Louis Riel and the North-West Uprising", NAC, RG 13, F2, Vol.819, p. 3175-78). The Notice, with a copy of the charges annexed (and numbered 1 to 6), confirmed that the emphasized words actually appeared in the original signed and sworn indictment. The Notice stated that "hereunto annexed is a copy of the Charges and Accusations against you for the Treasons therein set forth ...", and was signed by "B. B. Osler" and "G. W. Burbidge", two of the Crown prosecutors. The Notice referred to the charges in the plural, unlike the trial magistrate, Hugh Richardson, who dealt with the six charges as though they were only one charge (see section 1 of Chapter XIV). The first charge annexed to the Notice (relating to natural allegiance and Duck Lake) contained the above emphasized words. These emphasized words were subsequently omitted from the typed transcript of the trial undoubtedly due to a stenographic error. The typed transcript of the charges received from the NAC also contained a number of other errors ("Records of the Department of Justice", NAC, RG 13, Vol. 1421-24, file 202A). Reference is made to Chapter XIX concerning the Privy Council's statement, related to use of shorthand at the trial, that "no complaint is made of inaccuracy or mistake." It should also be noted that Crown counsel Osler in his address to the jury specifically stated that Riel

> ... is charged first as a **subject** of our Sovereign Lady the Queen ... **with levying war at Duck Lake**, Fish Creek and Batoche. [Emphasis added.]

He later referred to Riel being indicted under the *1351 Statute of Treasons* with respect to **"a person who levies war"**, [49] against the King. [Emphasis added.] In charging the jury, Magistrate Richardson also specifically stated that the charge of high treason laid against Riel "is that of levying war against Her Majesty." He then read verbatim section 4 of the *1351 Statute of Treasons* which deals specifically with levying war against the King in his realm. Richardson again stated that Riel was charged "with **levying war** upon Her Majesty **at the locality of Duck Lake** ... Fish Creek and Batoche." [50] [Emphasis added.]

The following is a specimen of the fourth treason charge:

> 4 That the said Louis Riel, then living within the Dominion of Canada and under the protection of our Sovereign Lady the Queen, not regarding the duty of his allegiance nor having the fear of God in his heart, but being moved and seduced by the instigation of the devil as a false traitor against our said Lady the Queen, and wholly withdrawing the allegiance, fidelity and obedience which he should and of right ought to bear towards our said Lady the Queen on the twenty-sixth day of March in the year aforesaid together with divers other false traitors to the said Alexander David Stewart unknown, armed and arrayed in a war-like manner, that is to say with guns, rifles, pistols, bayonets and other weapons, being then unlawfully, maliciously and traitorously assembled and gathered together against our said Lady the Queen most wickedly, maliciously and traitorously did levy and make war against our said Lady the Queen at the locality known as Duck Lake in the said the North-West Territories of Canada and within this realm, and did then maliciously and traitorously attempt and endeavor by force and arms to subvert and destroy the constitution and government of this realm as by law established, and deprive and depose our said Lady the Queen of and from the style, honor and kingly name of the Imperial Crown of this realm, in contempt of our said Lady the Queen and her laws, to the evil example of all others in the like case offending, contrary to the duty of the allegiance of him, the said Louis Riel, against the form of

---

[49]   *The Queen v. Louis Riel*, p. 65; 67.
[50]   *The Queen v. Louis Riel*, p. 343-44.

the statute in such case made and provided and against the
peace of our said Lady the Queen, her Crown and dignity.[51]

The charges averred that Riel's activities were "against the form of
the statute in such case made and provided." There was no specific
mention in the information and complaint that the statute in question
was the hoary *Statute of Treasons of 1351* passed in the 25th year of
Edward III's rule under the title "A Declaration which Offences shall be
Adjudged Treason". It was Chapter II of Statute 5. Chapter I was
entitled "By What Measures the King's Purveyors shall take Corn".
Hence, in the 1351 statutes taking corn preceded taking heads.

At least one of Riel's counsel was confused as to the statute under
which Riel's life was to be determined. On the first day of the trial (July
20, 1885) Thomas Cooke Johnstone (one of Riel's counsel) in arguing a
demurrer in open court as to the information, stated "As I understand it,
you are proceeding under 31 Victoria." Britton Bath Osler, senior
counsel for the prosecution (whose first name seemed most fitting for a
representative of Her Most Britannic Majesty), responded "You are
misunderstanding us then. 25 Edward III is the one." Edward III
became the 15 year-old King of England in 1327 and reigned until his
death in 1377. The statute 31 Victoria, under which Johnstone
mistakenly thought the Crown was proceeding, was the *1868 Canadian
Treason-Felony Statute*, Chapter 69, entitled "An Act for the Better
Security of the Crown and of the Government". Section 5 of this
Canadian Statute dealt with levying war as a treason-felony, not high
treason, and under section 5 the maximum punishment was life
imprisonment not death. This was a startling misapprehension for Riel's
counsel to make at the outset of a capital trial.

Some historians are confused as to the reference year of the *Statute
of Treasons*, stating it is 1352.[52] In the infamous Lord Haw-Haw case
referred to above, William Joyce was charged with high treason for
"adhering to the King's enemies...contrary to the *Treason Act*, 1351." In
A Concise Law Dictionary by Osborn,[53] the author discussed treason and
the *Treason Act, 1351*. When this *Treason Act* was passed it primarily
encompassed indignities and wrongs against the King, his consort, his

---

[51]   *Canada Sessional Papers*, (1886) No. 43, p. 15; *The Queen v. Louis Riel*, p. 5-6.
[52]   Thomas "A Judicial Murder-The Trial of Louis Riel", p. 37; Flanagan, *Riel
and the Rebellion* , p. 121; Friesen, p. 233.
[53]   P. G. Osborn, *A Concise Law Dictionary*, 5th ed, p. 317.

elder children, his Chancellor and judges. For example violating the King's eldest unmarried daughter constituted high treason. The Act also outlawed levying war against the King in his Realm (the crime with which Riel was charged), or adhering to his enemies in his Realm, or giving to them aid and comfort in the Realm, or elsewhere. As noted later in this text (with significance to the meaning of "Realm"), the *1351 Statute of Treasons* also made treasonous counterfeiting, and bringing false money into the Realm.

Unlike the situation when the *Statute of Treasons* became law, over time treason evolved, by judicial decisions, from an act of personal treachery against the King, his family and appointees to include seditious activities against the current governing authorities. This meant that the political regime in power at the time of the treason had an especial vested interest in the outcome of the trial over and above its normal role as enforcer of the peace. Exoneration of an accused charged with treason is tantamount to a censure of the government's activities or inactivities which led to the charge and a vindication of the alleged treacherous acts, results highly abhorrent to politicians in power.

If it had so chosen, or been directed to do so, the prosecution could have proceeded under a treason statute other than the Edwardian *Statute of Treasons*. The *Fenian Act* made it treasonable for an alien of a country at peace with Canada to endeavour to levy war against Canada. However, this would have imposed a burden of proof on the Crown to establish that Riel was an alien, which as Osler stated in his address to the jury, was "a responsibility the Crown did not choose to assume." Another treason statute that was available was the *1868 Canadian Statute* for treason-felony commented on above. About this Statute Osler informed the jury that "we have not thought it advisable to proceed under" that Statute.[54] What he did not divulge was that the inadvisability with respect to this Canadian Statute was that it made no provision for the death penalty, "a consummation devoutly to be wished"[55] by the Crown.

---

54   *The Queen v. Louis Riel,* p. 67.
55   Shakespeare, *Hamlet* Act III Scene I.

4.   THE TRIAL MAGISTRATE

Under Section 74 of the *North-West Territories Act, 1880*,[56] the Governor was empowered to appoint a barrister or advocate of five years standing in any of the Provinces to be a stipendiary magistrate within the North-West Territories. A stipendiary magistrate held office at the pleasure of the federal government and could be dismissed by it whenever it saw fit to do so. A stipendiary magistrate, as the name implies, was paid a stipend for his services, and was a minor official. Section 89 of the *North-West Territories Act of 1880* provided that an annual sum not exceeding $3,000 (not a small amount in those days) was payable to a stipendiary magistrate by the federal government. Pursuant to Section 76, a stipendiary magistrate was authorized to try certain crimes therein mentioned in a summary way without a jury. Under Section 76(5), a stipendiary magistrate, assisted by a justice of the peace with a jury of six men, was authorized to try "all other criminal cases". This was held to extend to the crime of high treason. Nowhere else in Canada was the conduct of a life or death treason trial entrusted to such a low-level official.

Hugh Richardson was the stipendiary magistrate in Regina who presided over the trial. Richardson was born in London, England in 1826. His family moved to the Toronto area while he was a child. Richardson was called to the bar of Upper Canada in 1847 and after practising law at Woodstock, Ontario until 1872, he worked as chief clerk in the Department of Justice in Ottawa for four years. He went to the North-West Territories in 1876. He became legal adviser to the Lieutenant Governor of the North-West Territories from 1876 to 1887 (a position he held throughout Riel's trial) and he was also appointed a stipendiary magistrate shortly after his arrival in the North-West. Richardson did not speak French. In the House of Commons Debates after the trial, Edward Blake the Leader of the Opposition restated his earlier objections to Richardson having been selected as the presiding magistrate in the trial of Louis Riel and stated:

> ... he is the legal adviser to the Executive of the North-West; he is so appointed during the pleasure of the Government; he is so paid a salary during the pleasure of the Government. He answers to the Attorney-General, the

---

[56]   *Statutes of Canada* 43, Vic. C.25.

> legal adviser of the Government in the North-West
> Territories; and it needs not to enlarge upon the relations
> and responsibilities of a Lieutenant Governor of the
> North-West Territories to a rebellion in the North-West
> ...it was an unhappy choice to select, of the three or four
> judges, the person who filled the position of the political
> adviser, the political law officer, to the Government in the
> Territories to be the judge in this particular trial. He is also
> the recipient of special favors.[57]

Blake then listed Magistrate Richardson's special favors. One of these favors listed was an additional salary, as legal adviser to the Lieutenant Governor. Blake also mentioned that "the judge chooses the jury panel". In these quotes Blake was disclosing his deep concern with the serious conflict of interest that Magistrate Richardson had in presiding at the trial of Riel. At the same time that Richardson was presiding at Riel's trial, he was a paid legal and political adviser to government officials of a government that was prosecuting Riel.

Prior to the Riel trial, there were incidents involving Richardson which indicated a bias on his part against the Metis.

In 1880, Richardson wrote to Colonel John Stoughton Dennis, the Deputy Minister of the Interior, suggesting prompt attention to Metis grievances because the half-breed population had been

> latterly subjected to the evil influences of leading spirits of
> the Manitoba troubles of 1870.[58]

Richardson's comments had cast the "leading spirits" as "evil" and, in the same letter, up to "no good". The main leading spirit of the "Manitoba troubles" of 1869-70 was, of course, Louis Riel.

Richardson was present at a meeting on March 12, 1885 at which North West Mounted Police Commissioner Acheson Gosford Irvine, Assistant Indian Commissioner Hayter Reed, and Lawrence Clarke (a Chief Factor of the Hudson's Bay Company) were also present. Clarke has been portrayed as an agent provocateur who, for personal reasons, wanted an influx of soldiers and resulting influx of funds to the North-West Territories. Clarke later contributed to the hostile environment by

[57]   *Debates of House of Commons, Session 1886*, Vol. 1, March 19, 1886, p. 241.
[58]   *Canada Sessional Papers* , (1885), 48 Victoria (No.116), p. 80-81.

falsely stating to a number of Metis that 500 NWMP were on their way to disband them and imprison Riel and others. [59]

At this meeting (between Irvine, Reed, Clarke and Richardson) the Metis situation was discussed.   The meeting, with Richardson's participation, concluded that in certain circumstances Riel should be arrested and that he and his followers should be prohibited from maintaining their senseless agitation. Shortly after, Commissioner Irvine sent a contingent of 100 constables from Regina to Fort Carlton.[60]

The following points made Richardson particularly unsuitable to preside over Riel's trial:

(i)   his malevolent categorization of the Metis leaders in the context of the "Manitoba troubles" of which Riel had been a leader;

(ii)   his participation in the meeting with Irvine, Reed and Clarke to discuss putting down the Metis agitation;

(iii)   his past position as an employee of the Department of Justice coupled with his past and continuing position as a legal adviser to the Lieutenant Governor of the North-West Territories;

(iv)   his holding office at the pleasure of Ottawa;

(v)   his knowledge that his stipends and "special favors" would be terminated if he no longer enjoyed Ottawa's pleasure;

(vi)   the fact that he was an Anglo-Saxon Orangeman;

(vii)   his total lack of experience in conducting a high treason trial.

Compounding this image of a non-objective, non-impartial, non-independent governmental appointee, adviser and magistrate with hostile preconceptions of Metis leaders was a question as to Richardson's judicial competence. The following are a few examples.

Prior to evidence being given in the trial, Riel's counsel (Charles Fitzpatrick and James Greenshields) in arguing that Richardson had no jurisdiction to try the offences against Riel, presented detailed historical facts and law to support their position. They dealt with the *Magna Carta* of 1215, judicial precedent, Lord Coke's interpretations, trial by jury, due

---

[59]   Don McLean, *1885, Metis Rebellion or Government Conspiracy?*, p. 97; Stanley, *The Birth of Western Canada*, p. 443 n. 69 (for a discussion relating to the 500 NWMP).

[60]   D. N. Sprague *Canada and the Metis, 1869-1885*, p. 172.

process of law, human rights, Imperial statutes, Canadian statutes, the British Constitution, the Canadian Constitution, etc., etc.   Crown counsel Christopher Robinson and Britton Osler were equally thorough in their comprehensive presentations.   At one point Richardson interrupted Greenshields to state "That has been repealed" referring to a statute of George IV cited by Riel's counsel to which Greenshields responded "Clause 5 has been repealed, but that is the only clause that is repealed."[61] Fitzpatrick summed up by contending the *North-West Territories Act of 1880* with respect to capital cases was *ultra vires* (beyond the powers) of the Canadian Parliament. After extensive and eloquent presentations by counsel (which in small print covers some 30 pages) Richardson ruled against the plea to the jurisdiction and Fitzpatrick's contention in eleven words: "Well, as I cannot hold that, I must sustain the demurrer."[62] No elaboration or reasons were given to counsel.

In his charge to the jury, Richardson did not instruct the jury that each of the first three counts required them to be satisfied that Riel was a British subject before he could be convicted on these counts. Neither did he instruct them that they could bring in a separate verdict on each of the counts. He lumped all six charges together. At one point he said "that any salient points that struck me as important … are brought to your attention."[63] He apparently did not think it salient to tell the jury that there was not a tittle of evidence presented in Court to prove that Riel was a British subject at the relevant times, and that this was a fundamental requirement of guilt on the first three counts.

Richardson presided at the treason-felony trials of the two "white rebels" William Henry Jackson and Thomas Scott (who was not the notorious Thomas Scott of the 1870 Red River Resistance). William Henry Jackson had served as Riel's personal secretary not long after Riel's arrival in the North-West Territories. There had been political lobbying by his family to have Jackson declared insane because of his peculiar ideas on religious matters and it succeeded.[64] Crown counsel Britton Osler and Jackson's own counsel concurred in pleading his insanity at the time of the uprising. However of three witnesses called

---

61   *The Queen v. Louis Riel,* p. 20.
62   *The Queen v. Louis Riel,* p. 41.
63   *The Queen v. Louis Riel,* p. 345.
64   Sandra E. Bingaman "The Trials of the 'White Rebels', 1885", *Saskatchewan History* Vol. XXV, Spring, 1972, p. 41 @ p. 44.

one was Dr. Augustus Jukes, the NWMP surgeon who had no expertise or training in the field of insanity. Jukes later testified as a rebuttal witness for the Crown at Riel's trial and gave a medical report on Riel's sanity to Prime Minister John A. Macdonald after Riel was found guilty (see Chapter XII section 2 and Chapter XXI).

In the Jackson trial, Jukes gave his opinion as to Jackson's "mental hallucinations" and "peculiar ideas on religious matters" after his imprisonment in Regina towards the end of June 1885. He gave no evidence as to Jackson's state of mind at the time of the uprising. An acquittal based on an insanity plea required proof that an accused was insane when the offence was committed, not at a later date. Jukes' evidence was mistimed and should not have been admitted in Jackson's trial. In that trial Richardson should not have permitted Jukes to so testify, and in his summing up should have instructed the jury to give no weight whatsoever to Jukes' testimony. The entire evidence as to insanity was brief and there was no vehement piercing cross-examination, as there subsequently was at Riel's trial. The facts lead one to the conclusion that either Richardson was ignorant of proper legal procedure or he was unquestioningly going along with Crown counsel and the members of Jackson's family who had conducted a lobbying campaign to achieve their desired outcome. Their lobbying had resulted in Jackson's case coming to the notice of both Edward Blake the leader of the Liberal Party and Alexander Campbell the Minister of Justice. Deputy Minister of Justice, George W. Burbidge, subsequently assented to the insanity defence. The jury quickly acquitted Jackson without retiring to the jury room.

In the treason-felony case of the other "white rebel" Thomas Scott, Crown counsel (including the ubiquitous Osler) presented a weak case. However Sandra Bingaman (who made a study of the two "white-rebel cases") observed that:

(i)   because of Richardson, proceedings were not kept at a very high level;

(ii)   misbehaviour by counsel on both sides was Richardson's final responsibility by not ordering them to desist in their "personal exchanges"; and

(iii)   he should also "be faulted for his charge to the jury."[65]

---

[65]   Bingaman, p. 52-53.

Richardson told the jury that the evidence supported a finding of guilty, but the jury found Scott not guilty in about 30 minutes.

In the trial of Chief Big Bear for treason-felony, Richardson displayed an ignorance of the law of treason in relation to the "constructive levying of war" and the "direct levying of war". The differentiation was vital to Big Bear's defence. Constructive levying of war required proof that the prisoner actually aided and assisted in the violence, whereas in a direct levying of war the prosecution need only prove that he was present with the insurrectionists. Crown counsel Osler had agreed with this interpretation by defence counsel Beverley Robertson in the treason-felony trial of Chief One Arrow a short time before.

In his charge to the jury in the Big Bear case, Richardson misinterpreted the law on a point crucial to Big Bear's chance for freedom. Richardson stated that fear of death was the only legal excuse for Big Bear being found in the rebel camp. However that was the law in relation only to the "direct" levying of war, not the "constructive" levying of war. Big Bear's witnesses and many Crown witnesses swore that he had on various occasions endeavoured to halt the strife, not aid it. The legal text (Archbold's *Pleading, Evidence, and Practice in Criminal Law*) on which Richardson was relying made clear that in "constructive" levying of war one who did not actually aid and assist in the violence was not a traitor, but merely a rioter. A disconcerted Robertson asked Richardson to summon the jury from the jury room to clarify the law to them, but Richardson's attempt to do so added to the jury's befuddlement. The result was that a weak Crown case resulted in a conviction and a sentence of three years imprisonment for Big Bear.

Because of the relatively primitive legal system in the North-West Territories, no appeal was allowed with respect to a magistrate's charge to the jury.[66] Richardson made one preposterous statement to Big Bear prior to sentencing the Chief. In addressing the Court, Big Bear frequently stated "when we owned the country". In sentencing Big Bear, Richardson (speaking with forked-tongue) told him that they never owned the land and that the land belonged to Queen Victoria. She had allowed the Indians to make use of it, but she wanted to make other use

---

[66]   *Senate Debates*, 1877, p. 320 (Hon. R. W. Scott, Secretary of State, stated that "the law was constructed for a primitive state of society.")

of it and that she gave the Indians the "choicest portions of the country".[67]

In the treason-felony trial of Chief One Arrow,[68] the distinction between direct levying of war and constructive levying of war continued to elude Richardson. With respect to this case an amusing incident is recorded in a letter of August 14, 1885 from Father Louis Cochin to Archbishop A. A. Taché concerning the translation of the treason-felony charge against Chief One Arrow. The rendition into Cree of the accusation against One Arrow farcically emerged as his having knocked off the Queen's bonnet and stabbed her in the behind with a sword. This so discombobulated One Arrow, who had never in his life set eyes on the Queen, that he asked the interpreter if he was drunk. [69] One Arrow cried out in astonishment when the interpreter told him that it was One Arrow that they were referring to. [70]

Other untoward incidents involving Richardson could be mentioned, such as his permitting hearsay evidence at the Riel trial. As well Richardson made certain prejudicial comments concerning Riel to the jury in his charge to them. Richardson's charge to the jury is discussed in Chapter XIV. There is a legal maxim that not only must justice be done it should manifestly and undoubtedly be seen to be done. The foregoing together with other significant matters detailed hereafter would lead many to conclude that, contrary to the legal maxim, justice was not only not seen to be done but was not done by having Richardson preside over the Riel trial. Justice manifestly and undoubtedly required that a magistrate with the lack of independence and biases that Richardson was encumbered with should not have participated in the Riel trial.

After the North-West Uprising trials, "liquor and horse stealing, property and contracts" were the subject of many of the trials presided over by Richardson.[71]

---

[67]   *The Regina Leader*, October 1, 1885, p. 4.
[68]   *The Queen v. Kah-pah-yak-as-to-cum* (One Arrow) CSP 1886, #52, p. 13.
[69]   Bob Beal and Rod Macleod, *Prairie Fire The 1885 North West Rebellion*, p. 309.
[70]   "Taché Papers", St. Boniface Historical Society Archives, p. T31965-68.
[71]   Louis Knafla and Richard Klumpenhouwer, "Lords of the Western Bench", *The Legal Archives Society of Alberta*, 1997, p. 158-59.

Chapter V

THE JURY AND ITS SELECTION

Riel, the French-speaking, Roman Catholic-reared, Metis was tried by an English-speaking, Anglo-Saxon, Protestant magistrate and a jury of six males, all English speaking, Anglo-Saxon Protestants. The jury was selected from a panel of 36 men who were not chosen randomly but were personally handpicked by Magistrate Richardson. Commentators differ on how many of the 36 were French. Stanley says one, Flanagan says two.[72]

Flanagan (an historian unsympathetic to Riel) pointed out the indisputable fact that the jurors chosen from the panel were men entirely of "British stock". He added that, as a result of the people from whom it was chosen, it was almost a foregone conclusion that a jury wholly of British stock would be selected. It was this entirely "British-stock" jury "of his peers" that had Riel's life in its hands. Flanagan also stated that it was highly dubious that unless the jurors were an ethnic microcosm of some larger population a fair trial was not possible, adding that this was never a principle of Canadian law.[73] Common sense as well as past trials of a number of African-Americans in the Southern United States by all-white juries are attestations to how highly dubious this unqualified assertion is in many cases. Chief Big Bear would undoubtedly not have been convicted by an ethnic microcosm jury consisting of only Indians. In fact the Supreme Court of Canada in overturning the conviction of an aboriginal man in British Columbia unanimously and sensibly ruled in June 1998 that because of evidence of widespread bias against aboriginal people in the community a realistic potential of prejudice was raised. As well "the law of evidence" may permit a judge to take judicial notice "where the basis of concern is widely known and accepted." Consequently, the Supreme Court laid down the law that both the prosecution and the defence may challenge prospective jurors about their racial views.[74] . Human nature was no different in the 1880s than it is on the eve of the new millennium. Section 11(d) of the *Canadian Charter of Rights and Freedoms*, which came

---

[72]   Stanley, *Louis Riel*, p. 418 note 29.
[73]   Flanagan, *Riel and the Rebellion*, p. 126.
[74]   *Williams v. Her Majesty the Queen*, [1998] 1 *Supreme Court Reports*, p. 1128.

into effect as part of the *Constitution Act, 1982* of Canada, provides that any person charged with an offence is entitled to "a fair and public hearing by an independent and impartial tribunal."

While the charges preferred against Riel were under the laws of Britain (i.e. the *1351 Statute of Treasons*), the trial procedure was under the laws of the North-West Territories. As noted earlier, the Canadian Government could have laid the high treason charges under the *Fenian Act*, a Canadian law also carrying the death penalty, but it chose not to do so. The result was that Riel's trial was governed by a hybrid of ancient substantive law and contemporary territorial procedural law.

The procedure for the conduct of the trial was set forth in the *North-West Territories Act of 1880* (43 Victoria, Chapter 25), a Canadian federal statute designed specifically for the North-West Territories. Section 76(1) to (4) of the Act gave a stipendiary magistrate power to try by himself without a jury certain crimes mentioned in those Sections. However a stipendiary magistrate was not qualified to sit alone to deal with criminal cases under Section 76(5) of the Act which, it was held, included treason. The Canadian Parliament, which had by the same Act authorized the appointment of stipendiary magistrates within the North-West Territories, decreed in its wisdom or otherwise that in a treason case (such as Riel's) a stipendiary magistrate was incompetent to act alone. Section 76(5) of the Act stated:

> In all other criminal cases, the stipendiary magistrate and a
> justice of the peace, with the intervention of a jury of six,
> may try any charge against any person or persons, for any
> crime.

This required that in addition to a jury scaled-down from the twelve-man requirement for criminal offences elsewhere in Canada, a justice of the peace had to team up with the magistrate on the bench. Hence Henry Le Jeune, a justice of the peace, sat next to Richardson throughout the trial. This resulted in a "wondrous strange" duo on the bench (a magistrate with a lower rank than a Queen's Bench judge, and an even more inferior justice of the peace) presiding over what Crown counsel Osler called "the highest crime known to the law".[75] There was no requirement for a justice of the peace to be a lawyer or one trained in the law. By Section 76, a stipendiary magistrate had magisterial functions appertaining to any justice of the peace, or any two justices of

---

75   *The Queen v. Louis Riel,* p. 64.

the peace. Le Jeune's presence on the bench was mere legalistic window-dressing. His participation was literally non-existent. He said nary a word from beginning to end and simply warmed a seat to meet the requirements of the law which did not entrust Richardson with the responsibility of presiding alone.

Section 76(9) authorized a stipendiary magistrate to summon prospective jurors from among such "male persons" as he may think suitable in that behalf. Women were not eligible to sit on a jury. One of the prospective jurors, Thomas Bull (a postmaster) asked to be excused, but was refused. Several jurors who were summoned did not appear.

Under subsections (10) and (11) of Section 76 of the *North-West Territories Act of 1880*, the accused had the right to peremptorily challenge up to six "persons", and the Crown had the right to challenge not more than four "jurors".[76] It appears that the 36 names on the jury panel were placed in a glass jar and slips of paper with the names of prospective jurors were extracted from it. Benjamin Limoges, the only French-Canadian on the panel according to G. F. G. Stanley, was not selected. Colonel Amyot, a colonel in the North-West under General Middleton (and also a member of Parliament for Bellechase, Quebec) read to the House of Commons answers to questions asked of F. X. Lemieux (one of Riel's lawyers) after the trial. Among other matters, Lemieux stated Limoges had fallen from a horse and "could not be present when the names of the jury were called over."[77] When the name of Michael Sullivan, an Irish Roman Catholic, was drawn from the jar the Crown quickly challenged him because he was not of "British-stock" or a Protestant. It was the only Crown challenge, while there were five for Riel. The end result of the Richardson - chosen panel and the Crown challenge was a six-man jury consisting of no Metis, no French, and no Roman Catholic members; in short a jury with little in common with the charismatic accused man.

A number of the witnesses in the trial were fluent only in French. François X. Lemieux, one of Riel lawyers, advised the Member of Parliament Colonel Amyot after the trial that the translators of English into French were not competent and had to be changed three or four

---

[76]   In using "persons" in one case and "jurors" in the other, the federal legislative draftsman breached a cardinal rule of legal drafting, i.e. consistency in the use of terms.

[77]   *Debates House of Commons*, March 11, 1886, p. 79.

times. He also stated that the translation of the evidence given in French was "mutilated, incorrectly reported, given in the lump ..."[78] Fitzpatrick and Greenshields objected to certain translations.[79] At one point during the direct examination of Father Vital Fourmond by F. X. Lemieux, Arthur Lewis (the interpreter from English to French) stated he did not feel qualified to correctly interpret Fourmond's evidence. This precipitated the amazing situation of Crown counsel Casgrain agreeing to translate the defence evidence and his law partner, defence counsel Fitzpatrick agreeing to translate the Crown evidence. This continued for a short time until Osler asked for a regular interpreter.[80]

Professor Stanley has written that a jury composed of half English and half French persons could have been constituted, and stated that in both the Jackson and Scott cases there were jurors with French names. Of course, the Crown was not as zealous in its proceedings against the 'white rebels', Scott and Jackson, neither of whom was convicted of the lesser charge of treason-felony, as it was in the case of Riel. Stanley suggested that, if the Riel jury had been made up as in these cases, this would have contributed to a diminution of the racial acrimony and political recriminations that ensued from Riel's finding of guilt by a purely English-speaking jury.[81]

The six jurors were Francis Cosgrove from Whitewood, Edwin J. Brooks from Indian Head, Henry J. Painter from Broadview, Walter Merryfield from Whitewood, Peel Deane from Broadview, and Edward Eratt from Moose Jaw. Cosgrove was elected foreman of the jury. Cosgrove, Merryfield, Deane and Eratt were farmers while Brooks and Painter were shopkeepers.

The size of the jury, the jurisdiction of a stipendiary magistrate to preside over a high treason charge and the venue of the trial were vehemently attacked by Riel's counsel before any witnesses were called. The arguments on the issues, which at times reached passionately eloquent levels, are discussed in Chapter VII.

---

[78]   *Debates House of Commons,* March 11, 1886, p. 78-79.
[79]   *The Queen v. Louis Riel,* p. 254.
[80]   *The Queen v. Louis Riel,* p. 240-41.
[81]   Stanley, *Louis Riel,* p. 418, n. 29.

Chapter VI

RIEL: BRITISH SUBJECT OR AMERICAN CITIZEN

The three counts of high treason based on Riel "being a subject of our Lady the Queen" and thereby owing her natural allegiance should not have been laid. Riel's lawyers should have made an application to the Court to dismiss these three counts for the simple reason that Riel was not "a subject of our Lady the Queen". The Crown failed to prove that Riel was a British subject. As well the judicial precedents, which stated in effect that a person who was born a British subject remained one until his death, were superseded by statute law. These matters were overlooked by Crown prosecutors, by defence counsel, by the presiding Magistrate and Justice of the Peace, and subsequently by some commentators. See for example a discussion of D. H. Brown's article in section 5(c) Chapter XVI.

With respect to the three high treason counts based on Riel being a British subject:

(i)   the Crown prosecutor should not have permitted them to be included in the charges;

(ii)   Riel's counsel should have made an application to have them dismissed at the outset of the trial;

(iii)   Magistrate Richardson should have applied the lack of evidence and the law to prohibit Riel's conviction on these three counts and he should have properly instructed the jury in this respect;

(iv)   the jury should not have brought in a guilty verdict as to these three counts. Since the law was not brought to its attention, the jury may be forgiven for having done so notwithstanding the legal maxim *"ignorantia juris quod quisque scire tenetur non excusat"* (ignorance of the law which everybody is supposed to know does not afford excuse);

(v)   the judges of the Appeal Court (the Court of Queen's Bench of Manitoba) should have applied the law, and the evidence (which they all claimed to have read) to prohibit Riel's conviction on these three counts.

The conviction of Riel on these three counts of high treason was improper and a gross miscarriage of justice. In Britain the judge-made law, which held that one born in the realm owed natural allegiance to the monarch unto death, was reversed by the *Naturalization Act of 1870* in the case of expatriation by a British subject. Under that law a British subject in a foreign state who voluntarily became naturalized in the foreign state was, pursuant to Section 6, deemed to have ceased to be a British subject and was regarded as an alien. The marginal note next to Section 6 reads "Capacity of British subject to renounce allegiance to Her Majesty." Section 6 of *The Naturalization Act, 1870* provided as follows:

> Any British subject who has at any time before, or may at any time after the passing of this Act, when in any foreign state and not under any disability voluntarily become naturalized in such state, shall from and after the time of his so having become naturalized in such foreign state, be deemed to have ceased to be a British subject and be regarded as an alien; ... [82]

In 1881 the Canadian Parliament adopted *The Naturalization Act, Canada, 1881*,[83] which in relation to expatriation was virtually a verbatim copy of the *British Naturalization Act of 1870*. The provisions in Section 9 of this Canadian Statute as to how a British subject naturalized in a foreign state could remain a British subject in Canada were inapplicable to Riel's situation. To remain a British subject in Canada after voluntarily becoming naturalized in a foreign state required that within two years after the *Naturalization Act* came into force a declaration had to be made and an oath of allegiance taken by that person.

It is not implausible to suppose that Magistrate Richardson may have had official dealings under the Canadian *Naturalization Act*. A Regulation was adopted, pursuant to the Act, by the federal government on December 19, 1883. Under this Regulation an alien who wished to become a British subject after a three year residency could apply in the North-West Territories to a Stipendiary Magistrate in the North-West Territories. If satisfied as to the facts the Stipendiary Magistrate granted a certificate of naturalization. Under section 2 of this 1883 Regulation, the Stipendiary Magistrate of the North-West Territories was required to keep a record of certificates filed with and issued by him. No evidence was presented at Riel's trial indicating that a certificate of naturalization

---

[82]   *The Naturalization Act, 1870 (U.K.)*, 33 Vic. c. 14, s. 6.
[83]   *The Naturalization Act, 1881 (Can.)*, 44 Vic. C. 13.

as a British subject had been issued to Riel by a Stipendiary Magistrate of the North-West Territories or by any other official.[84]

The term "disability" in Section 9 of the Canadian *Naturalization Act* was defined in Section 1 of the Act to mean "the status of being an infant, lunatic, idiot or married woman" (a sequence which belittled married women). Under this legal definition of "disability" none of the specified conditions applied to Riel particularly with respect to "lunatic", in light of the jury's non-acceptance of the insanity defence unsuccessfully pleaded by Riel's counsel, a defence which, as will be seen, Riel disavowed while vehemently proclaiming his sanity.

This Canadian Act was not declared in force until July 4, 1883,[85] but by its wording with respect to alienage under Section 9 it applied retroactively to naturalization in a foreign state. Section 8 of the Act was interesting. It provided that "an alien shall not be entitled to be tried by a jury *'de medietate linguae'*." The marginal note stated "Juries *de medietate linguae* abolished." *"De medietate linguae"* means a jury one-half of whom consisted of aliens. This has some similarity to the language law relating to juries in Manitoba discussed elsewhere herein. It may be that the 1881 Act was not in force in the North-West Territories in 1885. In any event the 1870 English Act was passed before the North-West Territories became part of Canada.

In the 1873 election the Liberal Party under the leadership of Alexander Mackenzie defeated Macdonald's Conservative Party. On February 11, 1875 Prime Minister Mackenzie (between the administrations of John A. Macdonald) introduced a resolution in the House of Commons to grant an amnesty to Riel for all acts committed by him during "the North-West troubles". This amnesty was conditional "on five years banishment from Her Majesty's Dominions." The amnesty covered the execution of Thomas Scott by Riel's Provisional Government in 1870. Today banishment or forced exile would be unconstitutional and unlawful under section 6(1) of the *Canadian Charter of Rights and Freedoms*, pursuant to which "every citizen of Canada has the right to enter, remain in and leave Canada." Riel was officially *persona non grata* in Canada when the resolution to banish him

---

[84]   *Statutes of Canada* 1884, Vol. 1& 2, p. 96-97, (December 19, 1883 Order-in-Council).

[85]   *Statutes of Canada*, 1884 Vol. 1 & 2 p. 92 and *Canada Gazette*, Vol. XVII, p. 2, (June 30, 1883 proclamation).

was adopted the next day. When the period of banishment expired in 1880, Riel was living in Montana. At that time he made up his mind to become an American citizen and signed a required Declaration of Intention to this effect. Some three years later on March 16, 1883 Riel became an American citizen by attending before Judge S. Wade in Fort Benton, Montana pursuant to which he received a Certificate of Naturalization declaring him to be a citizen of the United States of America.   The author obtained a copy of Riel's Certificate of Naturalization from the Provincial Archives of Manitoba.

In the affidavits filed on July 21, 1885 on motion for adjournment of the trial, one was sworn by Riel, a second by one of his counsel François-Xavier Lemieux and the third by Charles Fitzpatrick, another one of Riel's lawyers. The purpose for requesting the adjournment was to give time to arrange for certain witnesses to be called and, at least in Riel's view, for documents to be produced on Riel's behalf. Lemieux and Fitzpatrick wished to procure the attendance of certain specified alienists i.e. psychiatrists, as witnesses in an endeavour to prove Riel was insane.   Fitzpatrick's affidavit, as did Riel's, also wanted Gabriel Dumont, Michel Dumas and Napoléon Nault (three Metis fugitives then in the United States) to attend as witnesses to Riel's non-overt involvement and peaceful agitation but the subsequent defence strategy makes clear the defence counsel had no intention of arguing justification. For example F. X. Lemieux stated to the Court "I do not want to justify the rebellion."[86]

Greenshields, in requesting a trial adjournment, did refer to Riel's affidavit requesting the Montana fugitives as witnesses, but the trial transcript indicates the matter was not vigorously pursued.   In fact, Greenshields made a rather surprising comment concerning

> the evidence of the doctors from Quebec. This defence, we
> are instructed by others than the prisoner to make. [87]

In light of subsequent events this statement discloses that Riel's counsel intended to plead him insane. They would do so based, not on Riel's instructions, but on the instructions of "**others**". This astonishing disclosure meant that Riel's lawyers were not acting on his instructions but on those of some faceless unnamed persons. Riel in his affidavit specifically stated, among other matters, that he believed that among his

---

[86]   *The Queen v. Louis Riel*, p. 229.
[87]   *The Queen v. Louis Riel*, p. 48.

documents taken by General Middleton and his officers was his Certificate of Naturalization as a United States citizen, that this certificate was essential to his defence and by it:

> I can establish that at the time of the commission of the alleged offences I was a citizen of the United States of America, **and not a British subject**, as charged in the said information.[88] [Emphasis added.]

It was obvious from these affidavits that Riel and his counsel were at cross-purposes. In addition to his Naturalization Certificate, Riel wanted L. Vankoughnet, the Deputy Minister of Indian Affairs, and A. M. Burgess, the Deputy Minister of the Interior, to come as witnesses with various papers, petitions and documents. Lemieux and Fitzpatrick made no such proposal. The aim of Lemieux and Fitzpatrick in seeking an adjournment was to obtain witnesses to show that Riel was insane. Their affidavits made no request for, or any mention of, any documents whatsoever and in particular did not refer in any way to Riel being a United States citizen, or to his American Naturalization Certificate. Neither did the affidavits of Lemieux and Fitzpatrick refer to Riel not being a British subject under The *1870 Naturalization Act of Britain* or the *1881 Naturalization Act of Canada*. From the point of view of Fitzpatrick and Lemieux, these witnesses and documents would be totally irrelevant to the insanity plea they intended to pursue without Riel's authorization.

Riel's Naturalization Certificate was never produced at the trial. One of the Crown prosecutors, Christopher Robinson, stated

> With regard to the certificate of naturalization which the prisoner says is necessary for his defence, in our view the law is clear that the existence of that certificate would make no difference whatever ... [89]

Robinson added that the Crown prosecutors had received a telegram that very morning stating that the certificate or a certified copy of it was in Winnipeg, that it would be obtained and "they shall have the use of it."

These comments by Robinson have a dual significance. They indicated that he knew, or at least had an inkling, that Riel was a United States citizen, yet he persisted with the three charges alleging that Riel was a British subject. As well, the Certificate of Naturalization was

---

88   *The Queen v. Louis Riel,* p. 61-62.
89   *The Queen v. Louis Riel,* p. 55.

never produced at the trial, and nowhere in the Court proceedings did Riel's counsel bring up the matter, demand the Certificate be turned over, adduce it as evidence, or plead the invalidity of the three charges.

No evidence was presented at the trial to prove that Riel was a British subject nor to disprove his American citizenship. Richardson did not point out to the jury that there was no evidence whatsoever, presented in Court, to prove the specific allegation in each of the first three charges that Riel was "a subject of our Lady the Queen". Nor did he advise the jury that there was no evidence that Riel was a British subject who owed "our said Lady the Queen ... allegiance, fidelity and obedience."

The burden of proof was on the Crown to prove these allegations, which were of the essence. Failure on the part of the Crown to prove an essential element of a charge is legally fatal to the charge. A crown prosecutor's duty is not to seek a conviction at all costs but to seek justice. None of the crown prosecutors brought to the attention of the jury or the magistrate the lack of evidence or the law relating to Riel's status. This status was that of an American citizen and not that of a British subject. However, because Riel's counsel did not raise the issue or object in any way to Magistrate Richardson's charge, in being addressed the jury was not told either by Riel's counsel Fitzpatrick or by Richardson to consider the evidence, or lack thereof, on this point, and to throw out the charges. On these three charges Riel was convicted contrary to law and justice.

Chapter VII

JURISDICTION AND VENUE
OF THE MAGISTRATE'S COURT

Louis Riel was arraigned for high treason under the *1351 Statute of Treasons* on July 20, 1885 at 11:00 a.m. in Regina. Riel was taken to the improvised and crude courtroom by members of the North West Mounted Police. He was transported to the court disguised as a member of that police force. This was done because of a rumour widely afloat that Gabriel Dumont and a group of Metis would attempt to make a daring rescue of Riel. The "Mounties" were on guard and taking no chances. No escapade by Dumont occurred, and Riel proceeded to trial.

Regina at the time was a village with perhaps six hundred people and not long before its name was Pile o' Bones, a translation of "Wascana" an old Indian word. The arraignment took place in a smallish, make-shift, poorly-ventilated courtroom, in the office building of the Canada North West Land Company, a subsidiary of the CPR which was saved from bankruptcy as a result of the North-West Uprising. The Canadian Pacific Railway had transported troops from eastern Canada to the North-West to crush the uprising which led to Riel's trial and execution. The rented courtroom was jam-packed with court staff, the jury, lawyers (nine in all), reporters, interpreters, and a throng of curious spectators (including the spouses of General Middleton and Magistrate Richardson). They were there to gawk at the stately prisoner and to observe firsthand the *cause célèbre* which rivetted not only their community but the whole nation.

In the sweltering courtroom, the clerk of the court read the indictment to Riel who, standing in a dock perhaps four feet long and three feet wide, was surrounded by the standing room only crowd. When the clerk asked Riel if he was guilty or not guilty, before a response could be given, François X. Lemieux (one of the defence counsel) stated the defence was contesting the jurisdiction of the Court. Riel's plea to the jurisdiction read by Fitzpatrick in support of the motion essentially stated that the Court (composed of a stipendiary magistrate, a justice of the peace, and a jury of six) did not have jurisdiction to try offences punishable by death. The plea also stated that Riel should be sent to "Upper Canada" (curiously not Ontario as it had been called since 1867) or British Columbia for trial.

A lengthy argument as to the Court's jurisdiction ensued. It ranged from the lofty heights of the rights of man to the mind-numbing depths of chapter and verse of old and new statutes. The debate took up most of the rest of the day.

The defence's plea basically contended:

(i)   that the constitutional rights enshrined in the *Magna Carta* (the charter originally granted by King John in 1215) specifically as to trial by jury, took precedence over the *North-West Territories Act of 1880*; and

(ii)   that the Court as constituted did not have authority under that Statute of 1880 to try the case.

Fitzpatrick advanced the first point, Greenshields the second.

Fitzpatrick stated that the right of trial by jury constituted one of the fundamental articles of *Magna Carta*. He affirmed that under *Magna Carta* a trial by jury meant

> a trial by a jury of twelve men, impartially selected, who must unanimously concur in the guilt of the accused before a legal conviction can be made.[90]

Any law, i.e. the *North-West Territories Act 1880*, repugnant to any of these requirements was unconstitutional. Judgment by one's peers meant trial by a jury of twelve men according to the course of the common law.

Fitzpatrick pointed out that in a case of treason, since the Crown is a party to the suit, the appointment of the sheriff in England had been taken out of the King's hands and given to the people. He added "as Lord Coke says" this was to avoid suspicion that the sheriff would be interested and would return a "corrupt jury".

He argued that section 76(9) of the *North-West Territories Act, 1880* authorizing Richardson to select the jurors that Richardson thought suitable went to the basis of the jury system. With respect to a jury chosen in that manner, he asked:

> What does it mean, except that the jury is chosen not to try the case, but simply to register the decrees of the person who has chosen them. This is the position in which we now find ourselves.

---

[90]   *The Queen v. Louis Riel*, p. 11.

Fitzpatrick averred that this was not the law of the land, that there was the shadow not the substance of trial by jury, and that the jury was chosen by a method which made it as worthless as a dead body. He added, no doubt because the North-West Territories had no representatives in Parliament, that its people had not been consulted about whether they would be happy with a jury of six in treason or capital cases. He asserted that the Federal Parliament did not have constitutional authority to override the laws of England and the principles of the British Constitution.

After Fitzpatrick's animated peroration James Greenshields, another of Riel's Quebec counsel, stood to dispute the jurisdiction of the magistrate's court to hear Riel's case. He took the position that pre-Confederation British Imperial statutes remained in force in Canada and that the courts constituted by these Imperial statutes made the *North-West Territories Act 1880* unconstitutional and beyond the powers of the Federal Parliament to enact. He cited the *1859 Imperial Colonial Laws Validity Act* [91] to the effect that any colonial law (including one of Canada) repugnant to a statute of the British Parliament was, to the extent of the repugnancy, absolutely void and inoperative. He cited provisions from the Imperial statutes requiring that any offence subject to the death penalty must be tried in a court in Upper Canada or in British Columbia, not in the North-West Territories. Greenshields gave a careful, precise presentation bolstering it with legal textbook authorities. He then unflinchingly told Richardson to his face that the *North-West Territories Act 1880* made possible that:

> a government desirous of ridding itself of particular men in these Territories can, by **a servile creature appointed as magistrate,** with the absolute right to go out on the highway and streets and select his jury as he saw fit - might accomplish its ends in this way.[92] [Emphasis added.]

In response to this ostensible effrontery and monumental attack on magisterial independence Richardson responded, not in high dudgeon or

---

[91]   22-23 Vic., c. 63. Other *British Imperial Statutes* cited included 1-2 George IV, c. 66; 28-29 Vic. C. 23; and the post-Confederation *British North America Amendment Act of 1871.*

[92]   *The Queen v. Louis Riel,* p. 27.

with a stinging rebuke, but with the limp and almost acquiescent comment "Suit the jury to the occasion."[93]

Greenshields prefaced his remarks with an expression of defence counsel's utmost respect for the Court and the jury members. Consequently Richardson may have failed to appreciate that the phrase "servile creature appointed as magistrate" under the *North-West Territories Act* was most assuredly intended by Greenshields to apply to Richardson.   Of course Greenshields knew that Richardson was a government appointee under the Act holding office at the pleasure of the Government. Greenshields most likely knew that Richardson was a legal adviser to the Lieutenant-Governor of the North-West Territories, and that he had previously been a government employee in the Department of Justice in Ottawa.

Crown counsel, Christopher Robinson and Britton Bath Osler, took turns in responding to the plea of Fitzpatrick and Greenshields against the court's jurisdiction.

With respect to Fitzpatrick's contention concerning the jury, Robinson said that the right of a jury of any kind is not as fundamental a principle of the British constitution as the supremacy of Parliament. He added that the Federal Parliament is as supreme as the Imperial Parliament when it acts within the subjects entrusted to its jurisdiction. Robinson followed with a dissertation in chronological order of various statutes.[94]   In light of Robinson's argument, the author is of the view that those who cherish a guarantee of individual rights and fundamental freedoms should be thankful that the Trudeau Government insisted upon the *1982 Canadian Charter of Rights and Freedoms* in the repatriated Canadian Constitution. The Charter today guarantees these rights and freedoms in priority to the supremacy of Parliament and the provincial legislatures. Under section 1 of the Charter, this guarantee is subject only to such reasonable limits prescribed by law as can be demonstrably justified in a free and democratic society. Under section 33 Parliament or a provincial legislature has the right to opt out of certain Charter provisions for five-year renewable periods.

---

[93]   *The Queen v. Louis Riel*, p. 27.
[94]   E.g. *Rupert's Land Imperial Act*, 31 & 32 Vict. c. 105; 32 & 33 Vict. C. 3 (1869) Can.; 33 Vict. C. 31 (1870) Can.; 34 & 35 Vict. C. 28 (1871) Imp.; etc.

Without naming it, Robinson referred to the Connor case,[95] decided only a short time earlier. In this case the Court of Queen's Bench of Manitoba (on appeal from Magistrate Richardson and two justices of the peace) held that the jurisdiction of the North-West Territories court, with a jury of six, was valid in the case of a murder charge carrying the death penalty. Comment on the fortuitous timing of the judgment in the Connor case and Crown counsel Osler and Burbidge's involvement in it is given in Chapter XX.

Osler buttressed Robinson's argument and discussed powers which the Hudson's Bay Company previously had relating to the administration of justice, and that the statute 22 and 23 Vict. Ch. 26 relied on by the defence was inapplicable to the territories not in the possession of the Hudson's Bay Company. He asserted that the *North-West Territories Act 1880* did not clash with any Imperial statute and that it was the law. He referred to Britain's largest colony, India, and stated there was no grand jury or petit jury there, and that the law of treason in India was administered and tried by a stipendiary magistrate alone.[96]

Fitzpatrick replied at some length, concluding with the contention that the *North-West Territories Act 1880* with respect to the trial of cases subject to the death penalty was beyond the powers of the Federal Parliament.

After many hours of argument by counsel, Richardson ruled in eleven words "Well, as I cannot hold that, I must sustain the demurrer";[97] i.e. that the *North-West Territories Act 1880* was valid and that the court as constituted had jurisdiction to try Riel for high treason.

In view of the decision in the Connor case, made by the Manitoba Court of Queen's Bench (the appeal court for the North-West Territories) only seven days before Riel was charged it is incomprehensible that Riel's counsel could have expected any other decision. The appeal by Connor was from a murder conviction after a trial in a North-West Territories Court consisting of the very same Magistrate Richardson and Justice of the Peace Le Jeune with another Justice of the Peace Harry Fisher and a jury of six. Murder was a capital offence. The Manitoba Court of Queen's Bench had unanimously ruled

---

[95]   *The Queen v. Connor*, (1885) 2 *Manitoba Law Reports*, 235 (Man. Queen's Bench).
[96]   *The Queen v. Louis Riel*, p. 34-36.
[97]   *The Queen v. Louis Riel*, p. 41.

that the North-West Territories Court had jurisdiction in a capital offence case. Crown counsel Robinson pointed this out to Richardson and said this case was "a sufficient answer" and again "amply sufficient" to confirm the jurisdiction of the Riel court "unless my learned friends can point to some distinction between treason and murder."[98]

It almost seemed as though Fitzpatrick, Greenshields and Lemieux were simply not aware of the Connor case. As Riel said during the trial "My counsel come from Quebec, from a far province." But Johnstone later referred to the case as supporting a general demurrer to the information. Johnstone's reference to the Connor case is not surprising, since he had been one of the appellate counsel for the unfortunate Connor. However Fitzpatrick and Greenshields in addressing Richardson made no mention of the Connor case and made no effort to try to distinguish it from Riel's situation. Their lengthy arguments were doomed to failure before they started. Oddly, at no time during argument by any of the four counsel did Richardson himself refer to the Connor case, notwithstanding it was an appeal from the court over which he himself had presided. However, Richardson did refer to it twelve days later in his charge to the jury. This may be an indication that he himself was not aware of the results of the appeal of the Connor case at the time of the plea to the jurisdiction on July 20, but found out about it in the ensuing twelve days. Otherwise, instead of an eleven-word decision supporting the Court's jurisdiction without giving reasons he could have cited the Connor case at that time without waiting twelve days to "tell it to the jury".

Another subsequent indication that the challenge to the jurisdiction by defence counsel stood absolutely no chance of success was Richardson's mindset. Richardson in his remarks to the jury made comments which he himself correctly categorized as "strange". He said:

> It may strike you as strange, but ... I sitting here could not say whether they [counsel] were right or wrong in their opinions, and why? ... Having accepted a commission under the law, it would strike one as strange that I should take it upon myself without anything further to say that the Parliament of Canada had exceeded their power and should not have passed the Act.[99]

---

98   *The Queen v. Louis Riel*, p. 30.
99   *The Queen v. Louis Riel*, p. 346.

By these statements Richardson blatantly disclosed that he had abandoned a most elementary function for which he was appointed, namely adjudicating on the law. This astonishing admission that he should accept without question the law as decreed by Parliament made plausible Greenshields seeming implication, if not imputation, that Richardson was "a servile creature appointed as magistrate." Richardson's mental insularity ensured that he would peremptorily rebuff any constitutional assault on the federal law, and he did so in eleven words without explanation.

In the above quote Richardson said that he could not question Parliament "without anything further". Presumably he meant a decision of a court higher than his. Fortunately for his inability to "say whether they [counsel] were right or wrong in their opinions" he said that because of the Connor case (which he did not refer to by name) he was "not called upon" to question Parliament.

Osler was quite familiar with the Connor case. In the report of the judgment,[100] he is shown as lead counsel for the Crown assisted by J. A. M. Aikins. (For a profile of Aikins refer to section 3(a) of Chapter VIII.) It is not surprising to find Osler handling the Connor appeal a short time before he prosecuted Riel.   Prime Minister John A. Macdonald and Justice Minister Alexander Campbell dispatched him and Deputy Minister of Justice George W. Burbidge to Winnipeg for the appeal.[101] Dismissal of the Connor appeal was crucial to a trial of Riel in the North-West Territories so desired by Macdonald and Campbell. They knew from Robinson and Osler's letter of June 16, 1885 (see Chapter IV, section 2 and also Chapter X) that the trial would be before a stipendiary magistrate, a justice of the peace and a jury of six. This jury would be selected from a panel exclusively nominated by that magistrate.   As it happened the Chief Justice of Manitoba Lewis Wallbridge (who was to preside over the Connor appeal) was well known to both John A. Macdonald and to Justice Minister Campbell. In 1863, after a stint as solicitor-general, Wallbridge had succeeded Campbell as Speaker for the pre-Confederation Legislative Assembly of the Province of Canada and was Speaker during the administration of Paschal Taché and J. S. Macdonald and during the subsequent "Great

---

100   *The Queen v. Connor*, p. 235.
101   "Macdonald Papers", NAC Vol. 197 p. 82862-67, June 17, 1885.

Coalition". Wallbridge was an Ontarian all of his life until Prime Minister John A. Macdonald appointed him Chief Justice of Manitoba in 1882 at age 66. See Chapter XVII section 1 for a profile of Wallbridge.

At the improper bidding of Campbell the hearing of the Connor appeal was deferred by the Wallbridge-led court until Osler could appear so that the appeal could be "well argued". Shockingly, before the Connor appeal was heard Campbell told Macdonald that he had written "privately" to Chief Justice Wallbridge

> at the suggestion of Mr. Osler … urging the court should give as early a decision upon the point as they can.

As an article in *Canadian Lawyer* magazine expressed it

> This communication from the federal justice minister to a judge — a communication which materially affected the administration of justice in both the *Connor* and *Riel* cases — is a stunning revelation.[102]

Not long after this astounding message from the Minister of Justice to the Chief Justice of Manitoba, the Court of Queen's Bench of Manitoba refused Connor a new trial. In his Judgment Wallbridge stated it was "perfectly clear" that Parliament had

> conferred on the stipendiary magistrate with a justice of the peace, and the intervention of a jury of six, the power of try- ing a person for a capital offence.[103]

The other two appellate judges concurred. Justice Taylor, in his reasons, made a most condescending comment in relation to the aboriginal peoples who had lived in the North-West for many centuries and the Metis peoples who had lived and hunted on these prairie plains for many decades. He said:

> There can be no doubt that at the time of its occupation by English subjects the country now known as the North West Territories would fall within the description of an uninhabited country.[104]

This was a prevarication to match, if not surpass, Richardson's comment in Chapter IV, section 4 where he told Chief Big Bear that the

---

[102] Ronald L. Olesky, "Louis Riel and the Crown Letters", *Canadian Lawyer* magazine, February 1998.
[103] *The Queen v. Connor*, p. 239.
[104] *The Queen v. Connor*, p. 243.

Indians had never owned the land, the land belonged to the Queen and she had given them the choicest portions of the country.

After Riel pleaded not guilty, another of his lawyers, Thomas C. Johnstone, entered a written general demurrer to the information containing the charges. The gist of Johnstone's oral argument was that "The information is double", i.e. the overt acts laid in the last three charges were identical to the overt acts mentioned in the first three charges. He said that the first three charges were against Riel as a British subject, while the latter three were silent as to his nationality and should have declared that he was a subject of a foreign state at peace with Her Majesty. Crown counsel Burbidge stated in effect that the three latter charges were based on local allegiance, and that these were valid. Richardson overruled Johnstone. Riel was then asked to plead for a second time and again pleaded not guilty.

Chapter VIII

THE LAWYERS

There were nine lawyers in all involved in the Riel proceedings in Regina. The five Crown lawyers were Christopher Robinson, Britton Bath Osler, George Wheelock Burbidge, Thomas Chase Casgrain and David Lynch Scott. Four lawyers represented Riel; they were Charles Fitzpatrick, François-Xavier Lemieux, James Naismith Greenshields and Thomas Cooke Johnstone. The principal lawyers for the Crown and for Riel epitomized some of the underlying tensions pervading the prosecution of the Metis leader – Protestant versus Catholic; Anglo-Saxon versus French; Ontario versus Quebec. While not all-inclusive, there was a Conservative Party bent to the prosecution and a Liberal Party look to the defence. Prosecutors Robinson and Casgrain were Conservatives while Fitzpatrick and Lemieux were Liberals, as was Osler. The lead lawyers for the Crown, Robinson and Osler, who were both from Ontario, were older and more experienced in their legal profession than the principal defence counsel, Lemieux and Fitzpatrick, who came from Quebec. Robinson was a generation older than Riel's lawyers, while Osler had been born a dozen years before Lemieux. Fitzpatrick was a couple of years younger than Lemieux.

Justice Minister Campbell had assured Prime Minister Macdonald that great care would be taken to ensure that the prosecution would be well-done. The means by which this was to be carried out was by retaining outstanding senior lawyers, i.e. Robinson and Osler, to orchestrate the Crown's case backed up by the Deputy Minister of Justice. For image reasons a French-Canadian Quebec lawyer and a local Regina lawyer were added to the team.

Each of Robinson, Osler and Burbidge was a Queen's Counsel, not only in the literal sense of acting on behalf of the Queen; but also pursuant to their previous appointment as such. The honorific "Queen's Counsel", or "Q.C." for short, is awarded by the federal or a provincial government to lawyers with a certain degree of seniority. Originally a Q.C. was obliged to provide legal services to the Crown on request, but gradually this obligation disappeared. In addition to a prestige aspect, a Q.C. designation carries a few privileges, including the right to wear a silk gown in court. Appointments of Q.C.s today, in a number of provinces, may be based on such matters as political connections to the government awarding the title, being a nominee from a large law firm, on merit, or upon application. At the time of the trial, none of Riel's lawyers was entitled to this titular appurtenance.

The federal government had unlimited funds to seek out and retain prominent counsel and did so. The impecunious Riel, on the other hand, had been held incommunicado for a number of weeks prior to the trial and was shackled with a ball and chain for much of that time. He was in no position to pick and choose lawyers who would follow his instructions and defend him on the merits according to his express wishes. One of Riel's friends from his Montreal school days, Dr. J. B. Romuald Fiset (who had been a Liberal Member of Parliament) helped organize a committee to solicit funds for Riel's defence. This defence committee effectively hired three Quebec lawyers (Lemieux, Fitzpatrick and Greenshields) on Riel's behalf. Although relatively young, they were considered to be talented criminal lawyers. Fiset wrote Riel about the accommodations Fiset had made. In doing so he praised the abilities of Lemieux and Fitzpatrick. As will be discussed, these lawyers followed their own counsel, not Riel's, with a defence Riel unequivocally disowned, i.e. insanity, a defence almost certainly foredoomed to failure, thereby almost certainly leading inexorably to Riel's doom.

In Canada, unlike England, a lawyer may be both a barrister and a solicitor; the former pleads cases in court, while a solicitor performs mostly non-litigation work. The lawyers in the Riel case acted primarily as barristers, one of the oldest professions in the world. When the author first commenced his studies at the University of Manitoba Law School, the Dean, G. P. R. Tallin, told the class that the so-called oldest profession in the world ("ladies of the evening") was not a profession at all because a profession "puts service before reward".

The following are profiles on each of the nine lawyers.

1.   CROWN COUNSEL

(a)   Christopher Robinson

Christopher Robinson was the senior counsel at the trial. He was born at Toronto on January 21, 1828. He attended Upper Canada College and King's College in Toronto. He was a scion of Sir John Beverley Robinson. Christopher's father was a prominent member of the Upper Canada establishment. He was a member of the Family

Compact and an unswerving advocate of the imperial connection who became Chief Justice of Upper Canada in 1829. His son, Christopher, followed in his father's footsteps in becoming a lawyer in Upper Canada in 1850, although prior to launching his legal career he made a tour of England and Europe. He was appointed a Q.C. in 1863. At the time of the Riel trial in 1885 he was steeped in the law and enjoyed recognition as a top-flight advocate. As a result of his helpful role for the Crown in the Bering Sea imbroglio between Canada and the United States in the 1880s involving the fur-sealing industry, a knighthood was proffered to him but he did not accept it nor did he accept a judicial appointment.

While not timid Robinson's temperament was more reserved than that of Osler. It was said that his "style is not oratorical or declamatory, but rather conversational."[105] However his moderate disposition was accompanied by a first-rate intellect capable (in a non-emotional way) of examining and cross-examining witnesses and presenting a cogent, methodical summation of the evidence, in a persuasive, rational manner. It is worthy of note that it was the refined Robinson, not the sometimes overbearing Osler, who wrapped up the Crown's case in addressing the jury prior to the Magistrate's charge. He died on October 21, 1905 in Toronto.

(b) Britton Bath Osler

Britton Bath Osler was born in Tecumseh, Upper Canada on June 19, 1839. He was called to the bar of Upper Canada in 1862 and practised law in Southern Ontario. He became a Q.C. in 1876. He was a highly reputed criminal lawyer in Toronto when the highest law officer in the land, the Minister of Justice, called upon him to assume a lead role in the prosecution of Riel. Osler was then aged 46. An extant photograph of him at the time of the trial shows him to be wide-eyed (some might say almost pop-eyed), with a bald pate and droopy moustache à la General Middleton (and apparently a custom of the time), and robed in his barrister's gown. He was then at the peak of his abilities with courtroom skills finely honed by years of experience. While he was prominent in the law, several of his siblings achieved notability in their own right, particularly his brother William, a medical doctor who developed an international reputation.

---

[105]   "The Riel Trial", *Toronto Globe*, July 11, 1885.

In 1882 Osler, Dalton McCarthy (formerly of Barrie, Ontario), and others, established a law firm in Toronto called McCarthy, Osler, Hoskin and Creelman. The Irish born Protestant Dalton McCarthy had been John A. Macdonald's Ontario lieutenant. A powerful Conservative, he might have aspired to succeed the old warhorse Macdonald as Prime Minister if he had exhibited some discretion and political temperance. Instead he became an outspoken "leader of the anti-French, anti-Catholic, English rights movement of the late nineteenth century."[106]   One professor called McCarthy "the Conservative wheel horse among the Orange lodges of Ontario"[107]; another described him as "a vehement and reckless young man."[108] In Dalton McCarthy, Canada had its own form of McCarthyism long before the United States. One may speculate that McCarthy must have been pleased that his partner Osler had been selected to prosecute Riel, a symbol of all that was anathema to McCarthy.

It was this fiery bigoted individual with whom Osler set up shop in Toronto. McCarthy and Osler built up a successful law practice in short order, helped in part by obtaining as a client the western lands subsidiary of the CPR. This subsidiary was the Canada North West Land Company in whose Regina office building Riel was subsequently to be tried and sentenced to death. This CPR subsidiary referral came through the efforts of Osler's brother, financier Edmund Osler.

Descendant firms of the McCarthy-Osler firm continue today. Their current names are McCarthy Tetrault, and Osler Hoskin and Harcourt. Each is a well-regarded mega-firm (sometimes colloquially called a legal factory) with hundreds of lawyers based primarily in Toronto and, with the recent advent of interprovincial and international law firms, in other cities in Canada and abroad.

Osler's status within the Ontario bar was recognized by his election by his fellow practitioners as a bencher of the Law Society of Upper Canada. A bencher of a law society is somewhat analogous to a director of a corporation. The benchers are the governing body of a law society

---

106   Christopher Moore, *The Law Society of Upper Canada and Ontario's Lawyers 1797-1997*, p. 154.
107   Hardy, p. 403-04.
108   Donald Creighton, *The Story of Canada*, p.184.   Contrary to Creighton's words, McCarthy was not young; at the time referred to he was 50 years old.

and exercise regulatory powers over lawyers in areas such as discipline, competence and disbarment.

In reading the transcript of the Riel trial, it is evident that Osler was keenly intelligent, supremely self-confident, legally astute, and caustically haughty. He was a major strategist in preparation of the Crown's evidence. It was he who began the Crown's case by giving the opening address to the jury and he examined and cross-examined a number of trial witnesses.

He died at Atlantic City, New Jersey on February 5, 1901.

(c) George Wheelock Burbidge

George Wheelock Burbidge was the Deputy Minister of Justice of the federal government in Ottawa in 1885, the year Riel was tried. He was originally a Maritimer, having been born in Cornwallis, Nova Scotia on February 6, 1847. He was called to the New Brunswick bar in 1872. Alexander Campbell, the Minister of Justice, saw to it that Burbidge played a major role in planning and implementing the legal proceedings against Riel. As noted earlier, Justice Minister Campbell sent Burbidge with Osler to Winnipeg, while Riel was cooped up in a Regina jail. The Justice Minister's intention was to attain an outcome of the Connor appeal favourable to a trial in the North-West Territories of Riel by a court (found nowhere else in Canada) consisting of a stipendiary magistrate, justice of the peace and jury of six.

The desired precedent in the Connor case, with Osler as lead counsel, was handed down by the appeal court in Manitoba (headed by John A. Macdonald's appointee as Chief Justice, Lewis A. Wallbridge) one week before Riel was charged with treason.

Burbidge was an Ottawa mandarin – he served as Deputy Minister of Justice for a five-year period ending in 1887 and in that year was appointed a judge of the newly-formed Exchequer Court, now the Federal Court of Canada. Today that Court is sometimes disparaged as an institution with too many ex-civil servants and politicians with a federal bent on its bench and handling legal matters which could be capably dealt with by the various provincial superior courts. Some critics of the Federal Court occasionally call for its dissolution.

In the Jackson trial Burbidge was instrumental in **not** having the "white rebel", William Henry Jackson, convicted of treason-felony. He agreed that an insanity plea should be accepted by the Crown notwithstanding that there was an abundance of documentation and witnesses available to substantiate a persuasive case to prove treason-felony. The seemingly ubiquitous Osler, acting no doubt on Burbidge's instructions, presented no evidence whatsoever against Jackson as to treason-felony. The only witnesses called were those testifying as to Jackson's insanity.[109] Jackson was acquitted on the basis of insanity, and directed to be held in an insane asylum, from which he fled to the United States a few months later, living a long and sane life.

The acquittal of Jackson on an insanity defence may have given false hope to Fitzpatrick, Lemieux et al. that the selfsame defence on behalf of Riel, notwithstanding Riel's express instructions to the contrary, would be successful. However Burbidge and his political masters had no intention of playing the same game with Riel that they had with Jackson. Crown counsel successfully fought the Riel insanity defence with the utmost vigor, including intense cross-examination of the defence's alienists.

Several years after the events in the Regina courtroom, Burbidge wrote a text entitled *Digest of the Criminal Law of Canada*. Subsequently, in 1892, he was a co-author of the first statutory codification of Canadian criminal law.[110] This *1892 Criminal Code* included in one statute high treason, treason-felony, and the *Fenian Act* treason with respect to an alien of a foreign state at peace with Her Majesty levying or intending to levy war against the Queen. Prior to 1892 the three offences were found in three separate statutes. All charges were now referred to as indictable offences. It is interesting to note that in the section relating to lesser offences against Her Majesty such as breaking the public peace by e.g. throwing anything at the Queen the penalty, in addition to up to seven years imprisonment, included being "whipped once, twice or thrice as the court directs."[111] For the more serious offences, Burbidge and his collaborator did not carry through provisions for the draconian punishment of drawing and quartering and forfeiture of assets which, in earlier days, invariably ensued for high treason against the King under the *1351 Statute of Treasons*. For the lesser offence against the Queen personally a criminally-minded Canadian at the time contemplating *lèse-*

---

109   Bingaman, p. 45.
110   *Criminal Code of Canada, 1892* (55-56 Vict.).
111   *Criminal Code of Canada* 1892, Sections 65 to 69: 71.

majesté in Canada need not have feared a whipping since Queen Victoria never set foot in Canada.

Burbidge died at Ottawa on February 18, 1908.

(d) Thomas Chase Casgrain

Thomas Chase Casgrain was co-opted as a Crown counsel on the urging of Adolphe Caron, the federal Minister of Militia and Defence. Caron wanted a Quebecer on the prosecution team for political reasons. The junior counsel picked for this purpose was Casgrain who was born not in Quebec, but in Detroit, Michigan on July 28, 1852. His mother's maiden name was "Chase", hence his middle name. Casgrain was called to the Quebec bar in 1877. He originally practised law in Quebec City and while there he became professor of criminal law at Laval University. During the course of the Riel trial, Casgrain had his thirty-third birthday. At that time he was a partner in the same Quebec City law firm to which Defence Minister Caron himself belonged. This was rather intriguing since one of Riel's **lead** counsel, Fitzpatrick, was one year younger than Casgrain and was not only also a partner of Minister Caron's law firm (meaning that Casgrain and Fitzpatrick themselves were partners) but Fitzpatrick was married to Corinne Caron, the Minister's own sister. The trial witnessed the spectacle of two partners from the same Quebec City law firm appearing in Regina as counsel. Casgrain with a bevy of lawyers was attempting diligently to establish Riel's soundness of mind to secure his conviction with a view to his execution. Fitzpatrick with a group of lawyers was trying zealously to demonstrate Riel was a madman and to obtain his acquittal and committal to an asylum with a view to saving his life. Even more startling was that Riel (the man at the centre of the legal melodrama) ardently agreed with the prosecution's position as to his own rationality. He perfervidly disagreed with his own counsel's stance with respect to an insanity defence, which was to erupt into a very public display of discord, among Riel and his own lawyers, in open court.

The year after the Riel trial, Casgrain was elected to the Quebec legislature and was the Attorney-General of Quebec from 1891 to 1896. During his career he became bâtonnier-general of the bar of Quebec and of all the province. He was elected to the House of Commons in 1896. In 1897 he was appointed a Queen's Counsel. In 1897 he moved to Montreal where he resumed the practice of law. From 1911 to 1914 he was chairman of the International Joint Commission. He became Post-Master General of Canada in the Borden government in 1914, a position he held until his death on December 29, 1916.

It was said that as a lawyer he was the *vir probus*, the honest man, of whom Cicero spoke.[112]

(e) David Lynch Scott

David Lynch Scott was the fifth member of the prosecution team. An Ontarian by birth, he was born on August 21, 1845 in Brampton, Ontario then known as Canada West (and called Upper Canada until the *Union Act of 1840* united it with Lower Canada which was named Canada East). He received his early education in Brampton and his legal education at Osgoode Hall. Scott became a lawyer in Ontario in 1870. He carried on a law practice in Orangeville, Ontario from 1878 to 1882. He was mayor of Orangeville in 1879-80. He moved to Regina, North-West Territories in 1882 and continued his law practice there, becoming mayor of Regina in that same year. On January 11, 1885 he was the first person enrolled in the North-West Territories as a barrister. At the time of his retainer as one of the five Crown counsel for the Riel trial in 1885, Scott was the mayor of Regina, not a particularly grandiose position when only several hundred people then lived there. His middle name must have subliminally appealed to many members of the Orange Lodge in Ontario who wished to see Riel strung-up.

He played only a peripheral role in the trial, questioning three minor Crown witnesses and taking no part at all in cross-examination of defence witnesses or in the examination of the Crown witnesses called in rebuttal to testify as to Riel's sanity.

Scott acted as the main prosecutor in the trial of Chief Big Bear and also nine Cree Indians all charged with treason-felony. His conduct of these trials was not overly impressive and evidence of guilt was weak but all accused were found guilty very quickly.

Scott was appointed a Queen's Counsel in 1885. He became a Supreme Court justice in the North-West Territories in 1894. He moved to Alberta in 1905 where he continued as a judge, becoming Chief Justice of Alberta in 1921 when the Supreme Court of Alberta was split into two parts, the Trial and the Appellate Divisions. On this

---

112   Pierre-Georges Roy, *Les Avocats de Quebec*, (Levis, 1936) p. 80.

separation occurring Horace Harvey, the former Chief Justice of Alberta, became Chief Justice of the Trial Division but he was dissatisfied, asserting he was still entitled to be Chief Justice of Alberta. This fight over judicial primacy was taken to the Supreme Court of Canada, which ruled in favour of Harvey, not Scott.[113] With this ruling Scott was now the disgruntled one.   He hired R. B. Bennett, a prominent Calgary lawyer who later became Prime Minister, to appeal the matter to Canada's then court of last resort, the Judicial Committee of the Privy Council in England. The Privy Council held that Scott was indeed the Chief Justice of Alberta, not Harvey. It was an ephemeral victory for Scott.   He breathed his last breath soon afterwards at Cooking Lake, near Edmonton, Alberta.

2.   DEFENCE COUNSEL

(a)   Charles Fitzpatrick

Charles Fitzpatrick was undoubtedly the main counsel for Riel, notwithstanding he was then only thirty-one years old, and Riel's other lead co-counsel Lemieux was aged thirty-four.

Fitzpatrick was born on December 19, 1853 at Quebec City, Canada East (now the Province of Quebec).   Notwithstanding his relative youth he had a reputation as an outstanding criminal lawyer when he was retained to represent Riel. He was at the threshold of a remarkable political and judicial career which (except for Riel) eventually surpassed the attainments of every one else directly connected with the trial - the other eight lawyers, the magistrate, two additional lawyers on the appeal, and the three appeal judges in Manitoba. Fitzpatrick was to become a resplendent star in the legal firmament. Of the participants in the trial only Riel surpasses Fitzpatrick in historical notability.

Although both of his parents were of Irish ancestry (his mother's maiden name was Connolly), Fitzpatrick was raised and educated in a French-Canadian milieu and was fluently bilingual. He received his Bachelor of Arts degree (1873) and law degree (1876) from Laval University and was admitted to the Quebec bar on September 9, 1876. He practiced law in Quebec City, also acting as a Crown advocate from 1879 to 1887.

---

[113]   *Reference re Position of Chief Justice of Alberta re Harvey and Scott* [1922], 64 *Supreme Court of Canada Reports*, p. 135.

In 1879, Fitzpatrick married Corinne Caron, the daughter of Rene-Edouard Caron who had been mayor of Quebec City and lieutenant-governor of Quebec. Corinne was the sister of Adolphe Caron. In 1885 Adolphe Caron was the federal Minister of Militia and Defence in John A. Macdonald's administration, and the person in charge of military arrangements to crush Riel and quell the outbreak of hostilities in the North-West Territories. As noted herein, in 1885 Caron, Crown counsel Casgrain, and Riel's counsel Fitzpatrick were partners in the same Quebec City law firm. The author does not know if Riel was aware of this close professional affiliation among two of his adversaries and one of his own lawyers. This question is further discussed in Chapter XXII "Shortcomings of Riel's Lawyers" at section 3 "Fitzpatrick's Conflict of Interest".

With respect to the defence to be advanced on his behalf, Riel had been quite specific in a letter he wrote from jail to Fiset, Fitzpatrick and Lemieux one month before his lawyers arrived in Regina. Riel unequivocally stated his desire that "my trial should turn on the merit of my actions."[114] However after Lemieux and Fitzpatrick met with Riel on July 15th, they and Greenshields wrote Archbishop Taché at St. Boniface stating Riel "was not of sound mind". The die was cast and, as a consequence of an unsuccessful insanity defence, Riel was to die. Unbeknownst to and unapproved by Riel, his explicit wishes were to be disregarded and Fitzpatrick, Lemieux and Greenshields would pursue their own wishes i.e. an insanity defence after an erudite but failed attack on the jurisdiction of the Court. See Chapter XI in this respect. The strategy of Lemieux and Fitzpatrick may have appealed to clergy with whom they were in correspondence and to the Liberal party but it was an irreversible capital disaster for Riel.

Fitzpatrick took the lead in attacking the Court's legal competence, examining and cross-examining many witnesses, presenting objections and in making defence counsel's final address to the jury.

In his career after the trial, Fitzpatrick was elected to the Quebec legislature in 1890 as a Liberal and held his Quebec county seat until 1896. In 1891, he and Lemieux represented the recently deposed Quebec premier Honoré Mercier before a Royal Commission inquiring

---

[114]   Louis Riel, *The Collected Writings of Louis Riel*, , George F. G. Stanley ed, Vol.3 No. 3-065, p. 100 @ p. 102 (June 16, 1885 letter).

into corruption allegations relating to the Baie des Chaleurs Railway. Mercier was removed as premier by the lieutenant-governor of the province at a time when a lieutenant-governor was more than a simple figurehead. Fitzpatrick became a Queen's Counsel in 1893.

Fitzpatrick ran as a federal Liberal candidate in Quebec county in 1896 and won a seat in the House of Commons in the 1896 election which brought Wilfrid Laurier into power. Prime Minister Laurier immediately named Fitzpatrick solicitor-general of Canada, a post he held until 1902 when Laurier elevated him to the highest legal position in the land, Minister of Justice. He held this prestigious Cabinet portfolio until June 4, 1906, the date Laurier conferred on him one even more eminent, that of Chief Justice of Canada, the supreme judicial office in the country.

In 1907, shortly after he became Chief Justice, Fitzpatrick was appointed a knight commander of St. Michael and St. George ("KCMG"), a member of the second highest rank of a British order of knighthood. In 1911 he was appointed to the highest rank of knighthood, knight grand cross of St. Michael and St. George ("GCMG").

Fitzpatrick was Chief Justice of Canada for some twelve years. He resigned on October 21, 1918, and was promptly appointed lieutenant-governor of the Province of Quebec by the Conservative Prime Minister Robert. L. Borden. He retired on October 21, 1923. He died at Quebec City on June 17, 1942.

(b) François-Xavier Lemieux

François-Xavier Lemieux was born at Levis, Canada East (now Quebec) on April 9, 1851. He attended Laval University. He was admitted to the Quebec bar on July 24, 1872 when he was only twenty-one years old. He established his reputation as a criminal lawyer. In 1874 Lemieux married Diana Plamondon, whose father was M. A. Plamondon, a superior court judge. As a Liberal party candidate, he was twice defeated before being elected to the Legislative Assembly of Quebec on the third attempt in 1883. He sat as a member of the Quebec legislature until 1897 except for a one-year hiatus in 1893.

As mentioned herein, Romuald Fiset, who had been a teen-age school friend of Riel in Montreal, participated fully as a member of the Riel Defence Committee (of which there were many members) in arranging for Lemieux (as well as Fitzpatrick and Greenshields) to represent Riel. It was Fiset, Member of Parliament for Rimouski, who attended with Riel before the Clerk of the House of Commons on March 26, 1874 for the surreptitious swearing-in of Riel as the MP for Provencher on the second of three occasions that Riel was elected to Parliament. In his letter of May 22, 1885 to Riel, Fiset stated that it would be difficult to find better lawyers than Lemieux and Fitzpatrick. Fiset obviously intended no pun, but it is somewhat droll that Lemieux means "the best" in English. He also mentioned that Fitzpatrick was a brother-in-law of Militia-Minister Caron. Fiset and Lemieux were not only acquaintances, they were cousins.

Lemieux played a major role in Riel's defence. It was he who questioned the first defence witness in the absence of an opening address to the jury by the defence. He also had several barbed exchanges with Osler; as well there was a disconcerting and likely prejudicial in-court disagreement by Lemieux and Fitzpatrick with a chagrined Riel. This disagreement made stark how polarized Riel and his lawyers were concerning the basis of his defence. Lemieux and Fitzpatrick would brook no interference from Riel in the conduct of their self-contrived strategy of attempting to prove their own client was a maniac. Riel's lawyers seemed to have become almost manic about pursuing this defence of mania. The public dissension between Riel and his lawyers over their tactics is discussed in Chapter XI.

In the Debate in the House of Commons on March 11, 1886 with respect to the execution of Louis Riel, Colonel Amyot read from a document in which Lemieux gave answers to various questions put to him concerning the trial.[115] Lemieux answered questions relating to the fairness of the trial, the request for its delay, unavailability of witnesses and documents, lack of court decorum, the jury panel, etc. giving his views as to these aspects after Riel's execution. After the Riel trial, Lemieux carried on the practice of law and activities as a Quebec politician. In late 1891 he together with his Riel co-counsel Fitzpatrick, defended the recently deposed Premier of Quebec Honoré Mercier before a Royal Commission investigating bribery of the Quebec government by the railway contractors with the very subsidy that the Quebec government had granted to the Baie des Chaleurs Railway. On

---

[115]   *Debates, House of Commons*, 1886, p. 78f.

November 13, 1897, Lemieux was appointed to the Supreme Court of Quebec. On January 1, 1915 the King of England knighted him. He became Chief Justice of the Quebec Supreme Court on February 2, 1915 and continued as Chief Justice until he passed away at Quebec City on July 18, 1933.

(c) James Naismith Greenshields

James Naismith Greenshields was the third Quebec lawyer selected by the Riel Defence Committee. He was born in Quebec on August 7, 1852, and was called to the Quebec Bar in 1877.

In Riel's letter of July 16, 1885 from the Regina prison, written only a short time after he met his lawyers for the first time, Riel wrote to the Committee in Quebec and stated that the lawyers sent to him were first class and of "three nationalities". Lemieux was a French-Canadian, Fitzpatrick was an Irish-Canadian and Greenshields was an English-Canadian. In his letter of the same date to Prime Minister John A. Macdonald, Riel wrote that he had three conservative advocates, a French-Canadian, an Irishman (he didn't add "Canadian" which would have been more precise) and an English Protestant.

Greenshields was a young Montreal lawyer and, judging by his comments during the trial, he had a touch of chutzpah and fire. He aroused the ire of Robinson and Osler, both his seniors by a number of years. At one point he asserted that the defence's endeavour to obtain information had been "frustrated by the counsel for the prosecution or some one for the Government." This prompted Osler to stand up and declaim "you have no right to make such a statement."[116] Robinson added that Greenshields had "made some very strong and very inflammatory remarks."[117] Greenshields responded that he may have urged the adjournment application "with perhaps more warmth than the learned counsel, who seems much cooler, would have done."[118]

Greenshields played a conspicuous part in the proceedings. He argued (together with Fitzpatrick) the jurisdiction of the Court (see Chapter VII); he pleaded the case for an adjournment; he cross-examined key witnesses; he objected to Burbidge adducing hearsay evidence; and he protested improper translations of oral evidence. His

---

[116]   *The Queen v. Louis Riel,* p. 49.
[117]   *The Queen v. Louis Riel,* p. 57.
[118]   *The Queen v. Louis Riel,* p. 58.

participation, while not as extensive as Fitzpatrick's, was quite visible and involved.

In later years he became president and a director of a number of large Canadian corporations.

(d) Thomas Cooke Johnstone

Thomas Cooke Johnstone was the only non-Quebecer on Riel's defence team. At the time of the trial he was resident in Regina. He was born and educated in Canada West (now Ontario). He was called to the Bar of Ontario in 1876. He moved to Regina in 1882 after practicing law in Toronto for several years.

He together with John S. Ewart were legal counsel for John Connor in his appeal to the Manitoba Court of Queen's Bench. In the law report of the case, Johnstone is described as "of the North West bar." The Connor case is discussed in Chapter XX.

After moving to Regina, Johnstone carried on a law practice and also acted as the town's solicitor and as a crown prosecutor.

He was undoubtedly selected to assist Riel's Quebec lawyers because of his local connection to the trial site. However, his participation in the trial was minimal. He argued, without much enthusiasm, that the information containing the six charges of high treason was not sufficient in law. He entered a general demurrer based on the last three charges being identical to the first three, which alleged that Riel was a British subject. In advancing his proposition, Johnstone displayed a startling misunderstanding of the treason statute involved. He thought it was the Canadian treason-felony statute "31 Victoria", which made no provision for the death penalty in the circumstances alleged against Riel. This matter is discussed in Chapter XVI, section 1. Osler, not his co-counsel Lemieux or Fitzpatrick, put Johnstone straight by advising him that it was the *1351 Statute of Treasons*.

Johnstone was assigned to cross-exam John W. Astley, the third witness called by the prosecution. His tactics seemed to be to elicit from Astley an admission that Riel was erratic, a task in which he failed miserably. In answer to Johnstone's questions as to whether Riel was "excited" when interviewing Astley, who was then a Metis hostage, Astley said "Not that I could see, he talked reasonably, as rather a clever man." Later in response to Johnstone asking if he considered Riel's actions "eccentric", Astley responded "He seemed intelligent and in many respects a clever man."[119]   After Johnstone's cross-examination of Astley, he had no further vocal role in the trial, not one word.

An interesting anecdote concerning Johnstone is reported by one of the people charged with treason-felony as a result of the Saskatchewan Uprising.   Louis Goulet wrote that after he was summoned to appear a Winnipeg lawyer named "Clark" who was defending Thomas Scott had advised Goulet to elect for trial by a judge, without a jury.   The lawyer referred to by Goulet was actually Henry J. Clarke of Winnipeg.   As Goulet entered the courtroom, "Johnstone told me to ask for a jury trial."   Charles Nolin then told him "Don't listen to that guy, he's just looking for work."   Goulet elected for a judge without a jury, was granted bail and the charges were later dropped.[120]

Johnstone was eventually appointed a judge in the North-West Territories.   In 1902 when the Supreme Court of the North-West Territories was divided between Saskatchewan and Alberta, he continued on as a judge of the Supreme Court of Saskatchewan where he remained until his retirement in 1913.   On May 20, 1917 he died.

3.   OTHER LAWYERS INVOLVED IN RIEL'S APPEAL

There were two other lawyers, one for the Crown and one for Riel, who appeared as additional counsel on the appeal of Riel's conviction to the Court of Queen's Bench of Manitoba (the appellate court for the North-West Territories).   They were James A. M. Aikins and John S. Ewart, both of Winnipeg, the seat of the appellate court.   As Winnipeg trial lawyers of approximately the same age they were well known to each other.

(a)   James Albert Manning Aikins

James Albert Manning Aikins assisted Christopher Robinson and Britton Bath Osler as a Crown counsel in two hearings before the Manitoba Court of Queen's Bench relating to Riel.   One hearing was with respect to habeas corpus, the other was an appeal against conviction.   These cases are discussed in Chapter XVIII.   Aikins also appeared with Osler before the Manitoba Court of Queen's Bench on the appeal of the Connor case discussed in Chapter XX.

---

119   *The Queen v. Louis Riel* p. 106 and 108.
120   Guillaume Charette, *Vanishing Spaces, Memoirs of Louis Goulet*, p. 154.

Aikins was born on December 10, 1851 in Peel County, Ontario. His father was James Cox Aikins who as an Ontario senator was Secretary of State for Canada in two of John A. Macdonald's cabinets before Macdonald appointed him Lieutenant-Governor of Manitoba in 1882, a post which he held until 1888.

After attending Upper Canada College and the University of Toronto Aikins Jr. was admitted to the Ontario bar in 1878. He shortly thereafter moved to Winnipeg to practise law and became a Queen's counsel in 1884. He represented the Canadian Pacific Railway in western Canada until he was elected to the House of Commons as a Conservative in 1911. Aikins was the founder of the Winnipeg law firm now known as Aikins, MacAulay and Thorvaldson and which today is the largest law firm in Manitoba. He was one of the founders of the Canadian Bar Association. He was later knighted and was thereafter acronymically referred to as "Sir Jam". He was the son of the Minister of Revenue and son-in-law of A.W. McLelan, Minister of Marine and Fisheries, in John A. Macdonald's Conservative government. Both he and his father later became lieutenant-governors of the Province of Manitoba. When the author was a law student he articled in the Aikins MacAulay law firm.

"Sir Jam" was lieutenant-governor of Manitoba for the ten year period ended in 1926. On March 1, 1929 he died in Winnipeg.

(b) John Skirving Ewart

John Skirving Ewart appeared as defence counsel in the two Louis Riel hearings before the Manitoba Court of Queen's Bench sitting as an appellate court. In the law reports he is listed as counsel ahead of Lemieux and Fitzpatrick, unlike Aikins who is listed after Robinson and Osler. Ewart was a little older than Lemieux and Fitzpatrick, while Aikins was quite a bit younger than Robinson and Osler. Ewart also appeared as lead counsel with Thomas Cooke Johnstone in the Connor appeal discussed herein.

Ewart was born on August 11, 1849 in Toronto, Ontario. He was a nephew of Oliver Mowat. Mowat, a former pupil of John A. Macdonald and subsequently his lifelong bitter foe, was the Liberal Premier of Ontario from 1872 to 1896, when Wilfrid Laurier took him into his federal cabinet. At one point in the 1850s in the Parliament of Canada, Macdonald roared at Mowat "You damned pup. I'll slap your chops."[121]   Like Aikins, Ewart attended Upper Canada College, the preeminent boys school in Upper Canada. He became a lawyer in 1871 after studying at Osgoode Hall in Toronto. This was appropriate as Osgoode Hall was built by his grandfather. In due course he moved to Winnipeg where he practised law until 1904, a twenty-two year period in which he established a reputation as a distinguished barrister. He was also a bencher of the Law Society of Manitoba and editor of the Manitoba Law Reports. He became a Queen's Counsel in 1884. In 1889-90 Ewart and his partner James Fisher, whose law firm was called Fisher and Ewart, were active in the debate over the Manitoba School Question, a movement to abolish the dual system of schools under which separate schools were supported by public funds. This had been an essential component of Riel's requirements for the *Manitoba Act*, which brought Manitoba into Confederation as a Province in 1870. In this debate, Fisher and Ewart saw the movement as an injustice to Catholics, but their efforts were not successful. In 1890, Manitoba passed laws to not only abolish state support of Catholic schools, but also to do away with the right to use the French language in the provincial courts, the legislature and the bureaucracy. This also effectively revoked the entitlement of a Franco-Manitoban to have a trial in a provincial court before a French-speaking jury. In the last number of years the Franco-educational and language questions in Manitoba have been resolved to a certain extent.

Ewart moved to Ottawa in 1904 to be close to the Supreme Court of Canada before which he acted as counsel on many occasions. He also appeared before the Privy Council in England.

Ewart was an author in his later years, writing a number of legal articles and books and pamphlets including several relating to Canadian independence.

According to the Manitoba historian W. L. Morton, Ewart founded a "nationalist" tradition, i.e. non-provincial and anti-imperialist, in Manitoba with his book *The Kingdom of Canada and Other Papers*, published after he had moved to Ottawa.[122] Ewart died on February 21, 1933 at Ottawa.

---

[121]   Hardy, p. 56.
[122]   W. L. Morton, *Manitoba, a History*, p. 420.

Chapter IX

APPLICATION FOR ADJOURNMENT OF THE TRIAL

Immediately after Fitzpatrick and Greenshields' lengthy challenge of the Court's jurisdiction was magisterially dismissed in eleven words by Richardson, Johnstone rose to demur to the information (as discussed herein under "Thomas Cooke Johnstone" in the last paragraph of Chapter VII and subsection 2(d) of Chapter VIII). The demurrer (a plea raising a legal objection) alleged that there was a substantial defect in the indictment. After Richardson overruled the demurrer and Riel pleaded not guilty for a second time, Fitzpatrick stated that the defence was not then in a position to proceed with the trial and wanted until the following day to prepare affidavits supporting an application for adjournment. Robinson responded that the Crown reserved the liberty to oppose the adjournment.

The next day July 21, 1885 the defence submitted separate affidavits by Riel, Lemieux and Fitzpatrick upon which the application for adjournment was based.[123] These affidavits are also discussed in Chapter XXII, subsection 1(c) and convey the divergence between Riel's view of what was required for his defence and the view of Lemieux and Fitzpatrick. Riel's affidavit made clear that the witnesses and the documents he wanted were to show justification; in his words to

> prove that the agitation in the North-West Territories was
> constitutional and for the rights of the people of said North-
> West.[124]

There was not a hint of insanity in the affidavit. Lemieux, on the other hand, asked for the adjournment solely to arrange for the attendance of three alienists. An alienist is a psychiatrist, usually one who testifies in court. Nowhere in his affidavit did Lemieux state that he was calling these witnesses to testify as to Riel's insanity, but that was his unannounced intention. Fitzpatrick's affidavit also asked for time to bring the same three alienists to Regina and referred to Riel's past confinement in a lunatic asylum in Quebec. He stated that the Quebec alienists would prove that Riel had been insane for several years (i.e. in

---

123   *The Queen v. Louis Riel*, p. 59 to 64 (the affidavits).
124   *The Queen v. Louis Riel*, p. 61.

the 1870s) but he nowhere swore that he wanted these alienists, who had not seen Riel since the 1870s, to now testify as to Riel's insanity, although that was what he intended. He also referred to some of the witnesses Riel wanted and to information which could support a plea of justification. However later proceedings demonstrated that only a half-hearted attempt in this respect was made; and the defence counsel's main thrust throughout was the insanity plea. Fitzpatrick specifically stated to the jury in addressing them after the evidence was in "... no one of any nationality, of any creed ... can justify the rebellion ..."[125]

Riel and Lemieux requested a delay of one month, while Fitzpatrick asked for "sufficient time" to procure the witnesses.

Greenshields, followed by Fitzpatrick, presented arguments in favour of an adjournment. Greenshields said that Riel had only been arraigned for the first time on the previous day. He asserted the utter impossibility of making a defence without witnesses. He requested that the Court defray the expenses of obtaining the witnesses because Riel was "a man of little or no means." He stated that Gabriel Dumont, Michel Dumas and Napoléon Nault, who had fled to Montana, could give helpful evidence, particularly relating to Riel coming form Montana to assist the "half-breeds and citizens" in obtaining redress of their grievances. They would come to Regina on assurance of counsel that they would be protected. Dumont was of course the legendary buffalo hunter, and the Metis military strategist during the North-West Uprising. Fitzpatrick also wanted the alienists and all documents in the hands of the federal representatives, Burgess and Vankoughnet, brought before the Court. He asked for a one-month adjournment. As noted in subsection 2(c) of Chapter VIII, Greenshields mentioned that Crown witnesses had refused to talk to defence counsel; the witnesses said that they had been instructed not to do so.

Fitzpatrick reiterated the necessity of an adjournment to bring witnesses from Quebec. He added that he had received a letter, a copy of which he gave to Crown counsel, from a gentleman in contact with Dumont and Dumas. Fitzpatrick inferred from this letter that if they could be brought to Regina with immunity he could produce them in Court. He then said they would prove that if Riel had been listened to,

---

[125]   *The Queen v. Louis Riel,* p. 287.

not one drop of blood would have been shed. Osler objected and told Fitzpatrick to confine himself to the facts on the affidavit.

Robinson responded for the Crown. He commenced by chastising Greenshields for his departure from professional courtesy and etiquette and his tone and spirit.

He said it was Crown counsel's duty to oppose a postponement. He blasted as without precedent the thought that the Montana fugitives Dumont, Dumas and Nault should be brought to trial under protection and safe conduct.

As for the documents in Ottawa in the custody of the Deputy Minister of Indian Affairs, and the Deputy Minister of the Interior, he would oppose them as wholly inadmissible. As for correspondence found at Batoche, Robinson said these were "state documents" and the Crown would refuse their inspection on behalf of Riel to the extent they were treasonable correspondence or implicated others. He took this stance notwithstanding, as he said, they were "found in possession of the prisoner at Batoche."

Robinson said that Riel's certificate of naturalization as an American citizen would make no difference whatever in law, but he had telegraphed to Winnipeg for it where it was located as documents seized at Batoche had been forwarded to Winnipeg. Riel's American citizenship certificate was never again mentioned at the trial by any lawyer (Crown or defence) notwithstanding it would have amounted to proof that Riel was not a British subject, thereby invalidating three of the six charges against Riel.

As to Lemieux wishing to go to Quebec to obtain the medical witnesses whom he had expected to be in Regina at that time but were not, Robinson said that an application based on these grounds would not be listened to. He further stated that it must have been perfectly well known "the very moment the prisoner was captured" that Riel's trial would take place as soon as possible. That statement in relation to defence counsel was disingenuous. They were not retained on behalf of Riel until some time after his capture.

After Robinson seemingly rebuffed the defence's request, he abruptly announced that to obtain an impartial trial the Crown would accede to a one-week adjournment, and the Crown would pay the expenses of the witnesses.

Robinson then commented again on Greenshields' "very strong and very inflammatory remarks" concerning possible Crown witnesses, and said that counsel must always take their chances as to the reception they meet from witnesses and "they have no right to complain." Greenshields responded in the manner noted herein at Chapter VIII, subsection 2 (c).

Fitzpatrick then accepted the one-week postponement. Such a short adjournment was inadequate considering the time elements involved in the 1880s for getting witnesses from as far away as Quebec and Ontario and properly preparing them for trial. Osler interjected that the adjournment was peremptory and Fitzpatrick agreed. Richardson adjourned the trial to Tuesday July 28, 1885 at 10:00 am.

Robinson took a hard-line position on the adjournment application initially stating it was his duty to oppose it, and lambasting the defence with respect to the various points they had advanced. He may have done so because Riel, Lemieux and Greenshields had indicated they would require a month's postponement "in order to properly prepare for my defence" (Riel) and because if "we are forced on with this trial now we really have no defence to make" (Greenshields).[126] Lemieux stated in his affidavit that a delay of one month would give time to procure witnesses from Quebec and Toronto. Robinson may have come on strong with a view to intimidating the defence into accepting, without protest, the Crown's about-face assent to a one-week adjournment. If that was the case, Robinson was successful as Fitzpatrick, who had not pressed for a one-month adjournment, accepted Robinson's offer of a one-week delay without protest.

Some months later in the debates in the House of Commons after and concerning Louis Riel's execution, Mr. Cameron the member for Huron blasted the government as the perpetrator who, in effect, instructed Crown counsel to be harsh in responding to the adjournment application. He wanted to know why one month was not allowed. Cameron (a lawyer) said he knew the Crown counsel (referring to Robinson and Osler) and that they were gentlemen of honour and integrity. Cameron said "I know them too well to believe that they would have been parties to any proceedings of this kind." He further said that the "government instructed the judge and instructed the

---

126   *The Queen v. Louis Riel,* p. 45; 50 & 62.

counsel to press on the trial of this case" and not to give Riel an opportunity to prepare for his defence.[127]

Whether or not Cameron's castigations against the government were warranted, Riel's counsel did not vociferously demand a one month adjournment. Fitzpatrick reacted to Robinson's offer of one week by agreeing to it. As a result, the trial commenced seven days later, on July 28, 1885.

When Wilfrid Laurier (who was destined to become Prime Minister in 1896) subsequently spoke in the House of Commons debates referred to above, he said:

> It has been said that the trial was a fair one. I deny it... This man asked for a month's delay for his trial; he obtained eight days. Was that justice? Was that British justice? Was that giving fair play to the accused? ...
> Again when he asked for witnesses, was the request granted him? No, it was again refused.

Laurier said that when Riel asked that his papers taken from him at Batoche be turned over to his counsel the government refused for "Reasons of State". However, such an objection was not raised to tabling them in Parliament because, said Laurier, "such a reason would never have stood discussion in this public Parliament." [128]

With respect to obtaining the testimony of Dumont, Dumas and Nault in Montana (persons who Riel swore were "essential and material witnesses to my defence") one may ask why Riel's counsel did not apply to the court for a commission to have these witnesses examined in Montana. This procedure, if granted, would have authorized a person named in the commission to take the evidence on oath of Dumont, Dumas and Nault by interrogatories or *viva voce*, and their depositions to be read at the trial.

This procedure was even referred to by Mr. Rykert (a Member of Parliament and an admitted Orangeman) in a vitriolic, parliamentary diatribe he aimed at those who condemned the government for allowing Riel to be executed. In his speech, Cameron had quoted from page 166 of Archibald's text on Criminal Law that a "case may be put off for want of documentary evidence" and that "the most moral ground for

---

127   *Debates, House of Commons*, 1886 p. 105-08 (March 12).
128   *Debates, House of Commons*, 1886, p. 181 (March 16).

the delay is the absence of a material witness." Rykert in replying said that one found in the next line of that text that

> in the case of witnesses out of the country time is not granted, unless a commission is applied for to examine the witnesses.[129]

Riel's counsel never applied for such a commission.

---

[129]   *Debates, House of Commons,* 1886, p. 156; 166.

Chapter X

CROWN WITNESSES AND EVIDENCE

Riel's actual trial commenced at 10:00 a.m. on Tuesday, July 28, 1885. Following challenges to the jury panel, the six jurors (Francis Cosgrove, Edwin J. Brooks, Henry J. Painter, Walter Merryfield, Peel Deane, and Edward Eratt) were sworn in and empanelled. The trial could now proceed. "The charge is prepar'd; the lawyers are met; the Judge's all rang'd (a terrible show!)."[130]

Crown counsel Osler made the opening address to the jury. He referred to the six counts of high treason against Riel for levying war at Duck Lake, Fish Creek and Batoche and referred to three of the charges being based on Riel being a British subject i.e. natural allegiance, and the other three based on local allegiance. Reference is made to Chapter IV, section 3 for a discussion of natural allegiance and local allegiance. Osler stated that Riel was charged under the *Statute of Treasons* passed in the reign of Edward III i.e. in 1351. He defended the make-up of the court i.e. a stipendiary magistrate, a justice of the peace and a six-man jury. On June 16, 1885 Osler and Robinson gave the Minister of Justice a legal opinion that a trial for high treason before a stipendiary magistrate would be "anomalous and inappropriate".[131] They recommended to the Minister that either a special commission be created to conduct the trial or a law be passed empowering the government to have an accused tried anywhere in Canada. In light of this opinion Osler was hypocritical in telling the jury in the Riel trial that

> the ordinary courts organized in the land should be the
> courts in which justice is administered to the insignificant
> criminal, or to the one of greater prominence.

He added that "it is always to be avoided, if possible, the organization of special courts for special purposes."[132] The jury, of course, did not know of the legal opinion with the exact opposite advice which Osler and Robinson had given to Justice Minister Alexander Campbell only a few weeks earlier. This is understandable since

---

130 John Gay, *The Beggar's Opera*, Act III, xi, air lvii.
131 "Macdonald Papers", NAC RG13 Vol. 62, File No. 596, June 16, 1885.
132 *The Queen v. Louis Riel*, p. 67.

neither man nor angel can discern hypocrisy ... invisible,
except to God alone.[133]

Osler painted Riel as:

(i)   the mastermind behind the Metis Uprising;

(ii)   the one who threatened to carry out a "war of
         extermination";

(iii)   the one who ordered his men to fire on the police;

(iv)   the one who incited the Indians;

(v)   the one who levied war by his directions and his orders;
         and

(vi)   the one whose letters showed him as the person in
         authority.

Osler asserted that in performing these acts Riel did so, not to aid
the "half-breeds", but to use them for his own selfish ends; for his own
power and benefit; and to extract money for himself from the
government after which he was willing to leave the country. Osler
called Riel's followers "poor dupes" of this "leader and prophet of a
new religion" whose personal ambition and vanity and desire for power
and money, not any wrongs or grievances that existed, were the cause of
the matter, and that Riel did not care whose lives he sacrificed.

After Osler's opening remarks the Crown prosecutors called their
witnesses. Some, but not all of their witnesses, were cross-examined by
defence counsel immediately after each had testified. After the
testimony of the Crown witnesses, the defence lawyers called their
witnesses who were all cross-examined by the Crown lawyers.
Thereafter the Crown called witnesses in rebuttal and the defence cross-
examined some but not all of them. In all the Crown called two dozen
witnesses, the defence called five.

The cumulative objective of the evidence of the Crown witnesses
was to demonstrate that Riel:

(i)   was the instigator and the leader of the rebellious acts and
         the levying of war by the Metis at Duck Lake, Fish Creek
         and Batoche;

(ii)   was against constituted authority;

(iii)   was motivated by personal ambition, money, power and
         vanity;

---

133   John Milton, *Paradise Lost*, bk. iii, l. 682.

(iv)   duped the gullible Metis with his proclamation of a new religion and his status as a prophet; and

(v)   was a self-seeker who would abandon the Metis for cash.

A number of Crown witnesses gave strikingly similar testimony in a number of respects. For example Astley, Harold Ross, Peter Tompkins, his cousin William Tompkins, John B. Lash, Thomas Sanderson, and Thomas E. Jackson (older brother of William Henry Jackson discussed in Chapter IV, section 4) had each been held as a prisoner by the Metis. Each testified in direct examination that after the battle of Duck Lake Riel said that the police, under North West Mounted Police ("NWMP") Superintendent Major Leif Crozier, had fired first and Riel then told his men to fire on the police and, as most said, in the name of God. Some commentators have said that at the time Riel was on horseback waving a large crucifix back and forth. They also stated that on the day (May 12, 1885) that General Middleton's troops were routing the Metis at Batoche, Riel ordered Astley (one of the prisoners) to go to General Middleton. Riel instructed Astley to tell Middleton that if his troops massacred the Metis women and children the prisoners held by the Metis would be massacred. These Crown witnesses and another prisoner, George Ness, all indicated that by his conduct and speech Riel was in command of the armed Metis, and some of them said Riel was armed.

Lash, Henry Walters, Thomas Jackson and Sanderson (all prisoners of the Metis) and Dr. John H. Willoughby who was not a hostage, testified that Riel had talked about his plan to divide the country into seven parts. Different groups were to each receive one-seventh of the land e.g. the Indians, the half-breeds, the Poles, the Hungarians, etc.

Major E. W. Jarvis of the Winnipeg Field Battery identified various Riel and Metis papers, which then became exhibits.

Thomas Sanderson, who was held hostage by the Metis, testified that Riel asked him if it were true that 500 police were coming. Sanderson testified he told Riel "I guessed it was; that I thought there were 500 coming." In response to Greenshields' questions, Sanderson testified that while Riel said he would divide the country into seven parts, he did not say he expected foreign assistance or that he would play the Pope for the North-West Territories. Sanderson stated that

> by the way he spoke to me, the religion was just the same, anymore than he had cut himself from the Pope.

The last Crown witness, Robert Jefferson, identified a letter from Riel and the Exovedate to Chief Poundmaker in which the latter was asked to destroy Fort Battleford. One interesting bit of evidence given by a Crown witness, George Kerr, was that he attended a meeting in January, 1885 at which "there was a pretty good spread" and at which about 150 people were present including Riel. Kerr stated that at the meeting Riel proposed the health of Queen Victoria. Fitzpatrick showed a sense of humour in one exchange with Crown witness Peter Tompkins. Tompkins, who had been a prisoner in the cellar of a house, through the floor heard Riel say "Remember the Almighty, we have all got religion." In response to Fitzpatrick, Tompkins said this was "kind of cool advice coming through the floor at this time", prompting Fitzpatrick to respond "I suppose it would have been cooler if it had gone through an ice-house wouldn't it."[134]

At the trial, Crown witnesses gave evidence of the fighting at Duck Lake, Fish Creek and Batoche, including casualties sustained. Major Leif Crozier, Superintendent of the NWMP at Battleford, issued a proclamation several days before the battle at Duck Lake calling on the Metis to disperse but it had no effect. On March 26th Crozier with a party of police and volunteers was on his way to Duck Lake to get provisions. Crozier said that "a large party of rebels" met him. He stated his force was fired upon and several were killed and wounded. Fitzpatrick cross-examined Crozier who said he had advanced a short distance in front of his troops. He answered "yes" to a question that he was "met by one from the opposite side." He said that man appeared to be an Indian and that he heard the Indian was killed but he didn't see him drop.[135]

What Crozier did not say, because Fitzpatrick failed to ask him, was that on seeing two men with a white flag walking toward him to parley, Crozier asked "Gentleman Joe" McKay (a special constable of the NWMP and an interpreter) to advance with him to meet them. The two men were Isadore Dumont (Gabriel's brother) and Assywin (a Cree Indian). As they were talking, Assywin apparently tried to grab or turn away McKay's rifle. A number of writers state that McKay drew his pistol from his belt and shot and killed both Isadore Dumont and

---

134   *The Queen v. Louis Riel*, p. 127.
135   *The Queen v. Louis Riel*, p. 192-93.

Assywin then and there. Stanley indicates that McKay shot and killed Assywin and Dumont only after an order to fire from Superintendent Crozier. Similar accounts of these killings of Dumont and Assywin are found in a number of other sources.[136] On March 26, 1935 (the 50th anniversary of the Battle at Duck Lake) an interview with Gentleman Joe McKay was published in the *Prince Albert Daily Herald*. In this interview McKay said that "the shots I fired were the first in the rebellion ..." He declared that he "shot only after he had been ordered to do so by his commander, Major Crozier of the N.W.M.P."[137]

The killings of Dumont and Assywin at the Duck Lake parley by Special Constable Gentleman Joe McKay of the NWMP was the spark that ignited the North-West Uprising. McKay was acting under the direct orders of his superior, Major Crozier of the NWMP. The shocking fact is that Gentleman Joe McKay **was never called as a witness** at the trial of Louis Riel either by the Crown or by defence counsel. The Crown had no desire to call McKay as a witness because his evidence would have placed the blame for the initial bloodshed and the commencement of the North-West Uprising battles directly on the NWMP. Riel's defence counsel had no desire to call McKay as a witness because it did not fit within their preconceived defence strategy, which did not include self-defence or justification.

In the newspaper interview McKay also stated that Sergeant Brooks (of the NWMP) accompanied him and Major Crozier to the parley. During the parley, according to McKay, Major Crozier sent Sergeant Brooks back to the police and volunteers with orders to prepare for trouble. Sergeant Brooks was also not called as a witness.

A Crown witness at the trial, Thomas McKay (not Gentleman Joe McKay referred to above) testified that "the Indian talking to Major Crozier ... was killed when the firing began."[138] Thus the first killings of the North-West Uprising were initiated by the NWMP.

There was a short cross-examination of Crozier by Fitzpatrick that was noteworthy in its leniency. In his testimony Crozier was never asked and never volunteered the fact that the persons with him at the

---

[136]   Stanley, *Louis Riel*, p. 317; Beal & Macleod, p. 156-57; Maggie Siggins, *Riel a Life of Revolution*, p. 384; Howard, p. 390; Charlebois, p. 148.
[137]   "Survivors Recount Experiences ... ", *Prince Albert Daily Herald*, March 26, 1935.
[138]   *The Queen v. Louis Riel*, p. 95.

parley were Gentlemen Joe McKay and Sergeant Brooks. In his cross-examination of Crozier, Fitzpatrick also did not ask Crozier

(i)   who was present at the parley;

(ii)   who had fired the first shot at the parley ;

(iii)   on whose instructions the first shot was fired;

(iv)   specific questions as to the killing of Isadore Dumont and Assywin by Gentlemen Joe McKay:

(v)   who gave the order for the first shots that killed Dumont and Assywin during the parley;

(vi)   who gave the order for the first general volley of firing to commence; and

(vii)   if any of Crozier's men were killed during the parley.

The immediate result of the parley was one dead Indian, one dead Metis, no dead police, and the commencement of the North-West Uprising. Of course Fitzpatrick, like Lemieux, had no intention of attempting to justify the rebellion as he so stated in his address to the jury,[139] and questions along these lines would not assist him in pursuing the insanity defence.

Crown witness Hillyard Mitchell testified that on March 19th he had a long conversation with Riel. Riel stated to him that the response of the government to the petitions to the government about the grievances was not a proper reply and that 500 policemen were coming to shoot them. This was obviously a reference to the mischievous falsehood to this effect which Lawrence Clarke (a Hudson's Bay Company factor) told to a group of Metis, adding the 500 Mounted Police would quash the half-breed agitation.[140] According to Mitchell, Riel said he intended to bring Sir John to his feet, and in the Metis council room Mitchell was asked to propose to the police that they surrender Fort Carlton unconditionally. He further stated that Riel talked about a war of extermination if he could not come to terms with the government.[141]

Dr. John H. Willoughby testified that on March 1st he spoke to Riel at the house of a half-breed named Rocheleau whose Christian name he didn't remember. As a crowd of 60 or 70 mostly armed half-breeds drove up Riel said, according to Willoughby, he and his people

---

[139]   *The Queen v. Louis Riel,* p. 287.

[140]   Stanley, *Louis Riel,* p. 305.

[141]   *The Queen v. Louis Riel,* p. 162-67.

intended "to strike a blow to gain their rights." According to Willoughby, Riel added that the only answer they had received to their petitions to the government was "an increase of police", and that in one week the government police "will be wiped out of existence." Willoughby's testimony (which like that of other Crown witnesses appeared to be well-rehearsed) showed that Riel was in command, and alleged that Riel said that he would "rule this country or perish in the attempt."[142] In cross-examination, Fitzpatrick delved into what Riel had told Willoughby concerning the sub-division of the country and the different people (Irish, Germans, Italians, Poles, etc.) who would assist him in the rebellion. On questioning Willoughby, as to what Riel had said his religion was that formed the strongest branch of a tree, Willoughby replied "He said the Roman Catholic Church." Fitzpatrick was most likely not happy with this response since that was not the "new church" of Riel that defence counsel wished to bring out in support of their insanity plea.

The first time he was called Major-General Frederick Middleton stated that he was the commander of the Canadian home militia force, and at the request of Militia Minister Caron (the brother-in-law and law partner of Riel's defence counsel Fitzpatrick) he left Ottawa for the West on March 23, 1885. He testified as to the battle at Fish Creek, where "we lost 9 or 10 plus 40 wounded" on April 24th. The next month the battle of Batoche took place, where six of Middleton's soldiers were killed and 12 or 13 wounded, but the Metis were routed by his troops on May 12.

Riel was not captured by Middleton's troops but, rather than flee to Montana as Gabriel Dumont and others had done, he voluntarily surrendered. He likely did so under a deluded belief that he would be able to lay bare Metis and personal grievances and justify his actions in something akin to a state trial. Reference is made to Chapter IV, section 1. This belief was undoubtedly fostered by a letter that General Middleton wrote to Riel (during the battle of Batoche) in which Middleton testified he had written to Riel that:

> if he surrendered I would protect him **until his case was decided by the Canadian Government**. [Emphasis added.]

---

[142]   *The Queen v. Louis Riel,* p. 78.

Riel handed Middleton this letter on first being brought to him after his surrender.[143]

In cross-examination, Riel's lawyers attempted to lay the groundwork to later support the evidence of their witnesses that Riel was insane. Their cross-examination met with little success. The answers by John W. Astley discussed in section 2(d) of Chapter VIII to questions asked of him by Johnstone are one example.

Crown witness Jackson in responding to a question by Fitzpatrick about Riel's "new religion" answered "he spoke of religion merely as ordinary men do."[144] Fitzpatrick had Peter Tompkins confirm that he heard Riel making a speech in which he thanked the Lord and the Virgin Marie, St. Jean Baptiste, St. Joseph and other saints, and also that Riel gave praise to the angels after the victory at Duck Lake. However, hundreds of millions of Roman Catholics (particularly those raised in a religious milieu) pray to these same sacred figures with no suggestion that they have lost their senses except perhaps by atheists.

Defence counsel occasionally asked questions with respect to Metis grievances but since this aspect was quite secondary to their insanity defence they did so without much fervour and said on more than one occasion that they were not justifying the rebellion.[145]

In response to Greenshields' questions on cross-examination, General Middleton stated that Riel talked a good deal about his religion, that Rome was all wrong, and the priests were narrow-minded people, (sentiments undoubtedly shared by many non-Catholics including perhaps some of the six Protestants on Riel's jury). Greenshields, in an attempt to establish that Riel had fantastical religious views, received only negative replies from Middleton:

(i)   as to whether Riel said that he was a prophet;

(ii)   as to whether Riel said he was endowed with the spirit of God; and

(iii)   as to whether Astley told him that Riel wished as a condition of his surrender that he should be recognized as the head of the church he had formed at Batoche.[146]

---

143   *The Queen v. Louis Riel*, p. 184-85.
144   *The Queen v. Louis Riel*, p. 180.
145   *The Queen v. Louis Riel*, p. 229 and 287.
146   *The Queen v. Louis Riel*, p. 186.

General Middleton was one of the rebuttal witnesses subsequently called by the Crown to testify that Riel was not insane. This rebuttal evidence is discussed herein in section 2 of Chapter XII.

Captain George Holmes Young testified that he was the Infantry Brigade Major under General Middleton at Batoche, and that he seized a large number of papers and books from the house known as the Metis council chamber. Some of them were entered as exhibits including the letter of March 21, 1885 from Louis "David" Riel, Exovede and the Metis councillors to Major Crozier demanding that he surrender or face a war of extermination. Riel coined the term "Exovedate" to designate the Provisional Government on March 19, 1885. "Exovede" designated a councillor and was derived from the Latin meaning "one of the flock". Riel referred to this in his address to the jury.[147] Young said that he had known Riel "in the rebellion of '69 and '70". After his surrender, Riel was in Young's charge from May 15th to May 23rd. It is interesting to note that Young's father, Reverend George Young (a Methodist Minister) attended and prayed with Thomas Scott immediately prior to Scott's execution in 1870 by Riel's Provisional Government in the Red River Settlement. The Crown also called Young as a rebuttal witness.

Several other witnesses were called but the witness for the Crown who precipitated an open-court altercation between Riel and Riel's own counsel was Charles Nolin. Because of the unseemly and stunning open-court dissension, which erupted during Nolin's cross-examination (dealt with in Chapter XI) background information on the relationship between Riel and Nolin is presented. Nolin was Riel's cousin. Nolin had lived in the Red River Settlement in Manitoba in 1869 and had initially participated with Riel in the Metis political movement there. However animosity developed between them when Nolin and his Metis adherents voted against some of Riel's proposals in the Convention of Forty. This Convention was discussing the draft Bill of Rights for Manitoba's entry into Canada. They voted against Riel's insistence on provincial status and against the cancellation of the agreement between Canada and the Hudson's Bay Company for the acquisition of Rupert's Land to be replaced with a new agreement with the inhabitants of the North-West. Nolin and Riel had an angry confrontation and some time later Nolin became the leader of anti-Riel Metis in the Red River

---

[147]   *The Queen v. Louis Riel*, p. 322.

Settlement. Nolin abandoned his involvement in the agitation of 1870 when, as he said, he thought it had become unconstitutional. Nolin was appointed Minister of Agriculture in the Manitoba Government in 1875. He moved to the North-West Territories a few years later.

In the Riel trial in 1885 Nolin testified that he thought the presence of Riel in the North-West Territories in 1884 "would be good for the half-breeds" and that when Riel arrived Riel, his wife and children lived in Nolin's Batoche home for about four months. Apparently the lapse of time since the events in Red River had resulted in the dissipation or dormancy of the past hard feelings between the cousins. This amicable relationship eventually turned once more into one of enmity.

In September 1884 Nolin had been an advocate of violence if half-breed demands were not met, and Sergeant Harry Keenan of the NWMP thought Nolin was the most dangerous of the Metis because he favoured "tampering with the Indians".[148]

One cause leading to Nolin's anti-Riel attitude may have been that in January 1885 Riel pressured Nolin to withdraw his tender for telegraph poles on the government's Batoche line, a contract which would have been quite profitable for Nolin. Another likely more significant incident occurred after a long-delayed government response to the petition sent in December, 1884 by the half-breeds led by Riel to the government outlining their demands. On February 4, 1885 Lieutenant-Governor Edgar Dewdney received a telegram from Ottawa stating the government would establish a commission to investigate the claims of the half-breeds and would direct an enumeration of those who had not participated in a land grant in Manitoba. There was no mention of personal funds for Riel, which Father André had raised with Dewdney in January 1885. Dewdney affronted Riel by passing the government telegram on to Nolin and ignoring Riel. Riel saw the government response as a reluctance to deal with the Metis complaints and, undoubtedly, with him and his own expectations.

Riel thought of returning to Montana; the government would not deal with him or acknowledge him as a representative of the inhabitants of the North-West Territories. Perhaps he thought he was an impediment to their aspirations. However at a general gathering outside the church at Batoche on February 24 to discuss the government

---

148   Charlebois, p. 139; Stanley, *Louis Riel*, p. 412, note 41.

telegram, the meeting resoundingly made clear that Riel should remain and lead them. After this, Riel's non-combative attitude changed. He talked of setting up a provisional government and on March 5 a group of Riel adherents signed a pledge to "...save our country from a wicked government by taking up arms if necessary."[149] Some of the signatories went to see Nolin to have him sign the pledge. Only a few weeks earlier Nolin's wife Rosalie (the sister of Maxime Lépine, a staunch Riel supporter) had a remarkable (many Metis thought a miraculous) cure of a long-lasting incapacitating illness. Nolin and others attributed it to holy water from Lourdes, France being applied to his wife's body. The author recently visited Lourdes, and witnessed the intense devotion displayed by thousands of pilgrims from around the world. The deep faith of these pilgrims in the 1858 apparitional legend of Lourdes was undoubtedly matched by the faith of the Metis in 1885. In any event Father André capitalized on Rosalie's phenomenal return to health to extract a promise from Nolin that he would not participate in any violence. It was in the face of this promise, unknown to Riel, that Nolin was prompted to play for time when asked to sign the pledge. He recommended a novena (nine days of prayers and devotions) to end on March 19, the feast of St. Joseph, the patron saint of the Metis. After that, Nolin suggested, they could do what their consciences told them.

Reluctantly, Riel agreed to the novena. However at Mass at St. Laurent on March 15 at which Riel and other militant Metis were present, Father Vital Fourmond in his sermon denounced violence and declared that any one resorting to arms against the authorities would be excommunicated from the Roman Catholic Church. Riel was outraged and openly and vehemently remonstrated with Father Fourmond. This and an earlier altercation with Father André over formation of the provisional government led to a rupture between Riel (and his cohorts) and the Roman Catholic clergy.

However, Nolin was now on the side of the clergy, who encouraged him to attempt to form an opposing camp of Metis. Riel quickly got wind of Nolin's activities and on March 19 he had Nolin and two others arrested, a course which made clear to the clergy his determination to fight for what he told Father Fourmond were their

---

[149]   Louis Riel, *Collected Writings of Louis Riel*, George F. G. Stanley ed., Vol. 3, No. 3-194, p. 381-82.

"sacred rights". Nolin was tried by the Exovedate and found guilty and sentenced to death. Nolin then agreed to support the Exovedate and was freed. He was dissembling when he agreed to join with Riel and the others. A few days later he fled to Prince Albert, but instead of being welcomed he was unceremoniously clapped into jail by Captain Irvine of the NWMP who thought Nolin was a spy. Nolin was locked up for some four months, a deceitful pariah to many of his own people and an untrustworthy prisoner to those to whom he had defected. As in Manitoba in 1870, Nolin first supported Riel in the initial period and again subsequently became a turncoat. Nolin was "put at liberty" after going "to Regina to give [my] evidence in this case" for the Crown.[150]

With this background the stage was set for Nolin's cross-examination. It was also a prelude to the pernicious (for Riel) brouhaha, which flared up, in full public view, between Riel and his counsel whom Riel referred to as being "from Quebec, from a far province."[151] Crown counsel looked on with, perhaps, restrained delight at this damaging rift in open court before the wide-eyed jury. These events are the subject of the following Chapter.

---

[150]   *The Queen v. Louis Riel*, p. 204.
[151]   *The Queen v. Louis Riel*, p. 207.

Chapter XI

OPEN COURT DISSENSION BETWEEN RIEL AND HIS COUNSEL

Riel became increasingly unhappy with his Quebec counsel as he saw the line their cross-examination of Crown witnesses was taking. Riel gave express instructions to his counsel (Fitzpatrick and Lemieux) and to Fiset in his letter of June 16, 1885 in which he unambiguously stated that he wanted a trial based "on the merit of my actions" (see section 2(a) of Chapter VIII and section 1(a) of Chapter XXII). Contrary to these instructions, his counsels' questions were primarily directed towards supporting the subsequent insanity evidence they intended to adduce. On realizing on the first day of the trial that his lawyers were not following his instructions he (privately on that day) insisted to them that he be allowed to put questions to the witnesses,[152] but his lawyers would not permit this. The parade of Crown witnesses, prior to Nolin, gave strong evidence against Riel. He obviously felt his counsel were derelict in their cross-examination in which they mainly pursued traits or conduct which might tend to support their self-created insanity defence, while down playing or disregarding Riel's specific directions for a trial on the merits.

When Charles Nolin (Riel's hostile cousin) was called as a witness, it quickly became evident that he considered it payback time for the indignities he felt Riel had caused him. See the latter part of Chapter X for a discussion of the hostility between Riel and Nolin. His bitterness against Riel glared forth in his lengthy answers to the very brief questions asked of him during his examination. Nolin stated that about a month after Riel arrived in the North-West he showed Nolin a book he had written about destroying England, Canada, Rome and the Pope. Nolin also stated that Riel told him that he had a divine mission; that in December, 1884 Riel wanted money claiming the Canadian Government owed him $100,000 and that Father André was trying to get $35,000 for Riel, and that if Riel received it he'd go wherever the Government wished. Nolin added that Riel also said that with the money he would start a paper in the United States, raise nationalities, foreign armies would come into the country and he would destroy Manitoba and the

---

[152] *The Queen v. Louis Riel*, p. 211.

North-West and take possession of the North-West. Nolin told of Riel asking him to withdraw his tender to construct a government telegraph line.

Nolin testified that at a general meeting on February 24, Riel secretly arranged for five or six persons to say "no, no" when Riel told the meeting he was going to depart for the United States and that Riel never had any intention of leaving the country.

Nolin mentioned he had been asked to sign a paper to take up arms, but he suggested a novena instead. When the novena ended on March 19, Riel had four armed men take him prisoner. He was brought before the Metis council and, according to him, was acquitted by proving to the council that Riel had made use of the movement to claim an "indemnity for his own pocket." He then contrarily said he had been condemned to death when he was brought to the church where the council was meeting.

François-Xavier Lemieux cross-examined Nolin. Lemieux was successful in his early questioning, which indicated that Nolin acted with Riel when, according to Nolin, Riel plotted to deceive the people about Riel's pretended departure. Lemieux asked how Nolin could do so if, as he said, he had lost confidence in Riel. Lemieux also brought out that Nolin, after initially being a supporter, had been a defector of both the 1870 and North-West Metis movements led by Riel.

Lemieux then pursued questions aimed at incidents that might demonstrate signs of mental derangement on the part of Riel. Nolin stated that Riel:

(i)   considered himself a prophet;

(ii)   wrote and said that he was inspired;

(iii)   after his arrival showed Nolin a book written in buffalo blood; and

(iv)   said that after taking England and Canada he, Riel, would divide Canada and give different parts of it to different nations including the Prussians, the Irish, the Jews, and others.

Nolin stated that before the battle of Duck Lake he saw Riel going out with a crucifix about a foot and a half long. He further testified that when police were mentioned to Riel he became excitable and uncontrollable. He added among other things that he, Nolin, had "been put at liberty since [he] came to Regina to give his evidence in this case."[153]

An interesting, perhaps humorous, anecdote was told by Nolin to Lemieux during his cross-examination. Nolin said that one night he heard a noise in Riel's bowels and Riel asked him if he had heard it. Nolin answered in the affirmative whereupon Riel told him

> that that was his liver, and that he had inspirations that
> worked through every part of his body,[154]

after which Riel wrote on a sheet of paper and said that he was inspired. One might speculate that the noise could have been due to flatulence, not inspiration, and Riel's comment was simply designed to relieve a social embarrassment.

Lemieux omitted asking Nolin a number of pertinent questions such as:

(i)   why he continued to support Riel for more than six months after Riel had purportedly shown him the book, written in buffalo blood, relating to destroying England, Canada, Rome and the Pope;

(ii)   whether he had read any parts of the book and whether or not he could actually read; and

(iii)   why at one point Nolin said the Metis council acquitted him, but at another that he was condemned to death, etc.

When it appeared that Lemieux was finished with his cross-examination of Nolin, an extraordinary episode of great moment in the trial ensued.[155] The author of this text has paraphrased some of the following verbal exchanges. Riel jumped to his feet and asked Magistrate Richardson to permit him to question Nolin before he left the box. Riel said he had some observations to make before the court. His observations disclosed the monumental divergence between the defence Riel wished to present to save his life and the defence which his lawyers wished to pursue in an attempt to show that he was crazy. The sharp disagreement between Riel and his own lawyers over defending his life was laid bare with impassioned clarity for all present to witness.

Fitzpatrick, Riel's own legal counsel, immediately objected to Riel saying anything. Fitzpatrick told the court that defence counsel required

---

153   *The Queen v. Louis Riel*, p. 194-204.
154   *The Queen v. Louis Riel*, p.203.
155   *The Queen v. Louis Riel*, p. 205-15.

Riel to understand that anything done in the case must be done through them, that Riel was "now endeavouring to withhold instructions", that he must give them instructions **"and he must not be allowed to interfere."** [Emphasis added.] He said this notwithstanding the fact that he and the other defence counsel had ignored Riel's prior instructions to have a trial based on the merit of his actions and that they were pursuing an insanity defence that Riel had not authorized them to do and had specifically repudiated.

Richardson stated that the statute authorized Riel to defend himself personally or by counsel, but Fitzpatrick shot back that "Once he has counsel, he has no right to interfere." Riel interjected that his lawyers were trying to show that he was insane when Richardson abruptly told him to stop, and told him if he had questions for Nolin to tell them quietly to his counsel and they would ask them if they thought it proper to do so.

Crown counsel Osler, a clever fox, proclaimed that the Crown had no objection to Riel asking any particular question himself.

Fitzpatrick then told the Court that Riel was "actually obstructing the proper management of this case." Fitzpatrick said that Riel must be told not to interfere, "or else it will be absolutely useless for us to endeavour to continue any further in it." Richardson suggested that that was a matter between Riel and defence counsel. Fitzpatrick stated they were "entirely free" to throw up their brief and that they were considering doing so if Riel was allowed to interfere. He said that he had very little desire to have questions put which they did not desire to put, and asked what the Court had to do "with theories about inspiration and the division of lands", further than they had gone into it. This may or may not have indicated the nature of some of the questions Riel wished to ask, perhaps in clarification of prior testimony, but since Fitzpatrick threw the comment in without explanation his purpose in so doing is unknown.

After a suggestion by Crown counsel Robinson, concurred in by Fitzpatrick, Magistrate Richardson asked Riel, in five uninterrupted staccato exclamations, if he was defended by counsel. Riel answered:

> Partly; my cause is partly into their hands ... I want their
> services, but **I want my cause to be ... defended the best
> which circumstances allow.** [Emphasis added.]

Richardson fatuously replied "Then you must leave it in their hands." Riel eloquently countered:

> My counsel come from Quebec, from a far province. They have to put questions to men with whom they are not acquainted, on circumstances which they don't know ... they cannot follow the thread of the questions. They lose more than three-quarters of the opportunities of making good answers ...

Richardson told Riel he must leave the case in the hands of his advisers and he could speak at the proper time (i.e. after all evidence was in). At that time the law did not allow an accused to testify on his own behalf and anything he then said would not be evidence.

Riel persisted and said "The witnesses are passing and the opportunities." Richardson again told him if there was any questions that he wanted put to Nolin to tell his counsel and they would say whether it should be put. Riel responded "I have on cross-examination 200 questions."

Crown counsel Robinson reiterated that if his counsel agreed Riel could put any questions he pleased to Nolin, and later stated that the Crown would not object if Riel joined his counsel in examination or cross-examination of witnesses.

At Fitzpatrick's request, Richardson granted a brief adjournment. On re-convening, Fitzpatrick made a statement to the Court concluding with the comment that "the law says that when a man appears by counsel, that counsel must act for him during the whole trial." Lemieux remarked that if Riel insisted on questioning witnesses defence counsel objected, and that they would not continue to act in the case as counsel. Lemieux immediately followed this threat with an inconsistent, somewhat perverse, assertion that defence counsel thought it was "too late for [Riel] now to disavow or refuse." Essentially Riel's own counsel were telling him to shut up, to not interfere and to let them carry on with a lunacy defence that ran contrary to his specific instructions. Riel's lawyers had arrogated to themselves the manner in which Riel's fight for his life was to be conducted. Notwithstanding it was Riel's life at stake and not theirs they ignored Riel's desires. They acted, not in accordance with Riel's wishes, but pursuant to their own willful wishes and, presumably, the directions of the anonymous (to use Fitzpatrick's own words) "parties ... who were really our clients in this case."[156]   As Greenshields stated in his request for a trial adjournment:

> **This defence** [i.e. the doctors from Quebec who were to testify as to insanity] **we are instructed by others than the prisoner to make.**[157] [Emphasis added.]

Their actions and attitudes were unjust to Riel.

It was never disclosed who these real clients, who these "others", were whose instructions defence counsel was acting on, but these "others" also did not have their lives in peril. If Riel had known in advance that his lawyers intended to act on the advice not of him but of unknown "others", and that their defence strategy was to plead him insane without his consent he undoubtedly would have considered other alternatives. For example instead of surrendering himself for trial he could have fled to safety in the United States with Dumont and Dumas where he had United States citizenship.   Instead he had made a conscious decision to surrender in order to present the case of the Metis people and his own case before a Canadian court of law by, in his own words, a trial "on the merit of my actions".

As the verbal clashes continued between Riel and his own lawyers, Richardson again stated that if Riel insisted on putting a question the Court should not refuse him. Fitzpatrick said that Riel could only do so "after counsel have been refused."   Riel persisted and said he understood and knew that it was a matter of dignity for their profession, but he wished to be allowed to put questions. Richardson countered that he would not stop him but if Riel did so his counsel would abandon him at once. Riel asked Richardson if he could put the questions and have his lawyers advise him on procedure. Richardson offered Riel an opportunity to further instruct his counsel, but Lemieux said they didn't want that, that they had full instructions. (Only a few minutes earlier, Fitzpatrick had told Richardson that Riel was withholding instructions.)

Riel then made an elemental statement:

> The case concerns my good lawyers and my friends, **but in the first place it concerns me,** and, ... conscientiously I cannot abandon the wish I expressed to the Court, and I cannot abandon the wish that I expressed to retain my counsels ... [Emphasis added.]

---

[156]   *The Queen v. Louis Riel,* p. 50.
[157]   *The Queen v. Louis Riel,* p. 48.

Riel said he wished to retain his chances of doing the best for himself, and then to take the help "of those who are so kind to me" and that his counsel "ought" to help him. He asserted that he had been "insisting since yesterday" on the matter and that while he wished to retain them he could not abandon his dignity. He passionately proclaimed:

> Here I have to defend myself against the accusation of high
> treason, or I have to consent to the animal life of an asylum.
> I don't care much about animal life if I am not allowed to
> carry with it the moral existence of an intellectual being.

Richardson told him to stop. Richardson then said to Riel that if he had any question for Nolin, why couldn't he tell his counsel. The transcript then indicates there was a pause and after the pause Richardson said "Very well then, they don't think it proper to put it." Crown counsel Osler stated that the statute 7 William IV provided that the accused "shall make full defence by counsel". Instead of that 1836 English Statute Osler should have cited section 76(7) of the *1880 North-West Territories Act* which provided that after the close of the prosecution's case the person tried had the right "to make full answer and defence by counsel, attorney or agent."

Richardson then said an authority had been handed to him (without identifying who did so or the authority in question). Richardson said that the authority was to the effect that the court refused to let the defendant examine after a witness had been fully cross-examined by the defence lawyer, and that Riel was now in his counsel's hands. Riel asked about the right to make "full defence" (which Osler had just mentioned) and Richardson stated that Riel could address the Court after all witnesses were examined. Such an address was irrelevant to a "full defence"; it was not under oath and not evidence. At the time of the trial an accused was not allowed to give evidence. Riel said of his counsel that it would be "the coronation of their kindness" if they allowed ten questions. Richardson then asked counsel if they had any questions of Nolin and said "Let the re-examination go on."

The transcript does not identify which counsel asked the next questions of Nolin, but it was likely Crown counsel Casgrain. In answers to questions Nolin testified that Riel had separated from the clergy, that the half-breeds were greatly influenced by religion, and that

Riel succeeded in bringing the half-breeds with him by making himself appear as a prophet.

In re-cross-examination by Lemieux, Nolin testified that Riel gained influence by working against the clergy and making himself out as a priest, and that the ignorance and simplicity of the people were taken advantage of. At this answer Riel again stated that he himself wished to put a question to Nolin. Richardson said that if his counsel saw fit to put it, they would, and if not Nolin was discharged. Lemieux said Riel told him he'd only put questions by himself. Riel repeated his two wishes of defending himself and retaining his counsel.

Richardson and Crown counsel Robinson then both briefly summed up their views of the positions taken by Riel and his counsel. Riel asked if he had to keep silent and Richardson told him to inform his counsel what he wanted. Riel then asked if his counsel could insist on being his counsel "if I thank them for their services?" (i.e. if he fired them). Richardson said that at this stage he could not refuse to recognize Fitzpatrick, Lemieux and the others as having charge and the responsibility for the defence. Lemieux said: "We accept the responsibility." Riel once more tried to have the court accept his position. Richardson rebuffed him by stating that if his counsel did not continue Riel might have counsel assigned by the court to defend him, "and then he would be bound." Riel said "It is not against their dignity. I cannot see it in that light."

Richardson peremptorily ordered "Proceed with another witness, please." This brought an effective end to Riel's desire and attempts to be defended on the merit of his actions and to bring to public attention the grievances of and the injustices suffered by the Metis, and to demonstrate the gross neglect by the government in the matter. It also meant that his lawyers would now have free rein in their attempt to prove the Metis leader was a madman, a defence which was doomed to failure, a failure which led in due course to the hangman's noose.

Chapter XII

WITNESSES FOR THE
DEFENCE AND REBUTTAL WITNESSES

In the prior Chapter it was noted that Riel, in pleading with the Court to be permitted to ask questions, was told by Magistrate Richardson that Riel was in the hands of his counsel, after which Riel asked about the right to make full defence. Section 76(7) of the *North-West Territories Act* provided that he had the right "**to make full answer and defence**" by counsel, attorney or agent. Richardson's response to Riel's inquiry about a full defence was that he could address the Court after the witnesses were examined.[158] This reply, of course, had nothing whatsoever to do with a full defence. As well the "answer and defence" advanced by Fitzpatrick, Lemieux, Greenshields and Johnstone was not "full" in the sense that Riel wanted it to be i.e. Riel wanted a defence based on the merit of his actions.[159] He did not receive it.

Riel persistently attempted to have the right to ask questions of witnesses but the manner in which the verbal exchanges developed between him and his counsel and the Magistrate (outlined in the preceding Chapter) effectively foreclosed his efforts. His counsel viewed his endeavours as effronteries while specifically making clear they would abandon Riel if he insisted upon putting questions. His counsel also said it was too late for him to disavow or refuse their services. Their attitude was that they could abandon Riel, but he couldn't abandon them. The Magistrate, faced with a case that he said was beyond the ordinary run of cases (such as petty crimes and liquor offences) which he had dealt with in his whole career, initially said he would not stop Riel from putting a question but later reversed himself.

In response to Riel asking if he could dismiss his lawyers, Richardson said "I don't think at this stage I should refuse to recognize them as having charge and the responsibility for the defence."

Riel was a penniless prisoner. He was not paying his counsel. Fee-wise they were not beholden to Riel since they were receiving no fees from him. While a Committee was set up in Quebec to raise funds for the defence, Romuald Fiset, in a letter of May 22, 1885 to Monsignor

---

[158]   *The Queen v. Louis Riel*, p. 212.
[159]   See the first paragraph of Chapter XI.

Taché of St. Boniface, said that Lemieux and Fitzpatrick had offered their services gratuitously. The author of this book does not know if they received fees out of this defence fund, but they received no payments directly from the impoverished Riel. Although it seems extraordinary, considering the animosity that Macdonald had for Riel, a copy of this letter from Fiset to Tache is among the "John A. Macdonald Papers" in the National Archives of Canada.[160] In this letter Fiset told Taché that Fitzpatrick was the brother-in-law of the Hon. Caron (the Minister of Militia), as well as the fact that Lemieux and Fitzpatrick had offered their services free to act as Riel's lawyer. It seems strange that two young lawyers (with small children at home in Quebec City) would agree to act without payment for a man that they had never met, and agree to travel thousands of miles at a time when travel was much more arduous and lengthy than it is today. The offer of Lemieux and Fitzpatrick to act gratuitously when their was a defence fund for Riel also seems odd. Both lived in the same city as Militia Minister Caron, and one was the Minister's law partner and brother-in-law.

Instead of their loyalties being exclusive to Riel, their loyalties may have been split between Riel and the unknown "others" from whom they had taken instructions. See section 1(a) of Chapter XXII concerning these unknown "others". Riel, the pauper, faced with the Court saying in effect he couldn't fire his lawyers, and he couldn't ask questions, and with his lawyers threatening to abandon him, had become subdued. He never again attempted to ask a question or intervene in the proceedings. His yearning for a trial on the merit of his actions as he saw them, and as unequivocally conveyed to his counsel at the outset, was forever dashed.

In light of the failure of the insanity defence which Riel's lawyers adamantly insisted upon pursuing to the bitter end of the trial, Riel could have done no worse by demanding their peremptory dismissal and living or dying with the consequences. The demand, at the very least, would have caused a crisis in the proceedings, highly embarrassed his counsel and likely precipitated their withdrawal. Richardson, as he indicated, might then have assigned other counsel,[161] undoubtedly requiring an adjournment for this purpose. This may have given Riel an

---

[160]   "Macdonald Papers", NAC Vol. 107, p. 43105-06 , Letter of May 22, 1885 from Fiset to Taché.
[161]   *The Queen v. Louis Riel*, p. 214.

opportunity to have the tenor of the trial significantly altered in his favour.

1.   THE DEFENCE WITNESSES

The last witness for the Crown, in direct examination, completed his evidence at 6:00 p.m. on Wednesday, July 29, 1885.

The next day Thursday July 30 at ten o'clock in the morning defence counsel called the first defence witness. In contrast to the twenty-four witnesses called by the Crown, the defence were to call five witnesses in all. The main thrust of defence counsel's questioning of them was an endeavour to prove that Riel was insane. The five defence witnesses were examined and cross-examined in only a few hours on July 31, and after completion of their testimony the Crown had time on that very same day to call two of its own witnesses in rebuttal.

In this author's opinion, the cumulative evidence of the five witnesses called by Riel's lawyers did more to contribute to Riel's conviction than otherwise.

Two of the witnesses were unsympathetic Roman Catholic priests. One, Father Alexis André, considered Riel a "notorious character",[162] a "fool" and a heretic.[163] The other, Father Vital Fourmond, thought Riel was "insane or a great criminal".[164]

A third witness, Philip Garnot (a prisoner at the time of the trial), said he followed Riel against his will notwithstanding he acted as secretary of the Exovedate (the Metis council), signed Exovedate documents as such, and testified that he thought Riel was crazy.

The remaining two defence witnesses were medical doctors, called to give expert evidence that Riel was insane. Dr. François Roy stated that he was "not an expert in insanity",[165] while Dr. Daniel Clark gave answers which effectively established Riel's legal sanity, not the contrary. Defence counsel called Father Alexis André as the first defence witness.[166] Father André was the superior of the Oblate priests in the Carlton district and had been for seven years and had lived in the

---

[162]   "Macdonald Papers" NAC Vol. 107, p. 42995 –99, André to Dewdney, February 6, 1885.
[163]   *The Queen v. Louis Riel,* p. 232 and 234.
[164]   *The Queen v. Louis Riel,* p. 243.
[165]   *The Queen v. Louis Riel,* p.251.
[166]   *The Queen v. Louis Riel,* p. 226-35.

Saskatchewan country for twenty years. Questioned by Lemieux, he testified that prior to Riel's coming in July 1884 there was agitation among the French and English half-breeds. For some months after Riel's arrival there was constitutional agitation.

In response to direct questions from Lemieux, Father André testified:

(i)   as to the claims which the half-breeds had prior to the rebellion;

(ii)   that they held public meetings in which he took part;

(iii)   that three or four communications, resolutions or petitions were sent to the Dominion Government but only an evasive answer was received;

(iv)   that Monsignor Grandin received no favourable response to his own communication;

(v)   that the silence of the Government produced great dissatisfaction in the minds of the people; and

(vi)   that they had not received their land patents.

At this point Crown counsel Osler objected to this line of questioning. He said defence counsel was pursuing inconsistent defences – insanity and justification, that justification was no defence in law and if given in evidence "there would be the question of justifying the policy of the Government." Richardson said "It would be trying the Government."

Lemieux stated **"I do not want to justify the rebellion"**, [Emphasis added], but to show circumstances in the country justifying Riel in coming. Further verbal clashes took place between Osler and Lemieux, but Lemieux had André admit that since Riel's arrival a favourable answer had been received to some of the half-breed claims.

Shortly after Osler's objection, Lemieux abandoned questions of the type objected to by Osler. If, as Lemieux stated, he did not want to justify the rebellion, it is difficult to understand why he asked those questions in the first place. His statement to the Court that, if the people had confidence in Riel, Riel had a right to come and help them was both obvious and irrelevant once justification was ruled out. As well, Lemieux's line of questioning on that point was irrelevant to the insanity defence which he and his associates were imposing on Riel, a defence to which he quickly directed his questions.

Lemieux could have contested Osler's contention that one could not plead insanity and justification at the same time. See e.g. Chapter XIX in this respect. It could have been argued that whether or not Riel was insane the actions pursued, e.g. at Duck Lake, were in self-defence, etc. Even an insane man may defend himself.

Lemieux raised questions about Riel's attitude on religion and politics. André said that on these matters Riel lost all control of himself, that he was a fool, and that he did not have his intelligence of mind. He added that on politics, on the rebellion, on religion Riel stated things which frightened the priests, and all the priests met and unanimously decided that he was not responsible, he was completely a fool, and he could not suffer contradiction.

Although André was a witness for the defence, he was not a helpful one. André had been called

> a stocky Breton … an obstinate man with little constraint or
>
> etiquette … [with] an excellent heart and a true zeal.[167]

He had developed an antipathy towards Riel some months earlier. In early December 1884 he and Riel had a row over what Riel felt was the lukewarm attitude of the Oblate priests towards Riel's activities and the Metis crusade. A week later André had the first of two meetings with Riel, whom he undoubtedly considered a heretic, at which according to André the question of a cash indemnity for Riel (discussed hereafter) was raised. It does not strain credulity to contemplate that André could have been the instigator of the idea with a view to having his nemesis, and competition for allegiance of the Metis, return whence he came. In an undated letter written in January 1885 to Lieutenant Governor Edgar Dewdney, with whom he seemed to be on excellent terms, he referred to Riel as "the notorious Monsieur Riel".[168] He and Riel had exchanged words in March 1885 over Riel's desire to form a provisional government. Maggie Siggins pointed out that André "wasn't going to tolerate someone like Riel trespassing on his turf."[169] With this background, it is not strange that André's testimony was not sympathetic to Riel and was more helpful to the Crown than to the defence.

Thomas Casgrain commenced his cross-examination of Father André by inquiring as to meetings with Riel in December 1884 at which

---

[167] George Woodcock, *Gabriel Dumont*, p. 78.
[168] "Macdonald Papers", NAC RG . Vol. 107, p. 42954-57.
[169] Siggins, p. 351.

Riel claimed the Federal Government owed him money. André said that at meetings with Riel on December 12 and December 23, but not at any other time, Riel raised the matter. In the latter meeting, according to André, Riel claimed he was owed $100,000 but would accept $35,000 and he would leave the country. In response to a question that even if the government granted him $35,000 the half-breed question would remain the same André testified that Riel answered "If I am satisfied the half-breeds will be."

Casgrain's cross-examination of André on money matters was quite damaging to a defence based on insanity. If André was correct in his testimony, it portrayed Riel as clever and sane when it came to negotiating for government funds.

André testified that Riel wanted to change the mass, liturgy, ceremonies and symbols of the Catholic religion. Casgrain attempted to have André admit that a man with particular views on religious matters, and a great reformer of great religious questions, was not necessarily a fool. André would not concede this in relation to Riel saying he was an autocrat in religion and politics. André said that Riel exercised great influence over the half-breeds because he was so religious and appeared so devout, and did not admit his strange views at first. Lemieux, in re-examination, had André testify that with the least opposition Riel's physiognomy changed and he became a different man.

Father André's evidence to the effect that if Riel could get $35,000 from the Federal Government he would abandon the Metis was highly injurious to Riel. Richardson specifically referred to the $35,000 in his charge to the jury. Riel's lawyers adduced no evidence whatsoever to counter André's testimony on this point, which portrayed Riel as a money-grubbing self-seeker, not a champion of his people. This uncontested, one-sided version by Father André was undoubtedly one of the most prejudicial items of testimony in the trial. See also Chapter XVIII section 2 with respect to this $35,000, and with respect to Riel telling the jury he did not "speak of myself" until after the petitions had been sent to the Canadian Government.

The second defence witness was Philip Garnot, who was examined by Fitzpatrick.[170] He normally lived at Batoche but was in the Regina jail at the time of his examination. Fitzpatrick elicited from Garnot that

---

[170]   *The Queen v. Louis Riel*, p. 235-39.

Riel wanted Bishop Ignace Bourget (the Bishop of Montreal) to be Pope of the new world, that Riel wanted the people to acknowledge him as a prophet, that he made up prayers, that he would not stand contradiction and was irritable. Garnot also said that Riel told him that he was representing St. Peter. Garnot testified that in his presence Riel talked of dividing the country into seven provinces and seven different nationalities, and that he said he had a divine mission. Fitzpatrick questioned Garnot about Riel speaking of religion and the country, and whether Riel thought of the welfare of everyone except himself. Garnot (likely to the surprise of Fitzpatrick) said it seemed as if Riel

> was working in the interest of the half-breed population, and
> the settlers generally.

Garnot added that he thought Riel was crazy "because he acted very foolish."

Crown counsel Robinson, in a brief cross-examination, had Garnot disclose Riel's great influence over the half-breed population. Garnot said he only followed Riel because Riel came to him with armed men. He said the half-breeds looked to Riel as a leader and followed him, relying on his judgment and advice.

Nothing in the examination or cross-examination of Garnot elicited the fact that not only was he a member of the Exovedate but he was its secretary. As secretary he signed Exovedate documents in that capacity including the letter of March 21, 1885 to Superintendent Crozier of the NWMP threatening a war of extermination.

The third defence witness was Father Vital Fourmond an Oblate priest (like his Superior Father André) at St. Laurent.[171] Fourmond testified that he was personally acquainted with the facts upon which the other priests based their opinion as to Riel's insanity.

In response to a question from Lemieux he stated that before the rebellion Riel was affable, polite, pleasant and rational except when he was contradicted on politics and government. When contradicted he became a different man and would use violent expressions. Fourmond testified that when the rebellion commenced Riel became excited and lost control of his temper, and he often threatened to destroy all the churches. Fourmond carried on with his long, rambling, uninterrupted testimony leading the interpreter to state that he did not feel qualified to correctly interpret the evidence. This led to an extraordinary agreement

---

[171]   *The Queen v. Louis Riel*, p. 239-43.

by counsel that Casgrain would interpret the defence evidence and Fitzpatrick the evidence of the Crown. This carried on for awhile until Osler told the Court that the Crown wanted a regular interpreter.

Fourmond, in direct examination, recited a number of examples of Riel's heretical religious views, such as those he expressed relating to the Trinity, the Virgin Mary, the divine presence, Riel's desire to overthrow the Pope and have a new Pope appointed or appoint himself as Pope, etc.

Fourmond said that

> We [presumably the Oblate priests] made up our minds there
> was no way to explain this conduct but that he was insane,
> otherwise he would have to be too big a criminal.

Fourmond said that one of the facts on which he formed the opinion that Riel was insane at the time of the rebellion was that when Riel found out the clergy were against him he turned against the clergy. Fourmond also testified that Riel told some women that if they went to the priests the priests would kill them, and all of a sudden Riel passed from great rage and showed great politeness to him. Fourmond, in response to Lemieux's questions to this effect, said that in political and religious matters Riel was not sane. Another time, according to Fourmond, Riel got very excited and called him "a little tiger", supposedly because he had contradicted Riel. Lemieux asked Fourmond if Riel had shown him a book in which he had written prophecies in buffalo blood as to the future of the country. Fourmond said he'd heard of it, but never saw it, nor did Riel speak to him about it.

Casgrain cross-examined Fourmond who again said Riel became uncontrollable when contradicted. Fourmond said in response to whether Riel had asked for an oath of neutrality towards the provisional government that it was "a written promise concerning the exercise of the ministry" in such terms. Casgrain asked him if rather than saying Riel was a great criminal Fourmond would say Riel was insane, Fourmond answered that he did not say it, but he thought it.

Fourmond's evidence as to insanity was based primarily on Fourmond's views of Riel's heretical notions and his temper when contradicted. This evidence of supposed insanity was less than persuasive.

Dr. François Roy was the first medical witness to give evidence on behalf of the defence.[172] He was the medical superintendent of the mental hospital at Beauport, Quebec and had been for fifteen years. The asylum, owned by Dr. Roy and his partner, was an institution operated for financial gain.

Fitzpatrick conducted the direct examination of Roy who disclosed that Riel had been an inmate in his asylum for a number of months until his discharge in January 1878. He said that before Riel left the asylum he became cured "more or less". Roy stated that while at the asylum Riel suffered from megalomania, and described its symptoms many of which, he said, "are found in the ordinary maniac". He testified that those suffering from the disease were clever in discussions, tended to be irritable when their mental condition was questioned because they believe they are right, and they consider it an insult if one tries to bring them to reason again. The author of this text suggests that it is not improbable that these "symptoms" affect many rational people on occasion.

In response to leading questions from Fitzpatrick, Roy answered "yes" to pride, selfishness, egotism, and rapid change of affections being prominent features of the condition, but on matters not touching a patient's mania a patient will respond with reason.

Roy said that except for the immediately preceding day he had not seen Riel since January 1878 (over seven years earlier). Roy did not testify that he had personally examined Riel in Regina. He stated that based on the testimony of the witnesses he heard in Court "yesterday and today" Riel's mind was unsound on the occasions they described; that he was not the master of his acts; and Riel's symptoms were largely identical to those when he was at the Beauport Asylum.

In a leading question Roy was asked whether he believed that under the state of mind described by the other witnesses Riel was capable or incapable of knowing the nature of the acts which he did. Roy replied "No, I do not believe that he was in a condition to be master of his acts." He also agreed in response to another leading question that Riel "did not know what he was doing or whether it was contrary to law in reference to the particular delusion." These were Fitzpatrick's words, not those of Dr. Roy. Fitzpatrick was undoubtedly

---

[172]   *The Queen v. Louis Riel*, p. 243-56.

attempting to fit the evidence into the McNaghten Rules, relating to insanity, discussed hereafter in relation to Dr. Daniel Clark's evidence.

For some reason the Crown did not object to Fitzpatrick's leading questions. In the law of evidence, a leading question is one which directly or indirectly suggests the answer to the witness, or which puts a disputed matter to the witness in a form calling for a "yes" or "no" answer. Generally, leading questions may be asked in cross-examination, but not in examination-in-chief. It may be that while answering and listening to Roy, Crown counsel Osler felt confident that he was about to verbally pummel Roy, so much so that when Riel later addressed the jury he stated:

> I thank the lawyers for the Crown who destroyed the
> testimony of my good friend Dr. Roy.[173]

Osler commenced his cross-examination by having Roy confirm he was one of two proprietors of the Beauport Asylum, that the Asylum had 800 or 900 patients and the proprietors made money for themselves by keeping the patients. At one point, Dr. Roy told Osler he was a specialist to which Osler impudently shot back "You are quite a specialist in keeping a boarding house?" Defence counsel made no objection to this sarcastic comment.

Roy testified that at his Asylum he had previously looked after Riel, but Osler chastised him for not bringing Asylum books to verify Riel's symptoms at that time. In answer to Osler, Dr. Roy said that 25 to 30 patients were under his immediate treatment in 1877 (when Riel was there) and added that their treatment had more or less gone from his mind. Osler badgered Roy a number of times telling him to answer the question. On one occasion, being dissatisfied with Roy's response, Osler asked him four consecutive times what the leading feature of acute mania was. Roy rather unsuccessfully attempted to give as good as he got, telling Osler in relation to the number of Asylum patients "I do not know whether you have the right to ask those questions." When Osler asked if there were any other features of the disease Roy replied "I won't give you any."

Roy testified that one of the features of the disease was a fixed idea with a special ambition incapable of change by reasoning. In response to Osler's repeated pointed questions about leading features of the

---

[173]   *The Queen v. Louis Riel*, p. 316.

disease Roy, who may have become discombobulated by Osler's hectoring, made a stunning admission. He said to Osler "I am not an expert in insanity."

Osler asked Roy to tell him which symptoms of an unsound mind Riel had. Fitzpatrick intervened to state that if Roy did not understand the questions in English he should answer in French. Osler caustically retorted "If the man wants to hide himself under the French he can do so", and said the jury could decide whether the change was made at Roy's suggestion or that of his counsel. Section 94 of the *North-West Territories Act, 1880* permitted English or French to be used in court.

Dr. Roy, now speaking in French, testified that the evidence of Fathers André and Fourmond showed that Riel had symptoms of megalomania. Osler stridently riposted "That is no answer to my question."

Osler continued his grilling of Roy, again telling him he was not answering questions. Concerning one question, Osler insolently asked Roy "Have you not the capacity to understand it?" Fitzpatrick objected when Osler asked Roy about a man abandoning a non-controllable idea for $35,000. Osler protested to Magistrate Richardson that Fitzpatrick was interfering at a critical part of the examination and that he was giving Roy a cue as he had in regard to speaking French.

In answer to a question as to how he knew Riel had no knowledge of right or wrong during this time, Roy testified that Riel was under the influence of his delusions that he had a special mission to fulfill.

At one point Fitzpatrick objected to the translation being given, and he and Osler exchanged words.

Osler asked about the Mormon, Brigham Young. Roy thought Brigham Young was more or less insane. He told Osler that if he sent Brigham Young to his Asylum for a few months he would make a study of his case. Osler persisted in questioning Roy as to whether the evidence was consistent with a skilful fraud but he was not satisfied with Roy's answer. To one response Osler said "That is not an answer at all. Can you give me any answer?" Roy retorted "Put another question or in another way." Osler's animosity towards Roy shone through when he disdainfully and histrionically ended the cross-examination with

> If you cannot answer it in English or French, I may as well let you go. You can go.

Dr. Roy was a pivotal witness called by Riel's counsel with a view to proving Riel was demented. However his appearance in the witness box did not live up to the expectations that defence counsel had hoped for. Roy's outburst in response to Osler's ferocious cross-examination that he was "not an expert in insanity" undercut the force of his testimony. A number of other factors detracted from the weight of his opinion that Riel was of unsound mind. Until the previous day he had not seen Riel for many years. He based his opinion on Riel's insanity on evidence given by other witnesses since he did not conduct a personal examination of Riel prior to testifying; and he brought no medical records with him.

Roy also had difficulty speaking fluently in English and, after he changed to French during his cross-examination, the translation into English lost much of its impact on the jury. The jury heard Roy state that his opinion as to Riel's insanity was based on the witnesses heard that day and the prior day. This very brief period contrasted sharply with Roy's answer to Osler concerning Brigham Young (a 19th century American Mormon leader) where he said as to Young's prophetic inspiration that he would need to examine Young and study his case at his Asylum "for a few months". Dr. Roy heard various witnesses testify to Riel's heterodox religious views, particularly those concerning the papacy. Roy was a votary of ultramontanism. An ultramontane looked "beyond the mountains" i.e. the Alps, to Rome. Its followers, the ultramontanes, advocated the supreme authority of the Pope in matters of faith and discipline, and also advocated the subordination of the state to the Catholic Church. The doctrine of papal infallibility had been proclaimed in 1870 and the ultramontanes were zealous backers of the doctrine.

The evidence of witnesses such as Nolin, Garnot and Fourmond testifying as to Riel's strong antipathy to the Roman papacy would have shocked any ultramontane. Coming from Riel, a once devoted Roman Catholic, these views coupled with Riel's own unorthodox statements undoubtedly, subconsciously or otherwise, led Roy (a fervid ultramontane and Roman Catholic) to support the opinion that Riel was insane. It is not far-fetched to presume that Roy's opinion of Riel was strongly influenced by the heresies he heard attributed to Riel.

However, in the end result, the jury did not accept Roy's opinion.

The second alienist called in an attempt to prove Riel was insane was Dr. Daniel Clark.[174]   Clark, a medical doctor, was the Superintendent of the Toronto Lunatic Asylum, and had treated insane people for about ten years. He had appeared as an expert witness in lunacy cases on a number of occasions. As such he must have known that to establish a defence of insanity in a criminal prosecution the requirements set forth in the McNaghten Rules had to be met. Magistrate Richardson, in his charge to the jury, propounded the most important part of the McNaghten Rules as the law to the jury.[175]

The McNaghten Rules were formulated by the English common law judges after Daniel McNaghten was acquitted in his 1843 trial of shooting and killing Edward Drummond, the secretary of the Prime Minister, Sir Robert Peel. McNaghten mistakenly believed he was assassinating Peel. McNaghten had a delusional belief that Peel was persecuting him. The outrage that followed McNaghten's acquittal led to the common law judges being asked to answer a number of questions to elucidate matters relating to the defence of insanity. Their answers are referred to as the McNaghten Rules. The relevant part of the Rules stated:

> to establish a defence on the ground of insanity it must be
> clearly proved that, at the time of the committing of the act,
> the party accused was labouring under such a defect of
> reason, from disease of the mind, as not to know the nature
> and quality of the act he was doing or, if he did know it, that
> he did not know he was doing what was wrong.[176]

.   In almost all serious criminal offences, there is a presumption that *mens rea* is an essential ingredient required for conviction. *Mens rea*, Latin for "guilty mind", means a culpable state of mind or a knowledge of the wrongfulness of an act. A defence of insanity may be raised to rebut the existence of *mens rea*. The law also provided that the burden of proof of insanity was on the defence. To succeed with an insanity plea under the McNaghten Rules, the burden of proof was on the defence. In brief Riel's lawyers had to establish that due to a diseased mind Riel either did not know the nature and quality of the acts with which he was charged,

---

174   *The Queen v. Louis Riel,* p. 256-61.

175   *The Queen v. Louis Riel,* p. 348.

176   *McNaghten's Case* [1843-60] *All England Reports* 229 at 233 (House of Lords), 10 Cl. & Fin. 200; 8 E.R. 718.

or if he did that he did not know he was doing wrong. However, Clark not only failed to meet this onus, his testimony in this respect was a disaster insofar as proving Riel was insane.

While Clark did say to Fitzpatrick in examination-in-chief that a man who held the views and did the things that the witnesses in court said Riel did was of unsound mind, Clark gave answers to specific questions, which indicated that:

(i)   Riel knew the nature of the acts he committed; and

(ii)   Riel knew right from wrong in March, April, and May 1885.

March, April, and May 1885 were the months in which the charges alleged Riel committed various acts of high treason.

In cross-examination by Osler, Clark re-emphasized that Riel knew the nature and quality of the acts he was committing, and knew that it was wrong "subject to his delusions". Clark's answers to Fitzpatrick and Osler effectively and firmly ruled out the possibility of Riel's counsel relying on this expert witness to meet the insanity test required by the McNaghten Rules. On the contrary, Clark's answers supported the Crown's position that Riel was legally sane.

Further, Osler jumped on a reservation that Clark gave in his opinion to Fitzpatrick. When declaring that Riel was of insane mind, Clark qualified his answer by stating he assumed Riel was not a malingerer. Osler asked Clark if the facts were compatible with "a skilful shamming" by a malingerer. Clark answered "Yes I think so." Clark had never seen Riel prior to the trial. He testified that he examined Riel three times, once on the day of his testimony and twice on the prior day. Clark said that:

> in a cursory examination…it is impossible for any man to
> state from three examinations whether [Riel] is a deceiver or
> not

and to determine whether Riel was a sham he would have to have Riel under his supervision "for months [and] to watch him day by day." These qualifications significantly undermined Clark's assessment of Riel's mental state.

With respect to Clark telling Osler that Riel had told him that morning that Riel was a prophet and could foresee his acquittal by the jury, Osler had Clark admit that this could be consistent with fraud, an undiscovered fraud. In re-examination Fitzpatrick attempted to repair some of the damage by having Clark reiterate that Riel was capable of distinguishing right from wrong subject to his delusions. In doing so, Clark stated that Brigham Young was sound in mind. This contrasted with the evidence of the other defence alienist, Dr. Roy, who testified that Brigham Young "was more or less insane". On this weak note the defence closed its case.

Clark was a poor witness for the defence strategy of proving insanity because he obviously felt that the test set forth in the McNaghten Rules was unrealistic from an alienist's point of view. He made this clear:

(i)   when he told Osler he knew there was a conflict between the courts and the doctors;

(ii)   when he told Fitzpatrick "it is all nonsense to talk about a man not knowing what he is doing simply because he is insane";

(iii)   when he said in response to a question about whether Riel was able to judge what he was doing as either wrong or contrary to law that that was "one of the legal metaphysical distinctions in respect to right and wrong" that was dangerous;

(iv)   when he testified that within half an hour he could convince any lawyers who went to the Toronto Asylum that dozens in the institution "know right from wrong both in the abstract and in the concrete, and yet are undoubtedly insane"; and

(v)   when he testified as to Riel knowing the nature and quality of his acts and knowing right from wrong in March, April, and May 1885.

With respect to the law relating to insanity Clark, like Mr. Bumble in Charles Dickens *Oliver Twist*, thought "the law is a ass – a idiot", an asinine position to take in a court of law. He was unrepentant in his obstinate view of the law when in an 1887 article entitled "A Psycho-Medical History of Louis Riel" he wrote:

> Such knowledge [re the insane] would be laughed out of court by the legal profession, who can not discern any valid evidence that does not tally with a metaphysical and obsolete definition.[177]

---

[177]   *American Journal of Insanity*, Vol. 44, p. 33.

Clark's mind should have been sound enough to appreciate that it was irrational for him to expect that in the Riel trial his belief would prevail over the law as it then existed. Having said that, the McNaghten Rules were somewhat modified in Canada in the 1890s. Clark was batting his alienist's head against a legal brick wall (including Magistrate Richardson's subsequent charge to the jury) on each occasion that his testimony clashed with the McNaghten Rules. His pigheaded attitude resulted in a headache, not for him, but for Fitzpatrick and the other defence counsel in trying to prove Riel was insane.

However, the root cause of the headache was of defence counsel's own making. Since Clark was being called to prove Riel's insanity they should have thoroughly briefed him in advance of the trial as to the McNaghten Rules and determined if his evidence would be consonant with these Rules. As noted above, his answers (not only to Crown counsel Osler, but to Fitzpatrick) weakened, not strengthened, the insanity defence. Fitzpatrick should not have called Clark as a witness if he knew beforehand the answers Clark was to give as they related to the McNaghten Rules. If defence counsel had not briefed Clark and had no idea as to his views in this respect they were derelict in their duty. If they did know, it was appalling to call him as a witness to support an insanity defence.

After Riel's trial Clark gave lectures, wrote articles and gave interviews about Riel's "insanity". In one newspaper interview on November 18, 1885, Clark stated that Riel's mother was of "weak intellect" and that Riel's "father was a man with an ill-balanced mind and uncontrollable passions bordering upon insanity." [178] The author of this text located a letter to the editor of *The Toronto Mail* dated August 26, 1885 signed with the pseudonym "Alpha". Alpha referred to Riel's mother as a "semi-imbecile" and to Riel's father as "ill-balanced" and that his "hot-passions bordered on insanity".[179] There is an obvious similarity of language in the quotes from Dr. Clark's interview and in Alpha's letter. This strongly indicates that the same person made both of these quotes. These characterizations of Riel's parents by Clark were far-fetched utter nonsense, and give credence to Professor Flanagan's

---

[178] "Riel's Mental State, Opinions of Dr. Clark of the Toronto Asylum", *The Toronto Globe*, Wednesday, November 18, 1885, p. 8.
[179] *The Toronto Mail* dated Wednesday, August 26, 1885, p. 2, letter signed Alpha.

comment about Clark that before accepting anything reported by Clark one would want independent corroboration.[180]

William Lyon Mackenzie King, Canada's longest serving Prime Minister, was selected as the leading nation builder in Canada's history by *Maclean's* magazine on July 1, 1998. While in office King had visions, secretly communed with the world of spirits and was involved with spiritualism. It was perhaps fortunate for him that his sanity was not called into question by alienists such as Drs. Roy and Clark.

2.   THE CROWN'S REBUTTAL WITNESSES.

To rebut the defence's evidence of Riel's insanity the Crown called seven witnesses; i.e. two medical doctors, two army officers, a minister and two members of the North West Mounted Police.

While the defence's medical witnesses were not very convincing and had made only scanty observations or examinations of Riel, the rebuttal medical witnesses of the Crown also had meager opportunities to psychiatrically assess Riel. The skimpy scrutiny of Riel by the experts for each side, coupled with:

(i)   one (Clark) stating he would have to have Riel under supervision "for months" to determine if he was shamming;

(ii)   another (Roy, who had based his opinion as to Riel's unsound mind on witnesses he had heard in court for just over one day) saying with respect to the sanity of Brigham Young that he would need to study that Mormon leader "for a few months" at his Asylum; and

(iii)   a third (Wallace) having seen Riel for only half an hour;

calls into question the worthiness of their testimony for or against Riel's insanity. However as Magistrate Richardson pointed out in his charge to the jury, the defence had the responsibility of proving insanity, and that every man is presumed to be sane until the contrary is proved.

The Crown did not have a specific obligation to prove Riel was sane. This legal position was advantageous for the Crown since its first rebuttal witness, Dr. James M. Wallace, only saw Riel "for about half an

---

[180]   Thomas Flanagan, *Louis 'David' Riel:Prophet of the New World,* p. 16.

hour, that is alone, not in court."[181] This short period of time would manifestly be insufficient for a conclusive diagnosis of Riel's insanity.

Wallace was the medical superintendent for the Asylum for the Insane at Hamilton Ontario, an institution with over 600 patients. He had studied insanity for in excess of ten years and devoted nearly all of his time to the medical department of the Asylum.

Wallace testified in response to Crown counsel Osler's questions for about half an hour. He was present during the sitting of the court and formed an opinion as to Riel's mental responsibility. He stated he had not discovered any indication of insanity and that he thought Riel was of sound mind. In answers, which indicated he had been well briefed by Osler on the McNaghten Rules, Wallace said he thought Riel was capable of distinguishing right from wrong, and further that Riel was capable of "very acutely knowing the nature and quality of any act which he would commit."

In cross-examination, Fitzpatrick was able to attenuate the strong opinion given by Wallace. He had Wallace qualify his opinion that based on his limited examination it would be presumptuous to say Riel was not insane, and that he had been unable to discover any symptoms of insanity. At the same time he told Fitzpatrick that his opinion was "pretty fairly fixed" that Riel was not insane.

Fitzpatrick questioned Wallace on megalomania. Wallace stated that it simply applied to grandiose ideas, delusions such as a person believing himself to be a king or immensely wealthy. Fitzpatrick had Wallace extend the delusions to other categories, including a delusion that one is a great prophet or one is divinely inspired. Wallace would not accept many of the points Fitzpatrick was trying to establish. Fitzpatrick referred to French authors but Wallace firmly retorted "I don't want to hear of any French authors. I never read them." Fitzpatrick concluded his cross-examination on a rather irrelevant note, inquiring whether Wallace would put two or more lunatics together in the same ward.

The remaining Crown rebuttal witnesses were not experts in insanity. They were called to testify to the effect that each, on different occasions, had been with Riel over a number of days. They indicated that they had had rational conversations with Riel; and, except for the

---

[181]   *The Queen v. Louis Riel,* p. 262-68.

Minister Charles Pitblado who was not asked, stated from their time with Riel they had seen nothing which indicated he was of unsound mind. To the contrary, their evidence collectively indicated that in their opinion Riel was intelligent, clever and shrewd.

The jury knew that these witnesses were not experts in insanity. However statements such as that of Captain Holmes Young, who told Greenshields in cross examination "During the nine days I was living with [Riel] I would know if I was living with a lunatic", appealed to their common sense.

Dr. Augustus Jukes, senior surgeon of the North West Mounted Police (located at the Regina jail) and a medical doctor for thirty-five years, was called to the stand after Dr. Wallace.[182] He was examined-in-chief by Crown counsel Robinson. He admitted he had never paid special attention to insanity, but a number of persons of unsound mind had come under his observation at the Regina jail in the three preceding years.

Jukes stated that since about May 24 (some two months previous) he saw Riel almost every day at the Regina jail, and would speak to him on every occasion, and Riel in turn would talk to him. He said that he had never seen anything to indicate that Riel was insane or to cause him to question his mental condition. He also stated that notwithstanding this he had watched Riel very carefully to notice any appearance of unsoundness of mind since he had heard a rumour that the defence planned a plea of insanity.

In response to Fitzpatrick, Jukes said he had never specially examined Riel as a lunatic. He admitted that there were forms of insanity not discoverable except after considerable endeavours, and that one may converse with a man continually and not be aware of his insanity until one touched upon that point upon which he was insane. He added that his hearing was rather imperfect and he had not heard the translations from French into English as well as he wished, and he had heard nothing in court to satisfy him that Riel was of unsound mind. When Fitzpatrick inquired if a man might labour under the insane delusion that he had a mission, Jukes countered that would not necessarily imply that he was otherwise insane or incompetent "to be responsible for his own actions."

---

[182]   *The Queen v. Louis Riel,* p. 269-74.

Fitzpatrick used the archaic Latin word *quoad* (regarding) in posing two questions to Jukes. Fitzpatrick asked further questions dealing with "a man labouring under an insane delusion" that he was divinely inspired. In response, Jukes bested Fitzpatrick by retorting that some men with remarkable religious views had been declared insane

> until they gathered together great numbers of followers and became leaders of a new sect, then they became great prophets and great men.

He cited Mahomet. Mahomet, or Muhammad, of course is the Arab prophet who founded Islam and claimed he had visions in which he received from God the words of the Koran. Jukes stated that if Mahomet had failed in his endeavours, his beliefs "would have simply been regarded as a delusion of his own mind."

In response to Fitzpatrick, Jukes added that Riel's conduct was not like that of Mahomet, or the Mormons Joseph Smith and Brigham Young. Recurrent references to Brigham Young were surprising since, not only was Young a successful religious leader, he had been Governor of the Utah Territory for seven years in the 1850s. Jukes' opinion was that Riel was "a man of great shrewdness and very great depth."

Jukes testified that he had never spoken to Riel on religion or his alleged mission but based on much conversation and

> daily communication with [Riel] I have never spoken to him on a single subject on which he has spoken irrationally.

On this rather disadvantageous note, from Fitzpatrick's point of view, Jukes was finished and, it now being 5:00 p.m., the Court adjourned for the day.

The Court reconvened on Friday, July 31, 1885 at 10:00 a.m.

The Crown then called Captain Holmes Young (who had earlier testified for the Crown as noted in Chapter X) as a rebuttal witness.[183] Examined by Crown counsel Robinson, Young told the Court that Riel had been placed in his charge by General Middleton on May 15th, that Riel remained constantly in his charge day and night until May 23rd (a total of nine days) when Young delivered Riel in Regina. He said he and Riel conversed almost constantly and very freely, "on almost every subject connected with the rebellion", and that "there was an immense amount of conversation." According to Young, Riel told him

---

[183]   *The Queen v. Louis Riel,* p. 274-80.

he was not so foolish as to imagine that he could wage war
against Canada or Britain.

He hoped to Capture Major Crozier's force and use them as hostages
and

to compel the Canadian Government to consider the
situation or accede to his demands.

He said that if Riel wished time to answer him or to evade a point,
the conversation turned to religious matters. Riel told him that he
wished to purify religion in Canada and the North-West, and desired
local government of the Church in Canada.

Riel wrote the meaning of his mission in Crozier's notebook, saying

everyone had a mission, and that his mission was to
accomplish practical results.

This relatively modest "mission statement" conveyed no hint that its
proponent was demented. Many modern researchers, entrepreneurs,
and others could adopt it without difficulty.

Young averred that he observed nothing to indicate that Riel was
of unsound mind. He found that Riel's mind was fully equal to his, and
that Riel was "better educated and much more clever than I was
myself."

In cross-examination, Greenshields had Young admit that he had
no experience with the insane and no medical education. Greenshields
undoubtedly rued the question he asked Young about whether he
considered himself in a position to give an opinion as to sanity. Young
cogently replied:

I could not give a medical opinion, but I consider that during
the nine days I was living with him I would know if I was
living with a lunatic.

Greenshields asked another question the answer to which
weakened, rather than strengthened, his position. He asked if Riel had
explained what the practical results of his mission meant. Young
answered that Riel's explanation was that he worked to save the Metis
from annihilation by the Hudson's Bay Company and the Mounted
Police, although Riel evaded giving particulars.

There was a discussion of the word "Exovede" which appeared in
Young's notebook. It was from two Latin words "*ex*" meaning "from"
and "*ovede*" meaning "flock", indicating that neither Riel nor his
councillors were assuming authority, hence the Metis council was the
"exovedate".

That rather esoteric discussion concluded Young's testimony.

General Middleton followed Young in the witness box as the fourth rebuttal witness.[184] His prior direct testimony is discussed in Chapter X. General Middleton testified that Riel was in his custody for three or four days until May 19. On the first day Riel was in Middleton's tent for nearly the whole day and Middleton had conversations with him. Middleton asked Riel how he thought he would be able to wage war against Canada with England at its back. Riel answered that he didn't expect to beat them, but by showing a bold front he thought he would get better terms from the Government, and hoped to take hostages for this purpose.

On religious subjects, Riel told Middleton that Rome was wrong and corrupt, the priests narrow-minded and interfering. (It was views like these that doubtlessly contributed to the priests considering Riel insane.) Middleton classified as "excessively good" Riel's ideas expressed to him that "religion should be based on morality and humanity and charity", an assessment with which many would agree.

Middleton told the Court that he had not seen anything whatever to indicate any suspicion of Riel being of unsound mind. On the contrary Middleton found Riel to be

> a man of rather acute intellect. … quite able to hold his own
> upon any argument or topic we happened to touch upon.

Middleton concluded that Riel "was very far from being mad or a fool".

Greenshields asked three relatively innocuous questions in cross-examination, including having Middleton confirm he had never seen Riel prior to his surrender on May 15.

The next Crown rebuttal witness was Reverend Charles Bruce Pitblado, a Winnipeg clergyman.[185] He was on the steamer Northcote with Riel for almost three days on the Saskatchewan River, five days in all until Riel was delivered to prison in Regina. Pitblado spoke often with Riel as did Captain Holmes Young who was also on board the steamer. They had conversations on various subjects, including the rebellion and Riel's religious views.

Riel told him his chief object was to induce the Government to make a treaty similar to the one it had made with the half-breeds in Manitoba. He hoped to take hostages and then negotiate with the

---

[184]   *The Queen v. Louis Riel*, p. 280-82.
[185]   *The Queen v. Louis Riel*, p. 282-83.

Government, and this was his object at Duck Lake, at Fish Creek (where he also hoped the Indians would rise up to keep General Middleton's troops busy), and at Batoche.

Greenshields asked two questions in cross-examination, the latter establishing that Pitblado had never seen or met Riel prior to the day on which Riel's trip to the Regina jail started.

Captain Richard Burton Deane of the North West Mounted Police was the sixth Crown rebuttal witness.[186] He was in charge of the Regina jail and had had custody of Riel since May 23. He was a dour man with no music in his soul. He had no desire to chitchat with Riel and spoke to him chiefly on prison discipline (undoubtedly a matter close to his heart), Riel's diet, and "concessions as to liberty". He ensured that "All requisitions must be made to me."

Deane saw Riel frequently from first to last. He observed that Riel's "manner was most polite and suave" and he never altered it. He had seen "nothing whatsoever" to indicate that Riel was not of sound mind, rather Riel impressed him as "very shrewd". Deane was not cross-examined by Riel's lawyers.

The seventh and final Crown rebuttal witness was Joseph Piggott, a corporal in the North West Mounted Police. He testified he had had charge of Riel since May 22 and saw Riel many times a day, but didn't talk to him although he heard him speak often. In frequently observing Riel, he did not see anything to show his mind was unsound. He considered Riel of sound mind and a person who spoke "with reason and politeness".

Piggott was not cross-examined. Osler announced that the Crown's evidence in reply was closed.

This concluded the evidence and led to the next phase of the trial. This phase consisted of the addresses to the jury by defence counsel, by Riel and by Crown counsel, followed by the Magistrate's charge to the jury, the jury's verdict, Riel's post-verdict remarks to Magistrate Richardson and Justice of the Peace Le Jeune, and the sentence. These elements of the trial are dealt with in the three succeeding chapters.

---

[186]   *The Queen v. Louis Riel,* p. 283-84.

Chapter XIII

ADDRESSES TO THE JURY

Completion of the testimony of the witnesses was followed by addresses to the jury by defence counsel, by Riel and by Crown counsel in that order.

1. FITZPATRICK'S ADDRESS TO THE JURY

The next phase of the trial commenced with the address to the jury by chief defence counsel Charles Fitzpatrick.[187] He also addressed his remarks to "Your Honours". "Your Honours" in the plural included the wordless Justice of the Peace Henry Le Jeune who co-shared the bench with Magistrate Richardson. One may posit that Le Jeune, unlike Riel, would not have subscribed to the maxim of Francis Bacon that "silence is the virtue of fools". See Chapter V for a discussion of the requirement for a justice of the peace to co-preside with a magistrate.

Fitzpatrick's speech, which lasted over two hours, was emotional and flamboyant, at times high-minded and eloquent, and at times misguided and inaccurate. The main thrust of his presentation was directed to trying to prove that the evidence established Riel's insanity, a defence which Riel had bitterly repudiated. However before embarking on that task he sketched a picture:

(i)   of the praiseworthy citizen soldiers from the East and elsewhere who rallied around the flag of their country to suppress the rebellion;

(ii)   of the Metis and half-breeds, intermediaries between the Indians and the white men, preventing "brutality ... and ... fell designs" of the Indians and always on the side of civilization, mercy and humanity;

(iii)   of the "criminal folly and neglect [that] would have gone unpunished had there been no resistance";

(iv)   of the Government of Canada which "wholly failed in its duty" toward the North-West Territories; and

(v)   of the constitutional agitation and the sending of a deputation to Louis Riel, then a humble village schoolmaster in Montana with a wife and small children.

---

187   *The Queen v. Louis Riel,* p. 284-311.

Fitzpatrick early on told the jury that "no one of any nationality, of any creed...can justify the rebellion." He stated that treason is peculiarly an offence against the Government. Fitzpatrick made a mild complaint against the federal government. He stated that when he spoke of the Government "all parties are identical and the same in my eyes." He said the Government of Canada had wholly failed in its duty to the North-West Territories, but then added that the Government's faults "do not justify the rebellion."[188]

He pointed out the normal aspects of constitutional agitation were absent in the North-West Territories. The people there did not elect members of Parliament, or have a voice in its affairs or a representative to bring its grievances to Ottawa, 2,000 miles away, and had not since the North-West Territories became part of Canada some fifteen years earlier. He asked how on those facts they could endeavour to obtain redress of their wrongs by constitutional agitation. This argument seems rather odd when coupled with Fitzpatrick's earlier unqualified assertion that "no one" could justify the rebellion. He did not specify any alternative which the Metis might have pursued. Without discussing situations justifying a rebellion there are surely occasions when one might sympathize with the words written during the American Revolution by one future President of the United States to another. On January 30, 1787 Thomas Jefferson, in a letter to James Madison, wrote "A little rebellion now and then is a good thing." If the American Revolution had not succeeded, a number of American colonial rebels, including such notables as George Washington, Benjamin Franklin, John Adams and Thomas Jefferson may well have been charged by the English authorities with high treason. However, this did not come to pass, because as Sir John Harington wrote in his *Epigrams* some four centuries ago:

> Treason doth never prosper; what's the reason? For if it
> prosper, none dare call it treason.[189]

As he progressed in his argument to the jury, Fitzpatrick noted that Riel initially agitated by constitutional means until the beginning of March when an appeal to arms took place. Fitzpatrick then commented that he, Fitzpatrick, was treading "on dangerous ground". He told the

---

188   *The Queen v. Louis Riel,* p. 287.
189   Sir John Harington, *Epigrams*, bk. iv, No. 5, 'Of Treason".

jury that Riel was either a lunatic or entirely sane and responsible for all his acts. He stated that Riel's counsel had endeavoured:

> despite [Riel's] orders, despite his desire, despite his instructions, to make him out a fool.

He then startlingly asked whether if Riel was sane he had "any redeeming features in his character and in his conduct of this rebellion?" He pointed out that after the rebellion Riel did not act like a coward, play the sycophant or flee from justice, but voluntarily surrendered to face the consequences of his acts. Fitzpatrick, talking as if he were Riel, said "I fought for liberty, and if liberty is not worth fighting for, it is not worth having." Fitzpatrick did indeed "tread on dangerous ground" in discussing Riel's redeeming features "if he is a sane man", a phrase he used twice in this respect. If Riel was legally insane there was no need to discuss his redeeming features as a sane man.

Fitzpatrick stressed that Riel had redeeming features but maintained defence counsel were justified by the facts, borne out by the evidence, and that they

> were bound **in our instructions** [Emphasis added] as representing this man to say that he is entirely insane and irresponsible in his acts.

Only a few minutes earlier Fitzpatrick told the jury that defence counsel was endeavouring to prove Riel was a fool "despite his orders, despite his desire, despite his instructions." Now he was saying defence counsel "were bound in our instructions." None of Fitzpatrick, Lemieux, Greenshields or Johnstone disclosed who was giving them these instructions which were diametrically opposed to Riel's orders, desire and instructions. Keep in mind that ten days earlier when Greenshields made an application to adjourn the trial he stated:

> In addition to that, there is the evidence of the doctors from Quebec. **This evidence we are instructed by others than the prisoner to make**. [Emphasis added.]

Defence counsel had received their instruction from these mysterious "others" to prove Riel was *non compos mentis*. Defence counsel did not identify these "others" at the trial. Early (on June 16, 1885) Riel had written a letter to Romuald Fiset, one of the organizers of the Defence Committee in Quebec, and to his lawyers (Fitzpatrick and Lemieux) describing reasons for the uprising. Lemieux telegraphed back telling Riel "Your admirable letter ... creates great enthusiasm, great prospects." His lawyers said that Riel's folly was that "of loving his country too much."[190] However on July 15, 1885, one month later, Fitzpatrick and Lemieux interviewed Riel in the Regina jail, after which they immediately wrote to Archbishop Taché in St. Boniface saying Riel was not of sound mind. Riel's folly of "love of country" had suddenly become the folly of insanity. Why did they write to Archbishop Taché? Why did they discuss Riel's condition with Taché? These are only some of the many unanswered questions with respect to the defence counsel's handling of this case.

Fitzpatrick stated that Riel was a descendant of those Indians of whom the poet said "their untutored minds see God in clouds." He didn't name the poet, perhaps because of his surname. It wasn't Shakespeare, it was Alexander Pope in *An Essay on Man*.

Fitzpatrick referred to Riel's stay in Dr. Roy's Asylum in the 1870s and dealt with megalomania, symptoms of which he said are:

(i)   an extraordinary love of power and an extraordinary development of ambition;

(ii)   a belief that one is in direct communication with the Holy Ghost; and

(iii)   that one is naturally irritable, excitable and will not suffer contradiction.

Fitzpatrick outlined his view of the evidence supporting Riel's lunacy. These included on Riel's part:

- Riel's expectation that with four or five hundred Metis he could attack Canada (backed by England) and succeed in forcing his demand;
- his directly assailing the religious beliefs of the devout Metis, beliefs which formed an essential part of their natures, to achieve his object;
- not exercising prudence, caution and common sense by failing to lie low and "some day" he would have arrived at the highest pinnacle of his ambition;
- not siding with the priests since he knew they wanted to help him;
- if he was a deep, designing, cunning rascal of superior intellect he would have understood the Metis character better and that

---

[190]   Siggins, p. 416.

it was impossible for a crazy lunatic to eradicate their deeply rooted religion;

- his insane delusion that in the future he would control the North-West Territories;

- his conviction that he was called by God to chastise Canada and create a new country;

- his belief that he was inspired by God and in direct communication with the Holy Ghost;

- his belief (inspired by the Almighty) that he "will necessarily gain the victory"; and

- his delusion that with $35,000 he could carry out his mission, found a newspaper and rouse up foreign nations to help take possession of the country (see also Chapter XI and section 2 of Chapter XVIII).

Fitzpatrick briefly touched on the evidence presented by Drs. Clark and Roy and in doing so made several misstatements, discussed below. He mentioned the two priests (Fourmond and André) who thought Riel was a fool. He said that the Crown witnesses did not swear that Riel was not of unsound mind, but only they had not been able to discover any symptoms of insanity.

Fitzpatrick asked what proof there was that a number of Metis council documents were issued or that "an appeal was made to those savage hordes to rise in their fury." He chastised the Crown for not bringing Poundmaker, Big Bear and other Indians to testify in this respect, and Poundmaker to testify about a letter from Riel (i.e. Exhibit 9) asking the Indians to rise and face the enemy. He also said it was possible the doctors for the Crown had made a mistake.

In his peroration Fitzpatrick told the jury he left the case safely in their hands, knowing that right would be done and that Riel, "a poor confirmed lunatic", would not be sent to the gallows by them.

Professor George F. G. Stanley in his book *Louis Riel* called Fitzpatrick's speech "a good speech". This was a modest compliment for a speech which was filled at times with eloquent rhetoric but, as will be seen, it did not convince the jury. Riel himself in addressing the jury said that Fitzpatrick gave "a beautiful speech" before he proceeded to successfully argue against it, and demolish its validity.

On a couple of occasions during the address Fitzpatrick misspoke himself, on several others he made statements as to the Crown witnesses, Crown counsel, the magistrate, and other matters which might better have been left unsaid.

For example, Fitzpatrick told the jury that Dr. Roy had come to Regina "at the request of the Crown as well as of the defence for the purpose of giving evidence in this case." Crown counsel Robinson, in his address to the jury, stated he had to correct Fitzpatrick and that Dr. Roy "was not brought here on the part of the Crown." While the Crown had offered to assist in telegrams and expenses "Dr. Roy was not in any sense called as a witness for the Crown."[191]

Fitzpatrick told the jury that Riel said "I know I will necessarily gain the victory" (against the forces of Canada). However, to the contrary, Captain Young testified that Riel said "he was not so foolish as to imagine that he could wage war against Canada and Britain" but hoped to take hostages and compel the Canadian Government to consider the situation. General Middleton stated that Riel told him that he didn't expect to be able to beat [Canada and England] but hoped to take prisoners to get better terms.[192] Riel had succeeded with a similar strategy in Manitoba 15 years earlier. Although circumstances in the North-West Territories were different, Riel undoubtedly reasoned this strategy of taking hostages could work again, and help achieve in his words "practical results" and better terms from the government. This was a rational conclusion on Riel's part based on his experiences in Manitoba in 1869-70.

Fitzpatrick said that he noticed that his alienist Dr. Clark "was not very closely cross-examined." While an extensive number of questions were not asked of Clark in cross-examination, it was not necessary to do so since the right questions were asked and (from the Crown's point of view) the right answers received. Osler's cross-examination had been very precise in having Clark testify in a manner the effect of which was to destroy any defence of insanity under the McNaghten Rules (the provisions of which incidentally Fitzpatrick did not specifically address). As well, Osler had Clark essentially admit that Riel could be shamming and he could not say whether or not Riel was a deceiver.

Fitzpatrick made a rather specious comment when he asked "What interest have they [i.e. Drs. Roy and Clark] got in coming here and

---

191   *The Queen v. Louis Riel*, p. 302 and 332.
192   *The Queen v. Louis Riel*, p. 275 and 281.

perjuring themselves." Perjury is false testimony by a witness in a judicial proceeding, with the intent to mislead, knowing that the evidence is false. There was not a scintilla of evidence to indicate perjury in their testimony. An honest opinion honestly given is not perjury.

Some statements Fitzpatrick made to the jury, from Riel's point of view, would have been better left unmentioned, such as:

> I know that those gentlemen who were examined for the Crown tell the truth ... [except for Nolin] they did what they could do to get fair play;
> ... the evidence [of the Crown] is given to you by men who to the best of their skill and ability come here and tell you what they know;
> ... no more eminent, right-minded or fairer men in Canada could be found than they [Crown counsel] are;
> I speak under the direction of the distinguished magistrate who presides over this trial; and
> ... no one of any rationality, of any creed ... can justify the rebellion.

Why Fitzpatrick made these comments, questionable in several instances and unfavourable from Riel's perspective, is difficult to understand. Most of the Crown witnesses gave evidence not favourable to Riel's acquittal or to the attempt of Riel's counsel to prove his insanity. On the latter point the burden of proof was on the defence, not the Crown. Suggesting that the Crown witnesses were telling the truth was detrimental in these respects.

As for the fairness of Crown counsel, among other matters they opposed the defence's request for a one-month adjournment to permit witnesses and documents to be brought to Regina, initially opposing any adjournment whatsoever[193] and finally agreeing to one week. This short adjournment may have been one reason why it appeared that a star witness for the defence, Dr. Daniel Clark, had not been properly briefed, and why his evidence emerged as prejudicial to defence counsel's insanity plea. Crown counsel also opposed the calling of witnesses and production of documents that Riel swore were "essential and material" to his defence. They also refused releasing to Riel his own documents claiming they were state papers and they vehemently

---

193   *The Queen v. Louis Riel,* p. 53.

objected to any evidence of justification on Riel's part. As well Osler, unknown to Fitzpatrick, improperly suggested that Justice Minister Campbell write privately to Chief Justice Wallbridge (see Chapter XX). These various actions (so prejudicial to Riel) emanated from the men who were strenuously attempting to have Riel executed. Fitzpatrick, however saw these harmful acts as coming from men of whom there were none other in Canada "more eminent, right-minded or fairer."

The statement by Fitzpatrick to the jury that no one could justify the rebellion meant that if the insanity plea failed, as it did, Riel was left defenceless. Chapter XXII sets forth further more detailed discussion of shortcomings of defence counsel in their representation of Riel.

2.   RIEL'S ADDRESS TO THE JURY, THE MAGISTRATE AND THE JUSTICE OF THE PEACE

After Fitzpatrick sat down, Magistrate Richardson advised Riel that he could now speak to the jury. Before Riel could commence, one of his defence counsel (Lemieux) jumped to his feet and said to Richardson and Justice of the Peace Le Jeune

> I must declare before the court that we must not be
> considered responsible for any declaration he may make.

This antagonistic attitude towards their own client's speech was in keeping with defence counsel's prior opposition to Riel's cross-examining witnesses and with their stance on his sanity.

Riel had not given evidence during the trial. In 1885 an accused charged with high treason was not entitled to testify on his own behalf, but he was entitled to make a closing statement after the evidence was completed. However his statement was not evidence, and no questions could be asked.

Riel addressed his remarks not only to the jury but also to "Your Honors" i.e. Magistrate Richardson and the voiceless Justice of the Peace Le Jeune.[194] He apologized for his English, then asked the jury not to take as "a play of insanity" the prayers he then said asking God to bless the court, the jury, his and the Crown lawyers and all those who were around him.

He then launched into a remarkable speech in the hot, crowded courtroom. With eloquence and passion he talked of the Metis and their

---

[194]   *The Queen v. Louis Riel,* p. 311 to 325.

grievances, of how the "whites" in the North-West Territories were deprived of responsible government and public liberties, and of petitions to the Government to relieve the conditions of the North-West. He said "I believe I have done my duty."

Riel referred to his mission and said it was to aim at "practical results", a phrase he used seven times in his speech and a phrase that Captain Holmes Young, in his rebuttal testimony, confirmed Riel had used. Riel had told Young that this was his mission. Riel said that what he had done rested on the conviction that he was "called upon to do something for my country."

Riel recalled his work in Manitoba and how, with the help of others, he had obtained a constitution for Manitoba. He said at another point that he knew through the grace of God that he was "the founder of Manitoba". That was not an insane assertion. It is consistent with a statement on the plaque below the gigantic statue (pictured on the cover) of Louis Riel on the grounds of the Manitoba Legislative Buildings in Winnipeg adjacent to the Red River. The plaque reads in part:

> [Riel's] leadership inspired the creation of Manitoba as Canada's fifth province ... In 1992, the Parliament of Canada and the Legislative Assembly of Manitoba formally recognized Riel's contribution to the development of the Canadian Confederation and his role, and that of the Metis, as founders of Manitoba.

Riel then turned his rhetorical talent to the demolition of the insanity plea of his own lawyers, a task in which he was spectacularly successful. He pointed to the testimony of General Middleton and Captain Young who did not think him insane. He thanked Crown counsel for "destroying the testimony" of Dr. Roy. He asked a rhetorical question "As to religion, what is my belief? What is my insanity about?" and proceeded to answer it. He stated that he wished to leave Rome aside inasmuch as it was the cause of division between Catholics and Protestants. He looked to his children's children "shaking hands with the Protestants of the new-world in a friendly manner." He did not want the evils of Europe to be continued among the half-breeds or repeated in America and that work would take hundreds of years. Riel said he believed he was the prophet of the new world but that he was not trying to play insanity and he did not wish to set himself up as Pope. He said he could see "something into the future, we all see into the future more or less." He stated that the half-breeds as hunters could foretell many things. He had told Nolin there would be trouble in the North-West and told the half-breeds they would be punished. These matters had indeed occurred.

He said that if the jury sentenced him he would have the satisfaction of knowing that if he died he would not be reputed a lunatic. Riel "refused to compromise the validity of the Metis struggle for democracy in the West by saying he was insane."[195]

Riel in effect pleaded justification for his actions, something his lawyers did not do. He asserted that the

> agitation in the North-West Territories would have been constitutional, and would certainly be constitutional today if,
>
> in my opinion, we had not been attacked.

He told the jury that he had "acted reasonably and in self-defence." Riel castigated the Federal Government. He said that Parliament and the Cabinet did not provide representation for the North-West. Petition after petition had been ignored, the government had an absolute lack of responsibility "and therefore had insanity complicated with paralysis."

Riel said that if they accepted the defence plea of insanity, the jury should acquit him completely since he had been quarrelling with an insane and irresponsible Government. If they decided he was sane, he declared, they should also acquit him on the basis that having reason and a sound mind he acted reasonably and in self-defence, while it was the Government, irresponsible and insane, that acted wrong. Riel's words to the jury were:

> If you pronounce in favour of the Crown, which contends that I am responsible, acquit me all the same. You are perfectly justified in declaring that having my reason and sound mind, I have acted reasonably and in self defence, while the Government, my accuser, being irresponsible, and consequently insane, cannot but have acted wrong ... [196]

He added that if there was high treason, it was on the Government's part, not his. At this juncture, Magistrate Richardson interjected "Are you done?"

---

[195]   Don McLean, *Home from the Hill, a History of the Metis in Western Canada,* p. 236.

[196]   *The Queen v. Louis Riel,* p. 324.

Shortly before this Riel had told Richardson that while Richardson had acted according to his duty in appointing the jury "it is, in our view, against the guarantees of liberty."

Riel concluded by saying he had been neglecting himself for fifteen years; that his wife and children were without means; that he worked to better the condition of the people of the North-West; and that he had never had any pay. He ended by stating that he was putting his speech under the protection of God.

Riel's speech was a tour-de-force, one in which he had spectacularly preserved his self-esteem as a rational human being, but at a fatal cost. By an ironic twist of fate he had contributed to his own doom. His remarks made visibly clear to the jury that he was lucid, rational and sane, so much so that one juror Edwin J. Brooks subsequently told author William McCartney Davidson that Riel was no more insane than any of the others who addressed the jury.[197]

However, the gist of Riel's persuasive address had the effect of demolishing the only defence his lawyers had presented to the jury. Riel had satisfied the jury of his rationality. As for Riel's comments about the Metis being attacked and about self-defence and about an irresponsible Government, his lawyers on more than one occasion stated they were not justifying the rebellion, had presented no evidence in this respect, and did not advance it to the jury as a defence.

Riel's burning desire to show that he had "the moral existence of an intellectual being" (the phrase he used when he attempted to cross-examine witness Charles Nolin) succeeded so well that, in the jurors' minds, he completely undercut the injudicious defence strategy of Fitzpatrick, Lemieux and the other defence counsel. In this strange, topsy-turvy spectacle one beheld Riel arguing in favour of the Crown's position and against that of his own lawyers.

The repudiation by the jury of defence counsel's insanity plea, and no desire or attempt whatsoever on the part of the defence lawyers to plead justification, and possibly obtain an acquittal or a hung jury, left Riel defenceless and a guilty verdict inevitable. In the end result Riel would be hung, not the jury.

---

[197]   Davidson, p. 200.

3. CROWN COUNSEL ROBINSON'S ADDRESS TO THE JURY

After Fitzpatrick and Riel had concluded their addresses it was the turn of Crown counsel Christopher Robinson.[198] His remarks were quite dissimilar to those of Fitzpatrick, as were the two men themselves.

Fitzpatrick was a 31 year old Irish Catholic Liberal resident in Quebec City; Robinson was a generation older at age 57 and was an English Protestant Conservative living in Toronto, Ontario and called to the bar over a quarter of a century prior to Fitzpatrick's call to the Quebec bar.

Unlike the often-impassioned eloquence of Fitzpatrick, Robinson in his speech was dispassionate but incisive, wielding his words like a scalpel in dissecting the defence put forward by Riel's counsel. In a trenchant argument Robinson told the jury that there was no need for him to delve into the evidence in detail because there was no dispute, no contradiction, of the facts proved by the Crown. Defence counsel, he argued, had effectively admitted that the Crown case had been made out beyond all question. Accordingly he would address himself to the only defence which had been set up i.e. the insanity of Riel.

Before doing so Robinson touched briefly on comments the defence had made relating to justification of the rebellion, and said they must make their choice. They could not claim for Riel "a niche in the temple of fame and at the same time...a place in a lunatic asylum." This statement by Robinson was disingenuous. The defence had made an unequivocal choice. It is true that the defence lawyers initially made some irresolute attempts to introduce an element of justification, such as Greenshields' remarks about Riel when requesting an adjournment,[199] and some questions to Father André. However they had no intention of vigorously pursuing this matter and on more than one occasion proclaimed in open court that they were not seeking to justify the rebellion. From Riel's point of view, one may ask why not? If they were so determined to push an insanity plea, could they not have developed an argument in which insanity and justification could live together? See the discussion in this respect in Chapter XIX and in Chapter XXII subsection 1(c).

---

[198] *The Queen v. Louis Riel,* p. 325-43.
[199] *The Queen v. Louis Riel,* p. 47.

Robinson amassed an impressive display of evidence to support his contention that Riel was not a lunatic. He pointed out that neither the delegation to Riel in Montana in July 1884 nor the various meetings and thousands of people Riel addressed in the North-West from then to March 1885, nor the men who placed their lives under his control, had the slightest suspicion that he was insane. Indeed the scope of such a broad brush painted by Robinson of people who had seen and heard Riel might have directly (or indirectly through friends, neighbours and associates), extended to some if not all of the jurors.

As to the evidence of the medical experts Robinson said
> what medical men occasionally call unsoundness of mind and
> what may be insanity in law are two different things entirely.

He correctly pointed out that it was for the law to determine legally excusable insanity, implying that that was not the function of Drs. Roy and Clark.

As for Riel's supposed controlling mania of a sense of his own importance and power, Robinson reminded the jury that the witnesses Nolin and Father André testified that if Riel received $35,000 he would give up his power and his ambition and go away. Robinson contended that Riel was
> a man of strong mind ... unusually long-headed ... who
> calculated his schemes and drew his plans with shrewdness,
> and was controlled by no insane impulse.

As for Dr. Roy, Robinson found his evidence "unsatisfactory". Roy brought no registers or records from Riel's confinement in Beauport in the 1870s or as to why Riel was brought to the Asylum or how he came to be discharged. He also denied Fitzpatrick's comment that Roy was in any sense called as a Crown witness.

Robinson declared that judges had over and over again ruled "that insanity is not a question which is only decided by experts." He referred to Captain Young who testified "I think I should know if I had been living eight days [sic. Young actually said nine days] with a lunatic." He added that none of the medical men had observed Riel at the time when his state of mind was in question, whereas the Crown witnesses observed him and his demeanour at that very time. As well, Riel exhibited no unsoundness of mind after his schemes, hopes and desires had collapsed. That should have been the strongest test of an inherent weakness becoming apparent, but none did.

As for Fitzpatrick's argument that Riel started out with only constitutional agitation in mind, Robinson went through various items of evidence to dispute this and to show treason. Items cited by Robinson included the following:

- on March 3 Riel called sixty armed half-breeds "our police";
- on March 5 he told Nolin he had decided to take up arms;
- aspects of the evidence of Crown witnesses (Willoughby, Lash, Tompkins, Astley, Jackson, Nolin and McKay) and their statements implicating Riel;
- Riel's letter to Major Crozier demanding the surrender of Fort Carlton and Battleford failing which Riel and his followers would commence "a war of extermination"; and
- subsequent hostilities that broke out, bloodshed, and Riel's remarks after the Battle of Fish Creek "we must yet have another fight, and then our terms will be better."

Robinson quoted a letter to support his contention that Riel tried to raise up the Indians, and tried to have Poundmaker destroy Battleford. He disputed Fitzpatrick's argument that the Crown should have called Poundmaker as a witness to verify this, stating that that would have shown Poundmaker's complicity in the rebellion and this would not be "fair play".

Robinson concluded by saying the Crown had a twofold duty — impartiality and fair play for Riel on the one hand, and public justice on the other. He said that if fair play had not been granted and if the trial had not been impartial, Riel's life had been in the Crown's hands as much as the hands of the defence counsel. There was no mention at this point, or earlier by Fitzpatrick, of a number of matters which some would consider not fair play on the part of the Crown such as:

- the Crown's initial objection to the defence's request for an adjournment of the trial to obtain witnesses and documents followed by its consent to a seven day adjournment in lieu of the defence's request for thirty days;
- the attitude of the Crown with respect to the appearance of potential defence witnesses such as the Deputy Minister of Indian Affairs, the Deputy Minister of the Interior, Gabriel Dumont *et al*;
- the Crown's opposition to having petitions, documents and Riel's papers produced; etc., etc.

161

Robinson told the jury he was leaving the case in their hands with confidence. It was a confidence well placed. His speech, although significantly shorter then that of Fitzpatrick, masterfully marshaled evidence and argument that were persuasive to the jurors. He cited acts indicating that Riel had masterminded the rebellion. He pointed out that the only defence advanced was insanity. He then bombarded the jury with many examples to amply demonstrate that Riel was of sound mind. The jury agreed.

Chapter XIV

MAGISTRATE'S CHARGE
TO THE JURY AND THE VERDICT

Following the addresses to the jury by Fitzpatrick, Riel and Robinson, Magistrate Richardson addressed the jury at the conclusion of which the jurors withdrew to consider their verdict.

1. MAGISTRATE RICHARDSON'S CHARGE TO THE JURY

After Crown counsel Robinson had finished his presentation, Stipendiary Magistrate Richardson (with the mute Justice of the Peace Le Jeune sitting beside him) began the charge to the jury.[200] It was now in the latter part of the afternoon on Friday July 31, 1885.

Richardson advised the jury that it was his duty to place before them the law, to refresh their memory as to the evidence, and leave the jury to determine the outcome. He advised the jury that Riel had been charged with high treason "levying war against Her Majesty in her realms in these territories." He said the law was "founded upon a very old English statute ... passed in the reign of Edward III." He was referring to the *1351 Statute of Treasons,* from which he then quoted verbatim. He told the jury that high treason by levying war required an insurrection accompanied by force to accomplish an object of a general nature. He referred to Duck Lake, Fish Creek and Batoche as the localities where Riel was charged with levying war upon her Majesty.

Richardson told the jury that the Crown must prove that Riel was implicated or else he should be acquitted. If he was implicated, the jury must consider whether he is "answerable" (a favourite word Richardson used several times). Later Richardson told the jury that Riel must completely satisfy them "that he is not answerable by reason of unsoundness of mind." He then said he would read the evidence drawing to their attention his observations "which may be useful to yourselves in arriving at a conclusion." He read portions of the evidence until the Court adjourned at 6:00 p.m.

The Court reconvened at 10:00 a.m. on Saturday August 1 with Richardson continuing to read some of the evidence. He then digressed

---

[200]   *The Queen v. Louis Riel,* p. 343-49.

to discuss the question of jurisdiction of the Court notwithstanding that he had already ruled that he had jurisdiction (in eleven words after arguments by the Defence and the Crown covering thirty pages in the transcript). He stated that only "a few days before" the defence had contested the Court's jurisdiction, the Manitoba Court of Queen's Bench had confirmed the Court's jurisdiction established by federal law. That federal law had conferred on a stipendiary magistrate with a justice of the peace and a jury of six the power to try a person for a capital offence in the North-West Territories. The Manitoba Court of Queen's Bench was the appeal court for the North-West Territories with respect to capital offences. Richardson didn't mention that the appeal was the Connor Case discussed in Chapter XX and that he had been the presiding stipendiary magistrate.

Richardson said the jury must be satisfied that there was a rebellion and gratuitously added "as I think you must be." He said they must decide if Riel's implication had been brought home conclusively to them. If so, did the evidence relieve him from responsibility? Richardson discussed unsoundness of mind and said that until the day before he had never heard of megalomania. He counseled the jury that not every man pronounced insane by the doctors "is to be held free from being called upon to answer" for criminal offences.

He next referred to the evidence of Nolin and André and the $35,000 they testified Riel asked for which, according to the Crown, tended to show that Riel's scheme was to put money in his own pocket. Then he reminded them that witnesses had sworn that Riel became irritable when religion was brought up, but he added Riel's irritability had passed away when he was with Captain Young. "Does this show reasoning power?" asked Richardson.

As for the date of insanity, said Richardson, the defence fixed it as commencing early in March, but then Richardson stated as a bald fact "but threats of what he intended to do began in December." In doing so, Richardson failed to also state that only Riel's enemy, Nolin, so testified. Nolin had answered "Yes" to a leading and the final question asked of him by Crown counsel (unobjected to by Riel's counsel) after a number of immediately preceding questions concerning matters in March 1885, not December 1884. There was no elaboration or cross-examination on this point. Richardson also failed to point out that several Crown witnesses gave evidence to the contrary. George Ness testified he saw Riel frequently after August 1884 and prior to March 17, 1885. Ness testified he had heard nothing about taking up arms prior to March 17. George Kerr testified that in January 1885 he was at a public meeting at which Riel proposed the health of Queen Victoria. Thomas E. Jackson's evidence was that he had not heard up to March 1885 that Riel wished to resort to non-constitutional means and as an active participant he would "certainly" have heard if that was the case. Richardson also failed to mention that Nolin did not break with Riel until over two months after the date for which he answered "Yes" to the leading question concerning Riel's plan to take up arms.[201]

Richardson questioned why if Riel was insane those around him had not the charity to lay an information so he would be taken care of. He then said he was only suggesting it, it was not the law. Richardson told the jury he was called upon to tell them what insanity is in the eye of the law. He stated that the Crown must conclusively bring home against Riel the crime charged. If it did, Riel had the responsibility to relieve himself from the consequences of his acts.

Richardson then correctly stated the applicable provisions of the McNaghten Rules relating to the defence of legal insanity. He further instructed the jury that every man was presumed sane and to possess a sufficient degree of reason to be responsible for his crimes until the contrary be proved to the jury's satisfaction. Richardson quoted verbatim from the McNaghten Case in the words discussed at Dr. Clark's evidence in section 1 of Chapter XII, then stated "That I propound to you as the law." Richardson in effect told the jury that if the jury found Riel had conclusively made out a defence of insanity within the parameters of the McNaghten Rules, they must acquit him and declare it was on account of insanity.

He then added some highly prejudicial remarks:

> Not only must you think of the man in the dock, but you must think of society at large, you are not called upon to think of the Government at Ottawa simply as a Government, you have to think of the homes and of the people who live in this country, you have to ask yourself, can such things be permitted?

Richardson concluded by saying "the law which [he] is said to have broken has been in existence for centuries" (i.e. the *1351 Statute of*

---

[201]   *The Queen v. Louis Riel,* p. 142; 157; 177-78; 200-01.

Treasons) and a man coming into the country shall not say, "I will do as I like and no laws can touch me."

As noted, Richardson's charge contained a number of unfair and prejudicial comments, which indicated his bias in favour of a conviction. His remarks to the jury were also deficient in his failure to tell the jury that the Crown had the burden of proving (beyond a reasonable doubt) every essential element of an alleged offence such as high treason. If the Crown fails to prove an essential element of the offence the charge must be dismissed. A finding of treason-felony, which was not a capital offence, could not be substituted since, at the time, the concept of an "included offence" was not available.

Richardson dealt with the six charges as though they were one charge only. He used the singular for "charge" throughout his address to the jury. He did not deal with each count separately. He did not ask the jury to consider each of the six counts individually. Because of the British subject aspect, he should have dealt with each count separately. A count is a charge in an indictment. Osler himself told the jury that Riel "was charged under six counts."[202] Each count in an indictment was a separate indictment for the purposes of evidence and judgment. With respect to each of the first three counts, Richardson should have told the jury that Riel had been charged as "a subject of our Lady the Queen", in other words as a British subject. He should have advised the jury that, while they were at liberty to bring in a general verdict, they had the alternative of bringing in a partial verdict, such as a conviction on one or more counts and acquittal on others.[203] He should then have advised the jury that **none of the Crown or defence witnesses, not one single one, had testified as to where Riel was born or as to his being a British subject.** The jury, not being instructed otherwise, brought in one general verdict on the six counts, not a separate verdict on each count. Riel should never have been convicted of the three first charges. A fundamental constituent to the validity of these charges (namely that of being a British subject) had not been proved.

All six charges referred to acts "within the realm". In the formal context the word "realm" meant a "kingdom". The meaning of the "Realm" within the *1351 Statute of Treasons* is fully discussed in sections 2

---

[202]   *The Queen v. Louis Riel*, p. 65.
[203]   *Archbold's Pleading, Evidence & Practice*, 23rd ed., p.88; 215.

and 3 of Chapter XVI and demonstrates that the "Realm" did not extend to Canada. As such neither the North-West Territories nor Canada were a Realm within the *1351 Statute of Treasons* or otherwise. This was unequivocal under English law. With respect to levying war against the King or Queen, the *1351 Statute of Treasons* was, by its very terms, restricted to doing so "in his Realm". This contrasted with the treason of "giving [to the King's Enemies] Aid and Comfort in the Realm, or elsewhere." The "elsewhere" would have encompassed Canada, but Riel was not charged with aiding and comforting Queen Victoria's enemies. An argument could have, and should have, been made that the *1351 Statute of Treasons*, with its death penalty, did not apply in Canada, only in the British Realm. Since Riel's counsel did not raise the point one may perhaps understand, but not forgive, Richardson for not addressing the matter. He obviously did not know the law, which effectively determined that an English colony such as the North-West Territories and Canada were not part of the Realm within the *1351 Statute of Treasons*. A more detailed discussion of this aspect including the legal authorities confirming beyond doubt that Canada and the North-West Territories were not part of the "Realm", and that the Crown charged Riel under the wrong statute appears in Chapter XVI.

2.   THE JURY'S VERDICT

Magistrate Richardson completed his charge to the jury at 2:15 p.m. on Saturday, August 1, 1885. According to the August 3, 1885 edition of the *Daily Manitoban* newspaper published in Winnipeg and bearing a dateline "Regina, Aug. 1";

> The oath was administered to the guard to keep the jury
> without meat or drink, fire or lodging.

The message was clear – no creature comforts pending a verdict.

Riel was on his knees in the dock praying quietly when the jury returned to the crowded courtroom one hour later. The initial fluttery excitement of the spectators turned to a hush in anticipation of the verdict. The Clerk of the Court asked the jury "How say you, is the prisoner guilty or not guilty?" In so doing, the Clerk was obviously not asking for a separate verdict on each of the six counts. The Court, acquiesced in by Crown and defence counsel, did not treat each count as a separate indictment for the purposes of judgment. In response to the Clerk's question, the answer was "Guilty".

The foreman of the jury, Francis Cosgrove, then announced that he had been "asked by my brother jurors to recommend the prisoner to the mercy of the Crown." According to the *Daily Manitoban* article referred to above Cosgrove did so "while crying like a child." Richardson advised the jury that their recommendation of mercy would be forwarded in proper manner to the proper authorities.

After Richardson's comment concerning the recommendation of mercy, Crown counsel Robinson asked if Magistrate Richardson and Justice of the Peace Le Jeune proposed to now pass sentence. Richardson asked Riel if he had anything to say prior to passing sentence. At this point, Fitzpatrick asked Richardson and Le Jeune to note the objections which he had previously taken to the jurisdiction of the Court. Richardson, in noting the objections, told Fitzpatrick that he would understand why Richardson could not rule on it, a fatuous comment since he had disposed of Fitzpatrick's eloquent and far-reaching argument (in this respect) in eleven curt words at the outset of the case. In any event, if a *bona fide* challenge is made in court, it is the duty of the presiding official to rule on it.

Riel, obviously impatient, interjected "Can I speak now?"

Chapter XV

RIEL'S CLOSING STATEMENT AND THE SENTENCE

After the jury's verdict, and before Magistrate Richardson passed sentence, Riel made a final address.

1. RIEL'S LAST HURRAH

At last the eager Riel was to be given an opportunity to vindicate himself, apparently not appreciating that, regardless of his reasons, his oratory, his explanations, what he was about to say would bear not one whit on his fate at the hands of the soon-to-be "hanging judge" Richardson.

Before the words of his first sentence were complete, Richardson interrupted Riel. Riel had begun: "Your Honours, Gentlemen of the Jury ..." when Richardson butted in to say that there was no longer a jury, they had been discharged. Its members were still in their seats in the courtroom.

Riel's speech was lengthy, intelligible, emotional, rational and, finally, cathartic.[204] His final public words combined

(i)   elation at the verdict effectively confirming his sanity;

(ii)   his views on the history of the Red River Resistance of 1869-70 and its aftermath leading to the Saskatchewan troubles;

(iii)   the background to his idea of dividing the West into one-sevenths and a discussion of his plan for European immigration;

(iv)   his contribution to Manitoba and the Metis and, instead of reward, his mistreatment by the Government; and

(v)   his request for two commissions, one to determine if he was a deceiver, the other to have a trial of his fifteen year career.

Riel said at the outset of his speech "The court has done the work for me", thereby conveying the transparent implication that it was not his lawyers that did it. According to Riel what was done was to remove

---

204   *The Queen v. Louis Riel*, p. 350-71.

"the stain of insanity". He asserted that he would "cease to be called a fool". If he were to be executed, it would not be as an insane man.

He thanked the jury for recommending clemency, and later apologized for his English and not having the time to prepare what he was going to say.

Riel said it would be easy for him to make

> an incendiary protest … about the jury, their selection, about the one who had selected them, and about the competency of the court

but he would not do so since the Court proved him to be a reasonable man.

He said the Saskatchewan troubles were not isolated. They stemmed from the difficulties in the Red River in 1869. In the Red River after taking up arms and taking prisoners, a treaty was negotiated in 1870 which resulted in the *Manitoba Act* with one-seventh of the land being granted to the half-breeds of Manitoba. He said that in the North-West the people including the Indians had not "the means to be heard". Foreshadowing the multi-cultural society presently in Western Canada, Riel said his idea was to invite Italians, Irish, Danes, etc. to emigrate to the North-West and each be given "one-seventh" of the land. He added that if he had succeeded, as a public man he would have invited emigration from the different countries of the world. He asserted that he himself had Scandinavian, Irish, French and Indian blood. He declared that when they gave the land in Manitoba "we did not give it only for the Anglo-Saxon race."

Riel talked about the injustices he felt had been done to him:

(i)   the failure in Manitoba to grant him the promised amnesty. "I was outlawed, but no notification was sent to my house of any proceedings of the court";

(ii)   his expulsion as an elected member from the House of Commons twice;

(iii)   Government banishment from Canada for five years;

(iv)   not receiving his share of the Manitoba land grants;

(v)   not receiving an indemnity for his services in Manitoba;

(vi)   governing Manitoba for two months but having to flee like a bandit when General Wolseley arrived;

(vii)   helping the lieutenant-governor of Manitoba during the Fenian scare; and

(viii)   later having a $5,000 bounty put on his head by Liberal
          Leader Edward Blake of Ontario, now federal leader of the
          opposition.

During his discourse, Riel mentioned "it seems to me I have
become insane to hope [for justice]."

As Riel hesitated at one point, Richardson jumped in with "Is that
all?" Riel said he felt weak but carried on.

Riel asked that a commission "a special tribunal" be appointed to
try him. This was the same suggestion made by Crown counsel Osler
and Robinson to the Minister of Justice before Riel's trial, but Riel
wanted a trial on specific questions related to his Manitoba days and one
covering his entire career over the previous fifteen years. He also said
that he had been declared to be guilty of high treason and giving himself
as a prophet of the new world. He wished for the appointment of a
special commission of doctors to examine, not insanity, "but whether I
am a deceiver and imposter."

He stated that the previous night "the spirit that guides and assists
me" told him that a commission will sit and "You will see if I am an
imposter thereby." At least in this instance (with John A. Macdonald's
subsequent appointment of a medical commission to examine Riel), and
also in the idea of a western Canada populated by European immigrants,
Riel's vision was "prophetic".

Riel, now weary as were the spectators, closed his remarks by
saying

> If I have been astray, I have been astray not as an imposter,
> but according to my conscience.

2.   THE SENTENCE

Magistrate Richardson's condemnation of Riel was cold, callous
and concise.[205] He told Riel, as is sometimes done with a view to
reinforcing the correctness of a guilty verdict, that his counsel had
defended him with as great ability as they could have. He ignored the
fact that Riel utterly opposed his counsel's strategy of pleading his
insanity, that they disobeyed his instructions of having a trial on the
merit of his actions, and that they threatened to abandon him in mid-
trial.

---

[205]   *The Queen v. Louis Riel*, p. 371-72.

Richardson asserted that the jury had shown "unexampled patience". His reason for this statement is not clear; he may have really been referring to himself, since in both of Riel's speeches he prematurely asked Riel if he was finished.

Richardson told Riel that he had been found "guilty of a crime the most pernicious and greatest that man can commit" – high treason; that he had let loose the flood gates of rapine and bloodshed; aroused the Indians; and brought ruin on many families. Ignoring the fact that the half-breeds, both French and English, had beseeched Riel to come from Montana to the North-West to help them with their grievances, Richardson added "If you had simply left [these families] alone [they] were in comfort and many of them were on the road to affluence."

Richardson disdainfully disposed of Riel's final speech in a few words "For what you did, the remarks you have made form no excuse whatsoever." To Richardson Riel's words were a tale told, not by an idiot but by a traitor, "full of sound and fury, signifying nothing."[206]

As for the jury's recommendation of mercy Richardson gratuitously, insensitively but prophetically declared:

> I cannot hold out any hope to you … that Her Majesty will
> … open the hand of clemency to you.

The Magistrate then advised Riel to prepare to meet his end. He ordered that Riel be taken to the Regina jail until September 18th, and on that day taken to his place of execution "and there be hanged by the neck till you are dead, and may God have mercy on your soul." Hopefully, God had mercy on Riel's soul. Prime Minister John A. Macdonald, as discussed hereafter, had no mercy on Riel's body.

Under section 76(7) of the *North-West Territories Act of 1880*, the death sentence could not be carried out until "the pleasure of the Governor" was made known. This effectively meant that John A. Macdonald and his Cabinet would eventually determine that it was their "pleasure" that Louis Riel be hanged.

---

[206]   William Shakespeare, *Macbeth*, Act V, Scene v.

SECTION B

Legal, Judicial and Political Injustices

Louis Riel at the time of his trial

Louis Riel addressing the jury

Hugh Richardson, The Trial Magistrate

Chapter XVI

RIEL'S UNLAWFUL CONVICTION AND EXECUTION

Other chapters in this book provide overwhelming evidence of various injustices suffered by Riel pertinent to his court proceedings. These include the presiding magistrate's bias and lack of independence; judicial and political improprieties; deprivation of Riel's right to full answer and defence; and unauthorized and inadequate legal representation by his own lawyers. These matters are more than sufficient in themselves to demonstrate that, on an objective basis or otherwise, Riel was denied justice. However, there is a further legal argument that puts the final nail in the coffin of Riel's right to justice. An argument that should have been made at Riel's trial was that the charges against him were brought under the wrong statute and as a result NONE of the charges were legally valid and ALL of them should have been thrown out.

1. CHARGES LAID UNDER THE ENGLISH *1351 STATUTE OF TREASONS*

The charges as noted throughout this book and below, were brought under an English statute more than 530 years old, the *1351 Statute of Treasons*. This Statute entitled "A Declaration which Offences shall be adjudged Treason", is cited 25 Edward III, stat.5, c.2. It was passed in the twenty-fifth year of the reign of King Edward III of England. Edward III was the instigator of the Hundred Years War with France in 1337.

The charges against Riel were under the wrong statute; he should not have been convicted of any of the charges or executed under that statute. The rationale for this statement is that the *1351 Statute of Treasons* required that the accused "do levy War against our Lord the King **in his Realm.**" [Emphasis added.] As sections 3(b) and (c) of this Chapter conclusively demonstrate, the King's "Realm" was effectively the lands which comprised England and Wales and the narrow "four seas" described therein. The King's Realm decidedly did not include any of the lands of Canada.

The charges against Riel stated that his acts were "within this realm." The term "realm" in the context of Riel's charges bore no relationship whatsoever to the term "Realm" in the *1351 Statute of Treasons*. In the Riel charges the words "within the realm" were mere window-dressing, redundant and of no legal effect. Although of no great consequence, it is interesting to note that in the Riel charges "realm" is spelled with "r" in the lower case, whereas in the *1351 Statute of Treasons* "Realm" is spelled with an upper case "R".

An authority on English criminal law, Sir James Fitzjames Stephen (a High Court Justice) writing two years before Riel's trial, stated that the *1351 Statute of Treasons*

> ... is really a crude, clumsy performance which has raised as many questions as it can have settled, and which has been successful only when it was not required to be put in force.[207]

The reason for use of this hoary 1351 made-in-England legislation instead of the 1868 treason-felony statute passed by the Parliament of Canada (in which John A. Macdonald was Prime Minister) and containing the same offence concerning levying war against Her Majesty was plain and simple. Under the 534 year-old English law a convicted person would be put to death, while under the more recent Canadian law the penalty for levying war was only imprisonment, not execution. John A. Macdonald wanted Riel hanged, not imprisoned.

Crown counsel Osler confirmed more than once that it was the *1351 Statute of Treasons* under which Riel was indicted and the Crown was proceeding. Defence counsel Johnstone in demurring to the information indicting Riel stated "As I understand it, you are proceeding under 31 Victoria." The Statute 31 Victoria was the *1868 Canadian Statute* for treason-felony. Osler answered "You are misunderstanding us then. 25 Edward III is the one."[208] Later in his opening address to the jury, Osler stated "The prisoner has been indicted upon the statute of treason passed in the reign of Edward III."[209] Osler added that there were several Acts under which the Crown could have proceeded such as the *1868 Treason-Felony Act*, but thought it not advisable to do so. His unstated reason was that punishment under the latter Act for levying war against the Queen was only imprisonment, not death as in the case

---

[207]   Sir James Fitzjames Stephen, *A History of the Criminal Law of England*, Vol. II, p. 283.
[208]   *The Queen v. Louis Riel*, p. 42.
[209]   *The Queen v. Louis Riel*, p. 67.

of the of *1351 Statute of Treasons*. Magistrate Richardson, in his charge to the jury, confirmed that the charge (he used the singular) was founded upon the statute of Edward III. Richardson quoted verbatim from that *1351 Statute of Treasons* and then told the jury what was required to constitute the crime of high treason by levying war. He then advised the jury that the charge upon which Riel was on trial was under

> that statute, that clause of the statute, and it charges him with
> levying war upon Her Majesty

at Duck Lake, Fish Creek and Batoche.[210] There was no mention by the Crown or the Magistrate of Riel being charged under any other statute. This Chapter discusses several other English statutes and the *1868 Canadian Treason-Felony Statute* to demonstrate the inapplicability of the *1351 Statute of Treasons* to the charges against Riel.

2.   SCOPE OF THE CHARGES AGAINST RIEL

The indictment against Riel contained six separate charges. However Magistrate Richardson treated them as one charge in his instructions to the jury, contrary to the Notice to Riel of July 8, 1885 from Crown counsel Osler and Burbidge referred to in Chapter IV, section 3. All of the charges against Riel were identical except the first three were based on his being a British subject and the last three were based on his owing local allegiance to the Queen, and except for the locations of the acts charged i.e. Duck Lake, Fish Creek, and Batoche. Each charge was described as occurring "in the said North-West Territories of Canada and within this realm." The specific wording of each of the six charges, besides containing some antiquated and eccentric language, such as "being moved and seduced by the instigation of the devil", contained allegations that Riel:

   (i)   levied war against the Queen in the North-West Territories of Canada and within this realm;

   (ii)   endeavoured by force and arms to subvert and destroy the constitution and government of this realm; and

   (iii)   endeavoured to deprive and depose the Queen from "the style, honour and kingly name of the Imperial Crown of this realm."

---

[210]   *The Queen v. Louis Riel*, p. 343-44.

"Local allegiance", the exact wording of one of the charges, and use of the plural for the charges in the Notice to Riel dated July 8, 1885, are discussed in Chapter IV, section 3.

While the *1351 Statute of Treasons* contained a specific provision relating to levying war against the King in his Realm, it contained no provision equivalent to (ii) and (iii) above. However, strained judicial interpretation had subsequently extended the meaning of high treason to include taking up arms in an attempt to reform laws or remedy grievances.

It should be mentioned that in the Mulcahy case[211] an English court held that where several overt acts were charged in a count and a general verdict of guilty on that count is given such judgment will be sustained. The charges of treason-felony in the Mulcahy case were under the *British 1848 Treason-Felony Statute* and contained three separate counts each alleging several overt acts.

All charges against Riel referred to **"this realm"** in a manner which unequivocally meant either or both of the North-West Territories and Canada, but not England. This makes sense in one respect since none of the activities alleged against Riel occurred in England. However, from a legal point of view (as discussed below), this meant that Riel was charged and convicted under the wrong statute (that is the *1351 Statute of Treasons* carrying the death penalty). He could have been charged with the same offences under the made-in-Canada *1868 Treason-Felony Statute* under which the punishment was imprisonment, not death.

3. MEANING OF "REALM" IN THE *1351 STATUTE OF TREASONS*

There are numerous sources which establish beyond doubt that the term "Realm" in the *1351 Statute of Treasons* did not extend to Canada. Some of them are as follows:

(a) Joint Legal Opinion of England's Attorney General and Solicitor General

In April 1757, Sir Robert Henley and Honourable Charles Yorke, Attorney-General and Solicitor General respectively of England, were asked "in obedience to your Lordships' commands" to give an opinion

---

[211]   *Mulcahy v. The Queen,* 1868 *Law Reports, English and Irish Appeals,* p. 306.

with respect to two persons convicted of high treason in the "colony of Nova Scotia". The two persons had been convicted of high treason, and subject to execution under an Act of the Parliament of Great Britain, 1 Mar. c.VI, entitled "An Act that the counterfeiting of strange coins (being current **within this Realm**), the Queen's Highness Sign Manual or Privy Seal, to be adjudged Treason". [Emphasis added.] There were similar counterfeiting provisions in sections 5 and 6 of the *1351 Statute of Treasons.* The two men in Nova Scotia were counterfeiting and uttering Spanish dollars and pistareens in Nova Scotia.

On May 18, 1757 Messrs. Henley and Yorke delivered their joint opinion as Attorney-General and Solicitor General that the above Act of the English Parliament did not extend to Nova Scotia. The Act was not in force in Nova Scotia with respect to the counterfeiting because

> the Act is expressly restrained to the counterfeiting of foreign coin current **within the realm, of which Nova Scotia is no part.**[212] [Emphasis added.]

The opinion added:

> the proposition adopted by the Judges [i.e. of Nova Scotia], that the inhabitants of the colonies carry with them the statute laws of this realm, is not true as a general proposition, but depends on circumstances.

The foregoing makes crystal-clear that an English statute making an act treasonable "within the realm" had no application to acts in Nova Scotia, which if they had occurred in England would be treason, because Nova Scotia was not "within this realm" as contemplated by that treason statute. The exact parallel existed in the trial of Louis Riel. He was charged with high treason under a statute (the *1351 Statute of Treasons*) requiring that the offence occur in the "Realm". It is incontrovertible that, if the two accused in Nova Scotia were not in the "Realm" under an English treason statute, neither was Riel (in the North-West Territories) in the "Realm" under an English treason statute.

---

[212]   William Forsyth, *Cases and Opinions on Constitutional Law*, p. 2-3 reproduces the opinion of the Attorney General and Solicitor General.

(b) Definition of "Within the Realm"

In the 1652 edition of *Mare Clausum*, by Master John Selden, the definition of "within the realm" is stated as follows:

> *Intra regnum*, within the Kingdom, is by the same law taken, and that in the usual phrase for that which is *intra* (or as it wont to bee barbarously render'd *infra*) *quatuor maria*, within the four seas, to wit, the southern, western, eastern, and that northern sea which washeth both the sides of that neck of land whereby Scotland is united to England.
>
> ... *extra quatuor maria*, without the four seas, and *extra regnum*, without the Realm, do in our law books signifie the very same thing.
>
> Within the four seas and within the realm signified one and the same thing, ... out of the Realm, and without the four seas, becom one and the same also.[213]

According to Master Selden the Realm and the Kingdom are one and the same thing i.e. the *Regnum*. *Intra Regnum*, within the Realm, means within the four seas as described. Within the four seas encompasses England and Wales (and their adjoining narrow seas) but not Scotland or Ireland. England, Wales and these narrow seas and the Realm are one and the same thing. Anything *extra quatuor maria*, beyond the four seas, was not part of the Realm in 1351 (when the *Statute of Treasons* became law), or in 1652 (when Selden's *Mare Clausum* was published) or in 1885 (the year Riel was tried). Canada was not part of the Realm at the time of Riel's trial. It was *extra*, not *intra*, *quatuor maria*.

The renowned Sir Matthew Hale, who had been Chief Justice of the Court of King's Bench of England before his retirement in 1676, called Master Selden's *Mare Clausum* "a learned treatise".[214]

In his 1866 text *Martial Law in Time of Rebellion*, W. F. Finlason wrote that the "Realm" meant "England" alone, within the four seas, according to the legal phrase.[215]

In discussing the *1351 Statute of Treasons*, Archbold's text states that while Ireland, Scotland and the Channel Islands are not part thereof, "the realm of England comprehends the narrow seas and Wales." [216]

---

[213]   Master John Selden, *Mare Clausum*, bk. 2, Ch. XXIV, p. 387-89.
[214]   *Hale, De Jur*, Mar. Ch. 4.
[215]   W. F. Finlason, *Martial Law in Time of Rebellion*, p. 18.
[216]   *Archbold Criminal Pleading, Evidence and Practice*, p. 929.

(c)   Sir Matthew Hale's Interpretation of the "Realm"

Chapter XIV, Volume I of Sir Matthew Hale's celebrated book entitled *The History of the Pleas of the Crown*,[217] is entitled "Concerning levying of war against the King". Hale discusses the *1351 Statute of Treasons* in section III of Chapter XIV, entitled "En son realme". He states:

> *Ireland*, tho part of the dominions of the crown of England, yet is no part of the realm of *England, nor infra quatuor maria*, as hath been ruled *temp. E*.1. *Morrice Howard's* case: the like is to be said for *Scotland* even while it was under the power of the crown of *England* ...

Master Selden would not have been pleased that the phrase was "wont to bee barbarously render'd" as *"infra quatuor maria"* by Sir Matthew Hale. The phrase *"quatuor maria"*, meant the four seas described by Selden in section (b) above. The quote from Hale confirmed that a dominion of the crown of England, i.e. Ireland at that time, was not part of the realm of England. It should be mentioned that the 1544 *Statute of 35 Henry VIII*, c. 2 provided that a British subject could be tried in England for treason committed abroad if he was taken captive in England.[218] Since levying war outside the Realm was not treason and, in any event, since Riel was not a British subject, nor taken captive in England, that statute has no relevance to Louis Riel's situation.

(d)   *Statute of 36 George III*, Chapter VII (1795)

The discussion of the English and Canadian statutes in this subsection (d), and in subsections (e), (f) and (g) may seem somewhat legalistic. However the discussion is intended to further establish that the term "Realm" in the *1351 Statute of Treasons* did not extend to Canada.

On December 18, 1795 the Parliament of Great Britain passed a law entitled *An Act for the Safety and Preservation of His Majesty's Person and Government against treasonable and seditious Practices and Attempts (36 George III*, c.VII). This statute provided that a person convicted of the activities specified therein would be adjudged a traitor, suffer pain of

---

217   Sir Matthew Hale, *The History of the Pleas of the Crown*, p. 130; 154-55.
218   Sir William R. Anson, *The Law and Custom of the Constitution*, Vol. II, p. 292.

death and suffer forfeiture of lands, etc. as in cases of high treason. This included levying war against the King "within this Realm".

One of the activities for which one would be declared a traitor and be executed was an attempt to deprive or depose the King, his heirs and successors from:

> the Style, Honour or Kingly Name of the Imperial Crown of this Realm, **or of any other of His Majesty's Dominions or Countries.**[Emphasis added.]

The addition after "Realm" of the words "or of any other of His Majesty's Dominions or Countries" attests to the fact that these other Dominions and Countries, such as those in Canada and Australia, were not part of the Realm. If they were part of the Realm, insertion of other "Dominions and Countries" in the Statute was superfluous and pointless.

The same statute of King George the Third also contained non-treasonous provisions. These were "High Misdemeanors". For a second conviction, in addition to the usual punishment for high misdemeanors, one was liable

> to be banished this Realm, or to be transported to such Place as shall be appointed by His Majesty for the Transportation of Offenders.

Transportation consisted of sending felons away to a penal colony, e.g. to Australia, usually to be kept there in hard labour. The statute specifically provided that if an offender who had been banished from the Realm "or transported beyond the Seas" was afterwards at large within "any Part of the Kingdom of Great Britain" without lawful cause before expiration of his term, he would be executed. This is verification that when an offender was banished from the Realm, he was banished from all parts of Great Britain. Since "beyond the Seas" was beyond the *"quatuor maria"* described by Master Selden and outlined in subsection (b) above, transportation "beyond the Seas" was transportation out of the Realm. The "Realm" and lands "beyond the Seas", such as Australia and Canada, were mutually exclusive. Neither Australia nor Canada were part of the Realm. They were lands "beyond the Seas".

One of the three elements of the charges against Riel (as described above in paragraph (ii) of section 2 of this Chapter was that he did "attempt and endeavour by force and arms to subvert and destroy the constitution and Government of this realm." In 1885, the year of Riel's trial, there was no specific statutory provision in Canada or the United

Kingdom, which made this an offence. However a "strained" judicial interpretation undoubtedly extended the reach of the statute to the meaning of "levying war against the King" to include "popular risings … against the established law and government."[219] The wording of the 1795 statute referred to the high misdemeanor offence of inciting "hatred or contempt" of the "Government and Constitution of this Realm" (without mention or inclusion of "any other of His Majesty's Dominions or Countries") i.e. without inclusion of Canada. The charges against Riel did not specify that he incited hatred or contempt but referred to the use of "force and arms" against the constitution and government "of this realm" (meaning Canada). Unlike the wording of the charges against Riel there was no reference in the 1795 statute or in the *1351 Statute of Treasons* to "force and arms" in relation to "the Constitution and the Government."

As noted under section (f) below, this 1795 statute was repealed in 1848 except as to offences against the Person of the Sovereign and as such had no relevance to the charges against Riel. It is discussed here to illustrate that the "Realm" is distinguished from the King's other "Dominions or Countries". It also illustrates that the language described in the charges against Riel (attempt to depose the Queen) referred to in paragraph (iii) of section 2 of this Chapter is similar to that found in this statute (repealed in this respect in 1848). In neither case is such language found in the *1351 Statute of Treasons*.

(e) *Statute of 57 George III*, **Chapter VI (1817)**

On March 17, 1817 the *Statute 57 George III*, c. VI was passed by the British Parliament making "perpetual" certain parts of the 1795 statute (referred to in subsection (d) above). These included the traitorous offences mentioned in subsection (d) of levying war against the King "within this Realm" and acts intended to deprive or depose the King from the "style" etc. of the Imperial Crown "of this Realm, or of any other of his Majesty's Dominions or Countries." The punishment of death and forfeiture of lands, etc. as in cases of high treason was continued for these offences. These offences were two of the specific elements alleged against Riel in each of the six charges against him

---

[219]   Thomas Pitt Taswell-Langmead, *English Constitutional History from the Teutonic Conquest to the Present Time*, p. 395.

except, of course, the "realm" referred to in Riel's charges was the realm of Canada. It was not the "Realm" referred to in these British statutes, nor was Riel charged under these 1795 or 1817 statutes.

As noted in subsection (f), the 1848 treason-felony statute of the United Kingdom repealed most provisions of both of the *1795* and the *1817 George III* statutes discussed under subsection (d) and this subsection (e). The provisions not repealed related only to offences against the "Person" of the Sovereign and re-classified a number of formerly traitorous offences carrying the death penalty (such as levying war against Her Majesty) to felonies no longer punishable by the death penalty, but only punishable by transportation or imprisonment. It did not, however, repeal the *1351 Statute of Treasons*.

This *1817 Statute of George III* also distinguishes between the "Realm" and the "other Dominions or Countries", thereby effectively distinguishing between England and Canada.

(f)   British *Statute of 11 & 12 Victoria*, Chapter XII (1848)

This statute entitled *An Act for the better Security of the Crown and Government of the United Kingdom* (often called the Treason-Felony Act) was passed by the British Parliament on April 22, 1848.

This 1848 Act did several things:

- (A) it repealed the 1795 and 1817 Statutes of George III, discussed in subsections (d) and (e), except as to offences against the "Person" of the Sovereign;
- (B) it reclassified as felonies certain offences under those statutes that were previously punished as high treason carrying the death penalty, and provided that these offences were now punishable only by transportation or imprisonment and not death; and
- (C) it declared that the offences against the Person of the Sovereign extended to and were in force "in that part of the United Kingdom called Ireland."

This statute was passed at the time of the Irish potato famine. It has been said that the treason-felony laws were "primarily directed against, and applied to the Irish."[220]

---

[220]   Sir Leonard Radzinowicz, *A History of English Criminal Law*, Vol.5, p. 419.

The offences against the "Person of the Sovereign" that were not repealed and were continued in force by this 1848 statute were those relating to:

> compassing, imagining, inventing, devising, or intending Death or Destruction, or any bodily Harm tending to Death and Destruction, Maim or Wounding, Imprisonment or Restraint of the Person of the heirs and Successors of his said Majesty King George the Third, and the expressing, uttering, or declaring of such Compassings, Imaginations, Inventions, Devices, or Intentions, or any of them.

The offences which formerly carried the death penalty but which were now declared to be felonies subject to a punishment of transportation or imprisonment (but not death) included:

(i)   acts "within the United Kingdom or without … to deprive or depose our most Gracious Lady the Queen, Her Heirs and Successors, from the Style, Honour, or Royal Name of the Imperial Crown of the United Kingdom, or of any other of Her Majesty's Dominions and Countries"; and

(ii)   "levying War against Her Majesty, Her Heirs and Successors, **within any part of the United Kingdom**" in order by force to compel changes in measures, intimidate or overawe Parliament, etc. [Emphasis added.]

Both paragraph (i) and the substance of paragraph (ii) appeared in the charges against Riel but there was no reference, nor could there have been, in the Riel charges to the United Kingdom.

There was no reference in this 1848 statute or in the *1351 Statute of Treasons,* as there was in the charges against Riel, to an

> attempt and endeavour by force and arms to subvert and destroy the constitution and Government of this realm.

In repealing a number of provisions of 36 George III, Chapter VII the *1848 Statute of Victoria* did not restate the language relating to "the Government and Constitution of this Realm." However, this language from that long repealed 1795 statute was specifically used, many years after its repeal, in the charges against Riel. As a result of the *1848 Statute of Victoria,* the *1795 Statute of George III* was revised. If Riel had been subject to and charged under this 1848 statute, there were no provisions under which he could have been tried for treason and executed based on the facts alleged against him, since none of the allegations related to the Person of the Sovereign.

185

The references to "the Realm", in the previous English statutes such as the *1795 and 1817 George III Statutes,* were replaced by "United Kingdom" in this 1848 statute. In the offence in paragraph (i) above "United Kingdom" is followed by "or of any other of Her Majesty's Dominions and Countries." This further emphasizes the fact that the "Realm" did not include England's overseas Dominions and Countries. In 1848 the "United Kingdom" had now become coincident with the "Realm" of the previous statutes, and does not include any of the Queen's other Dominions and Countries, such as Australia and Canada.

The offence under paragraph (i) above (deposing the Queen) applied to acts within the United Kingdom **or without**. The offence under paragraph (ii) above was specifically restricted to levying war "within any part of the United Kingdom", **not outside of it**. If Riel could have been charged under this 1848 Statute, there would have to have been proof of wrongdoing against Riel. Such proof would have had to demonstrate that he intended and did overt acts in the North-West Territories to deprive or depose the Queen from the style, etc., of the Imperial Crown in the United Kingdom or in the North-West Territories. If this 1848 British statute had applied in Canada, the acts with which Riel was charged would have been only felonies (not treason) and the penalty was not death, but transportation or imprisonment.

There was nothing whatsoever in the testimony given at Riel's trial that dealt separately with those parts of the charges which specifically alleged against Riel that he attempted to deprive and depose the Queen

> of and from the style, honor and kingly name of the Imperial
> Crown of this realm.

In the arguments of Crown and defence counsel, and in Magistrate Richardson's charge to the jury, there was no discussion whatsoever of the fatal difference in the meaning of the term "Realm" in the *1351 Statute of Treasons,* and the term "realm" as used in the Riel charges.

Crown counsel Osler, as noted in section 1 of this Chapter, stated unequivocally that Riel was indicted under the *1351 Statute of Treasons.* None of Osler, Fitzpatrick, Magistrate Richardson or anyone else at the trial (other than the misguided defence counsel Johnstone) referred to the charges against Riel being laid under any other statute. The hapless Johnstone, as noted in section 1, referred to the *1868 Canadian Treason-*

Felony Statute and was promptly told by Osler that Johnstone was wrong and that the proceedings were under the *1351 Statute of Treasons*.

The *1848 Statute of Victoria* did provide in effect that the *1351 Statute of Treasons* remained in force and nothing "enacted" by it was in any manner affected. For a similar provision refer to subsection 4(b) of this Chapter.

(g) Canadian *Statute of 31 Victoria*, Chapter LXIX (1868)

On May 22, 1868 Canada (which then consisted of the Provinces of Ontario, Quebec, Nova Scotia and New Brunswick), passed a law almost identical to the English *1848 Treason-Felony Statute* discussed in sub-section (f) above. The Canadian statute had the same title as the 1848 English Statute, namely *An Act for the better security of the Crown and Government* except it omitted the words "of the United Kingdom" at the end.

This Canadian law is known as the *1868 Treason-Felony Statute*. In brief it provided that compassing, intending, etc. the death of the Queen accompanied by an overt act, etc. was treason carrying the death penalty; so too was the conduct of an officer or soldier in Her Majesty's Army unlawfully corresponding with the Queen's enemies, giving them advice, etc. Riel was charged with none of these capital offences. The statute further provided that substantially the same offences as those described in paragraphs (i) and (ii) of the preceding subsection (f) were felonies (not treason) subjecting the offender to imprisonment (not death). Under the *1868 Canadian Treason-Felony Statute*, felony (i) i.e. (attempting to deprive or depose the Queen from the style ... of the Imperial Crown ...) applied within Canada or without, while felony (ii) applied to levying war against Her Majesty within any part of the United Kingdom or Canada. These were substantially the same offences for which Riel was tried for treason and condemned to be hung under a statute more than 530 years old, the *1351 Statute of Treasons*. However, the 1351 statute contained nothing remotely equivalent or similar to the language referred to in paragraph (i) of subsection (f) (although the charges against Riel did). As for the verbiage in the statute relating to the offence in paragraph (ii) (relating to levying war) to compel changes or to intimidate Parliament by force, there was none of this language in the *1351 Statute of Treasons*. The *1351 Statute of Treasons* simply stated "if a Man do levy War against our Lord the King in his Realm."

There was also absolutely nothing in the *1351 Statute of Treasons* under which Riel was charged referring (as Riel's charges did) to the traitorous

> attempt and endeavour by force and arms to subvert and destroy the constitution and government of the realm

Hence the charges against Riel contained two allegations of treason that were not specified as treason in the *1351 Statute of Treasons* under which (as discussed in section 1 of this Chapter) the Crown was proceeding. Strained judicial interpretation had extended the words of the 1351 statute beyond their plain meaning.

The *1868 Canadian Treason-Felony Statute* did not use the term "Realm", as did the *1351 Statute of Treasons* and the Riel charges. It referred to levying war "within any part of the United Kingdom or Canada." Canada, of course, was not part of the United Kingdom and this legislative distinction is confirmatory. As discussed in subsection (f), "United Kingdom" replaced the previous use of the word "Realm" in the *1848 Treason-Felony Statute of Victoria.* The *1868 Canadian Statute* in distinguishing between Canada and the United Kingdom in relation to the non-treasonous felony of levying war was effectively distinguishing between Canada and the Realm. This further confirmed that Canada was not part of the "Realm" referred to in the 1351 Statute of Treasons.

Crown counsel Osler on two occasions confirmed that the Crown was not proceeding against Riel under the *1868 Treason-Felony Statute;* nor was it proceeding under the *Fenian Act.* The *1868 Canadian Statute* had a provision virtually identical to the *1848 Treason-Felony Statute of the United Kingdom.* The former Statute provided in effect that nothing in the 1868 statute lessened the force or in any manner affected anything enacted by the *1351 Statute of Treasons.* This meant that the *1351 Statute of Treasons* was in force in Canada. However, the only relevant provision in relation to Riel was the one stating it was "Treason" (not "High Treason"):

> if a Man do levy War against our Lord the King **in his Realm.**[Emphasis added.]

This literally meant that for Riel to be convicted of treason under the *1351 Statute of Treasons* he would have had to levy war in the King's Realm. The King's Realm was within the *"quatuor maria"*, or four Seas described by Master Selden at subsection (b) of Section 3 above. The Statute of Treasons was the very Statute that Crown counsel Osler said Riel had been indicted under, and which Magistrate Richardson referred to, quoted from and applied in his charge to the jury. The term Realm was changed to the "United Kingdom" in the *1848 Statute of Victoria* discussed in subsection (f) above. Only if Riel had levied war in the Realm could he have been validly and justly convicted under the *1351 Statute of Treasons*.

Use of the term "realm" in the charges against Riel was spurious. In the Riel charges, there is no doubt that "realm" referred to "Canada". It certainly did not refer to the *"quatuor maria"* or to England which in 1885 (the year of Riel's trial) was the only "realm" covered by the *1351 Statute of Treasons*. It was totally unnecessary in the charges against Riel of levying war to add the words "and within the realm" after "in the said North-West Territories of Canada." It added nothing and was misleading in relation to the true meaning of "Realm" in the *1351 Statute of Treasons*. Insertion of "within the realm" in the Riel charges was of no effect in bringing the charges with respect to Riel's activities in Canada under the *1351 Statute of Treasons*.

Riel, of course, could have been validly charged under the *1868 Canadian Treason-Felony* Statute with levying war against the Queen in Canada or with intending to deprive or depose her from the style, honour and royal name of the Imperial Crown. Refer to subsection (f) of this section for a discussion of this matter. However, under this Canadian statute these charges were only felonies, not treason, and the punishment was only imprisonment not death. This Canadian law passed in 1868 by a Parliament headed by Prime Minister John A. Macdonald was not good enough for the Prime Minister's purposes. He turned to an ancient English statute with a view to having Riel executed, but in so doing he achieved an invalid and unjust result.

4.   ARGUMENTS AS TO APPLICABILITY OF *1351 STATUTE OF TREASONS*

It is beyond question that the "Realm" encompassed by the English *1351 Statute of Treasons*, under which Riel was charged, did not include Canada. However some may contend that the point is irrelevant because levying war under the *1351 Statute of Treasons* applied in Canada even if Canada was not part of the Realm, i.e. not part of England.

Proponents of this view may cite the high treason conviction in Ireland in 1849 of William Smith O'Brien. They may also refer to section 1 of the *1868 Canadian Treason-Felony Statute*. As well they may argue that provisions in pre-colonial statutes of a general character (such as the *1351 Statute of Treasons*) appropriate to the state of affairs of a colony, applied therein. The following discussion deals with each of these points.

(a)   The William Smith O'Brien Case [221]

In the heart of Dublin, Ireland lies O'Connell Street, the splendid main avenue of the city. This broad way is divided down its middle by a wide pedestrian boulevard. In several places on the boulevard there are statues to commemorate historical figures of Ireland. When the author and his wife were strolling down this boulevard recently we encountered a larger-than-life monument of William Smith O'Brien. This statue (within a stone's throw of one of James Joyce, the greatest English-speaking novelist of the twentieth century) was mounted on a high pedestal with a plaque identifying Smith O'Brien, his treason conviction, and other particulars.

William Smith O'Brien was an Irish patriot who led a group of men in Tipperary, Ireland against the authorities there during the Irish potato famine, a time when absentee English landlords were dispossessing their Irish tenants from the land. As a result of their activities, Smith O'Brien and others were charged with levying war against the Queen under the *1351 Statute of Treasons*. Smith O'Brien was convicted of high treason and sentenced to death on October 9, 1848. Fortunately for him, his sentence was subsequently commuted to transportation and he was shipped to Australia. He was eventually pardoned and returned home where he died on June 16, 1864.

Smith O'Brien appealed his conviction for high treason on a number of grounds, none of which succeeded. His counsel argued, among other matters, that Ireland was not part of the realm and consequently levying war in Ireland was not treason. The House of Lords dismissed this part of the argument in only two sentences. The judgment stated:

> **This objection depends upon the construction of the statute of Henry VII**, passing by the name of Poyning's Law. **By that statute** we think that those acts which were treason in England by the statute of Edw. III. were made treason in Ireland if committed there, and we cannot deem it

---

[221]   *O'Brien v. The Queen*, [1849] 9 *English Reports*, 1169.

necessary to say more upon the subject than that **the terms of the statute** admit of no doubt.[Emphasis added.]

The *Statute of Henry VII* (commonly called Poyning's Law) was an Irish statute, not an English one.[222] It was passed in Ireland in 1495 in the tenth year of the reign of Henry VII. It enacted that all statutes of late made in the realm of England relating to "the public weal" were to be deemed good and effectual in the law and

> be accepted, used and executed in this land of Ireland ...
> according to the tenor and effect of the same, and ... that
> they and every of them be authorised, proved and confirmed
> in this land.

Smith O'Brien's counsel admitted that the *1351 Statute of Treasons* was transferred to Ireland by Poyning's Law.

This case is distinguished from the circumstances of the Riel case on several grounds. The House of Lords in its judgment stated specifically that it was Poyning's Law (a statute enacted in Ireland, not England) which made acts, which were treason under the *1351 Statute of Treasons,* treason in Ireland if committed there. The Lords did not state that the *Statute of Treasons* itself, or by itself, made the levying of war in Ireland treason. Without Poyning's Law there would have been no treason in Ireland under the *1351 Statute of Treasons* and Smith O'Brien would have been acquitted. This is further confirmed by the House of Lords stating that the question raised by Smith O'Brien's counsel "depends upon the construction of the *Statute of Henry VII,* passing by the name of Poyning's Law." If the *1351 Statute of Treasons* of England in and of itself had applied in Ireland (which was then part of the United Kingdom but not part of the realm) it would have been unnecessary for the House of Lords to construe the Irish statute. Poyning's Law was positive and precise in stating that the law was to "be accepted, used and executed in this land of Ireland." It was the specific, positive provisions in the Irish Poyning's Law, not the *English Statute of Treasons,* which validated in Ireland the treason offences under the latter statute. Archbold succinctly states "The operation of this statute [the *1351 Statute of Treasons*] was extended to Ireland by Poyning's Act."[223]

---

[222]   *10 Henry VII,* c. 22 (1495).
[223]   *Archbold's Pleading, Evidence & Practice,* 23rd ed., p.929.

(b)   Section 1 of the *1868 Canadian Treason-Felony Statute*

This statute is discussed in subsection 3 (g) above.   One of its provisions, section 1, provided that nothing in the statute
> shall lessen the force of or in any manner affect anything enacted by

the *1351 Statute of Treasons.*

Unlike Poyning's Law discussed in subsection (a) above, section 1 of the *1868 Canadian Treason-Felony Statute* was not a declaration or positive enactment. Section 1 did not affirmatively ordain that the *1351 Statute of Treasons*
> be accepted, used and executed in [Canada] … according to the tenor and effect of the same.

The House of Lord's stated that it was Poyning's Law, an Irish statute, which made acts, which were treason in England under the *1351 Statute of Treasons,* treason in Ireland.   The specific direct declaratory provisions of the Irish Poyning's Law did so.   There was no statute passed in Canada that was similar to the Irish Poyning's Law.

Section 1 of the *Canadian 1868 Treason-Felony Statute* was not an affirmative, direct enactment of the *1351 Statute of Treasons* as a Canadian law. It was a negative statement. It did not decree that the *1351 Statute of Treasons* shall be accepted, used and executed **in Canada** according to its tenor and effect.   There was no mention whatsoever of Canada in section 1.   Ireland had been specifically mentioned in Poyning's Law. What section 1 amounted to was an indirect, unassertive provision that the *1868 Canadian Statute* did not lessen the force and effect of the 1351 English *Statute.* This could be interpreted as meaning the *1351 Statute of Treasons* was in force in Canada. This would mean that section 4 of the *1351 Statute of Treasons* was in force in Canada. Section 4 provided that it was treason "if a Man do levy War against our Lord the King in his Realm."

Thus, by section 1 of the *1868 Canadian Treason-Felony Statute,* the law in Canada made it treason for a man to "levy war against the King in his Realm", i.e. to levy war against the King in England, not in Canada. The Realm (as conclusively established in section 3 of this Chapter) was England only, not Canada.   The idea that when the *1351 Statute of Treasons* became law in Canada it made it an offence **in Canada** under that Statute to levy war against the Queen in **England** (the "Realm") is a correct one.   This is precisely what Section 5 of the *1868 Canadian*

Treason-Felony Statute did – i.e. it **made it an offence in Canada** to levy war against the Queen **in the United Kingdom**. The two Statutes are consistent in this respect. Legally, if Riel had traveled to England and levied war against Queen Victoria in England, and escaped to Canada, he could have been charged with an offence, under Section 5 of that 1868 Canadian Statute. As well Riel would have been guilty under section 4 of the *1351 Statute of Treasons* of an offence in Canada if he had traveled to England and levied war against the Queen in England.

Section 5 of the *1868 Canadian Statute* was also specific in making it an offence to levy war against the Queen in Canada. There was no provision in the *1351 Statute of Treasons* making it an offence to levy war against the Queen in Canada, the offence with which Riel was charged thereunder. As noted previously the offence under the *1868 Canadian Statute* was a non-capital felony, whereas the offence under the *1351 English Statute* was treason carrying the death penalty.

The provision in section 12 of the *1351 Statute of Treasons* is additional confirmation that the offence against Riel of levying war in Canada was not valid under that Statute. Under section 12 only the King and the Parliament of England could declare new treasons. In 1885, the year of Riel's trial, there was no outstanding declaration by the King and Parliament of England that levying war against the King **in Canada** was treason (carrying the death penalty).

The discussion in section 5 below entitled "Strict Interpretation of Penal Laws" further bolsters the conclusion that levying war as provided in the *1351 Statute of Treasons* (under which Riel was charged, convicted and executed) did not apply to acts of Riel in the North-West Territories or in Canada. See also the last paragraph of subsection 5(c) below.

(c)   Applicability of Pre-Colonial English Statutes in Canada

Although far-fetched, some may be inclined to contend that the provisions in pre-colonial statutes of a general character, such as the *1351 Statute of Treasons,* applied to activities of colonists in possessions and colonies acquired during the colonial era. This would be so even for those parts of the pre-colonial statute which by their very words were restricted to the Realm, and there were no colonies in contemplation when they became law. The rationale for this view might be that it was appropriate to the state of affairs of a colony which would otherwise be without such laws. As well, one might argue, this position was further strengthened in the case of a statute, such as the *1351 Statute of Treasons*, which was declaratory of the pre-existing common law.

This hermeneutical and judicial elasticity and extension of plain words of statutes to apply to matters definitely not contemplated by them brings to mind Humpty Dumpty stating "in a rather scornful tone" to Alice

> When I use a word it means just what I choose it to mean, –
> neither more nor less.[224]

In fact in 1885, at the time of Riel's trial, there was a statute enacted in Canada dealing with treason and felony. It was the *1868 Canadian Treason-Felony Statute* passed by the Parliament of Canada. Riel could have been charged under it. It was not necessary to have an ancient imported statute used for this purpose, unless of course the purpose was death to the alleged malefactor.

If levying war in Canada had carried the death penalty, John A. Macdonald and his cohorts undoubtedly would have preferred to prosecute Riel under the *1868 Canadian Statute*. However, since Riel could not be executed under this *1868 Canadian Statute*, Macdonald had to resort to one made in another country five hundred and thirty-four years earlier to achieve his objective of having Riel executed.

As for the argument that the treasons referred to in the *1351 Statute of Treasons* were declaratory of the common law this is irrelevant. Sir Matthew Hale is referred to in subsection (c) of section 3 of this Chapter. Hale was the author of another classic English law text *Pleas of the Crown* written in 1678.[225] At page 10, Hale stated that the *1351 Statute of Treasons*:

> reduced and settled all treasons; and by that means all
> Treasons that were before are reduced.

In other words treasons at common law prior to 1351 ceased to exist at common law. They were put into a different form, a statute. Only those statutory treasons referred to in the *1351 Statute* existed as of its date.

The pre-colonial common law of a general character, in the case of treason, was not in force in Canada.

---

[224]   Lewis Carroll, *Through the Looking Glass*, Chapter 6.
[225]   Sir Matthew Hale, *Pleas of the Crown, a Methodical Summary, 1678*, p. 10.

5.   STRICT INTERPRETATION OF PENAL LAWS

If the *1351 Statute of Treasons* intended that levying war against the King was to apply outside the Realm, as well as within the Realm, it would have specifically said so. It specifically so provided in the treason offence immediately following (i.e. adhering to the King's enemies in his Realm, giving to them "Aid and Comfort in the Realm, **or elsewhere.**"[Emphasis added.]   There was no "or elsewhere" provided for in the offence of levying war. This war offence only applied in the Realm.

In the high treason trial in 1917 of Sir Rodger Casement under the 1351 Statute of Treasons for his adhering to the King's enemies elsewhere than in the King's Realm (i.e. Germany) the following quote appears:

> Thus, every species of aid or comfort, in the words of the statute, which, when given to a rebel within the realm, would make the subject guilty of levying war; if given to an enemy, whether within or without the realm, will make the party guilty of adhering to the King's enemies.[226]

This quote gives one explanation for why there was no provision relating to levying war outside the Realm in the *1351 Statute of Treasons*. In that statute what would be levying war in the Realm in that situation amounts to adhering to and aiding and comforting the King's enemies when done outside the Realm. Riel was outside the Queen's Realm but he was not charged with adhering to and aiding and comforting the Queen's enemies outside the Realm.

The *1351 Statute of Treasons* (25 Edward III, Chapter II) was declaratory of the existing common law relating to treason. It specified which acts or conduct were henceforth to be treason. It further provided that if a "supposed Treason" not specified came before any Justices:

> the Justices shall tarry without any going to Judgment of the Treason, till the Cause be shewed and declared before the King and his Parliament, whether it ought to be judged Treason or other Felony.

---

[226]   *The King v. Casement* [1917], *1 King's Bench* 98, p. 120-121 referring to 1 East, P.C. 78.

The marginal note in the statute reads "New Questions of Treason shall first be decided in Parliament." As noted in the above quote from Sir Matthew Hale's *Pleas of the Crown*:

> 2. The Statute of 25 *E*.3. reduced and settled all Treasons;
> and by that means all Treasons that were before are reduced.

Whatever treason offences existed at common law prior to the *1351 Statute of Treasons* were wiped out and no new treasons could be declared, except by the King and his Parliament. In other words, no treason of levying war "against our Lord the King **outside his Realm**" was valid unless declared by the King of England and his Parliament. At the time of Riel's trial there was no such outstanding declaration.

(a)   Strict Construction of *1351 Statute of Treasons*

Many statutes require interpretation to determine their legal meaning and effect. One of the statutory rules of interpretation that applied for most of the 19th century was that penal statutes must be strictly construed. This rule required that all elements prescribed by a penal statute, whether material or not, morally, which would constitute the offence must be established. So wrote a leading authority on statutory interpretation, former Chief Justice Sir Peter Benson Maxwell, in his landmark 1875 text.[227] However two years before Riel's trial, Maxwell published his second edition modifying his previous writings. In the 1883 edition he stated that the rule requiring strict construction of penal statutes "was more rigorously applied in former times." In his second edition Maxwell stated that a judicial interpreter must now, honestly and faithfully, give the Legislature's language "its plain and rational meaning", and promote its object.

Also in this second edition, Maxwell wrote that "it is unquestionably a reasonable expectation" that a legislature would not leave to "mere doubtful inference" a matter such as

> the infliction of suffering, or an encroachment on natural
> liberty and rights

but would "manifest [its intention] with reasonable clearness".

He also wrote that it was "not competent to a Court to extend" words of a statute if the Legislature had failed to use words "sufficiently comprehensive" to prohibit all cases intended to be prevented by the

---

[227]   Sir Peter Benson Maxwell, *On the Interpretation of Statutes*, p. 240.

mischief. In dealing with the "degree of strictness applied to the construction of a penal statute" he wrote that this in large part depended
> on the severity of the statute. When it merely imposed a
> pecuniary penalty, it was construed less strictly than where
> the rule was invoked in *favorem vitae* [i.e. in favour of life]. [228]

Construction of a statute was to be more strictly construed in favour of an accused whose liberty or life were to be adversely affected than for an accused who could suffer only a financial penalty. Interpretation of statutes should be highly favourable to personal liberty.[229] In a penal statute omission of provisions should not be added nor construction strained. Sir Fortunatus Dwarris wrote
> A penal law then, shall not be extended by equity; that is,
> things which do not come within the words, shall not be
> brought within it, by construction.[230]

This is similar to the above quote from Maxwell as to the incompetence of a Court to extend insufficiently comprehensive words of a statute.

In 1887, two years after Riel's trial, Lord Esher, Master of the Rolls, stated:
> If there is a reasonable interpretation which will avoid the
> penalty in any particular case we must adopt that
> construction … That is the settled rule for the construction
> of penal sections.[231]

In the third edition of Hardcastle's 1901 text, there is the following sentenced based on an 1898 judgment:
> Where an enactment imposes a penalty for a criminal
> offence, a person against whom it is sought to enforce the
> penalty is entitled to the benefit of any doubt which may
> arise on the construction of the enactment.[232]

Hardcastle's text also referred to an 1882 case in stating:
> Where there is an enactment which may entail penal
> consequences, you ought not to do violence to the language

---

[228]   Maxwell, 2nd ed., p. 318-21.

[229]   Lord Abinger, *Henderson v. Sherborne*, (1837), 2 *Meeson & Welsby*, p. 239.

[230]   Sir Fortunatus Dwarris, *A General Treatise on Statutes: Their Rules of Construction and the Proper Boundaries of Legislation and of Judicial Interpretation*, p. 634.

[231]   Tuck & Sons v. Priestner, [1887] 19 Q.B.D, p. 638.

[232]   Henry Hardcastle, *A Treatise on the Construction and Effect of Statute Law*, p. 457. *London County Council v. Aylesbury Dairy Co.* (1898), 1Q.B. 106 @ 109.

in order to bring people within it, but ought rather to take care that no one is brought within it who is not brought within it by express language.[233]

(b) Examples of Strict Construction of Penal Statutes.

There are numerous examples of penal statutes being interpreted strictly and in favour of an accused who would otherwise incur punishment or death. A few examples are:

(i)   Dwarris at page 634 of his text refers to a statute of Edward 6. Under that statute, theft of horses (in the plural) was a capital offence. According to Dwarris "the judges conceived that this did not extend to him that should steal but one horse." Maxwell referred to the same statute at page 321 of his second edition. The law was subsequently amended.

(ii) Maxwell states that formerly a capital felony indictment against a person for assaulting another at a certain time and place, and feloniously cutting or robbing him, failed because there was no mention in the indictment that the cutting or robbing was done at that certain time or place.[234]

(iii) Dwarris at page 634 refers to Bacon's Maxims in stating that if the law prescribed the loss of a right hand for an offence, and the offender had previously had his right hand cut off, the letter of the law would not be extended to loss of his left hand.

(c) Review of Riel Case With Respect to Strict Construction

From the foregoing, and other examples which could be cited, it was beyond doubt at the time of Riel's trial that the *1351 Statute of Treasons* had to be strictly construed. Every element of the charges against Riel, which constituted the offence, had to be established. No omissions, if any, or strained interpretation of the 1351 Statute under which Riel was indicted, were permissible or lawful, the more so in the case of a capital offence.

However the exact opposite occurred. The *1351 Statute of Treasons* was obviously applied as though the "Realm" in the Riel charges

---

233   Hardcastle, p. 457. *Rumball v. Schmidt* (1882), 8 Q.B.D. at p. 608.
234   Maxwell, 2nd ed., p. 321 referring to 2 Hale, 178, *R .v. Bank*, Cro. Jac. 41.

encompassed not just the *"quatuor maria"* i.e. England,[235] but also Canada, "a Dominion beyond the Seas". The interpretation of this penal statute was not strictly construed and its application was false.

Interpreting the words "the King in his Realm" (in the *1351 Statute of Treasons*) to mean "the King in his Realm **and in Canada**" was prohibited and wrong [Emphasis added]. In the Riel trial such an interpretation was all the more perverse and unjust considering the fact that the death penalty was involved, the most severe of all penalties.

With respect to levying war (the offence with which Riel was charged), the *1351 Statute of Treasons* required that the war be against the King "in his Realm". If Riel had levied war in England, i.e. in the Realm, he could have been lawfully convicted in Canada under the *1351 Statute of Treasons*. The idea that the *1351 Statute of Treasons* could subsequently be interpreted to make it an offence in Canada to levy war against the Queen in England is sound. This is precisely what the *1868 Canadian Treason-Felony Statute* did when it was enacted. The *1868 Canadian Treason-Felony Statute* (under which Riel was not indicted because he could not have been executed under it) contained a provision making it a Canadian felony, punishable by imprisonment not death, to levy war against the Queen in the United Kingdom as well as in Canada.

Strict construction of a severe penal statute does not permit the extension of the King's "Realm" to mean "or of any other of the King's (or Queen's) Dominions and Countries." The latter phrase followed the term "Realm" for certain specified offences in the statutes of 36 George III; 57 George III; and 11 and 12 Victoria discussed in subsections (d), (e) and (f) of section 3 of this Chapter. If the term "Realm" automatically encompassed these other "Dominions and Countries" there would have been no need to indicate that these specified offences (which did not include levying war) were offences in these other Dominions and Countries, such as Canada and Australia.

The severity of the *1351 Statute of Treasons* was beyond question. It had to be construed, as Maxwell said, "in *favorem vitae*", in favour of life. It was not competent to a court to extend the words of the statute respecting levying of war in the King's Realm to levying war "outside the King's Realm". It was not competent to construe the *1351 Statute of*

---

[235] In the *1848 Treason-Felony Statute of Victoria* discussed above the term "Realm" from previous statutes was changed to "United Kingdom". It also referred to "that part of the United Kingdom called Ireland."

Treasons to extend to levying war in Canada. Levying war in the King's Realm can not be construed to extend to lands not within the King's Realm.

There is an article entitled "The Meaning of Treason in 1885" by D. H. Brown, which discusses the law of treason in the year in which Riel was tried and convicted.[236] The author of the article correctly stated that Riel was indicted under the *Statute of Treasons* of Edward III. However he did not specifically address the point of whether the *1351 Statute of Treasons* is applicable to "levying war" **outside the Realm**. He stated the statute makes no mention of "crimes against the realm" and adds "that is, against the king in his political capacity." This categorization of "realm" is totally inapplicable to the meaning of "Realm" as used in the *Statute of Treasons* and as discussed herein.

There is nothing in the article which confirms that "if a Man do levy War against our Lord the King in his Realm" (section 4 of the *1351 Statute of Treasons*) this means "if a Man do levy War against our Lord the King outside His Realm" e.g. Canada. The fact that the judges (as the article points out) subsequently judicially extended the plain meaning of the words of the statute to include political armed resistance to the public order of the realm as treason is not relevant to the meaning of Realm in the *1351 Statute of Treasons*. The judicially expanded treason of levying war was still restricted to the "Realm". It was not extended to Canada. The Maclane and McMahon cases, which the article cited, are irrelevant to this point. Neither Maclane nor McMahon was charged with levying war under section 4 of the *1351 Statute of Treasons*. Maclane was charged with compassing the King's death, an offence not limited to the Realm; McMahon was charged as a United States citizen under a statute of Upper Canada. In any event the 1866 McMahon case was superseded by the *Naturalization Acts* of Britain (1870) and of Canada (1881) discussed in Chapter VI. Brown's article did not discourse upon the *1868 Canadian Treason-Felony Statute* discussed in subsection 3(g).

As for English statutes, to the extent they may have been in force in Rupert's Land as of 1670 they had to be read according to their provisions. As noted elsewhere Crown counsel Osler and Magistrate Richardson both made clear in their addresses to the jury that Riel was

---

[236]   D. F. Brown, "The Meaning of Treason in 1885", *Saskatchewan History*, Vol. 28 (Spring), 1975, p. 65-73.

charged with levying war under the *1351 Statute of Treasons*. Richardson actually read verbatim section 4 of that Statute, dealing with levying war in the King's Realm.[237] In this respect the inapplicability outside the Realm (England) of the levying war provision of the *1351 Statute of Treasons* has been discussed herein as has the strict interpretation of severe penal statutes.

With respect to subsection 4(b) of this Chapter, one may note that section 1 of the *1868 Canadian Treason-Felony Statute* actually referred to the "twenty-fifth year of King Edward the Third". It did not refer to the 25th year of his "reign" (as did the later statute RSC 1886, c. 146, s. 9 enacted the year after Riel's execution). King Edward III's twenty-fifth year was the year 1336, while the twenty-fifth year of his reign was 1351 i.e. the year of the *Statute of Treasons*. Although unnecessary to do so, one could argue that on a strict interpretation of the *1868 Treason-Felony Statute* this discrepancy further confirms that the *1351 Statute of Treasons* was not applicable to the charges against Riel in Canada.

6.   SUMMARY

- Riel was tried under the *1351 Statute of Treasons* with levying war against the Queen in the North-West Territories.

- Levying war under the *1351 Statute of Treasons* was only treason if it occurred in the King's "Realm".

- The King's Realm meant *"intra quatuor maria"*, within the four narrow seas adjacent to England and Wales.

- Neither the North-West Territories nor Canada were part of the King's Realm.

- The word "realm" used in the charges against Riel was irrelevant and of no effect. The "realm" referred to in the Riel charges was Canada, not the King's Realm (i.e. England, Wales, and the four narrow seas).

- Those parts of the charges against Riel referred to in paragraph (iii) of section 2 of this Chapter relating to endeavouring to deprive and depose the Queen from the style etc. of the Imperial Crown were not specifically mentioned as offences under the *1351 Statute of Treasons*. They were non-capital felonies, not capital treason offences under the *1868 Canadian Treason-Felony Statute*. Further,

---

[237]   *The Queen v. Louis Riel*, p. 67 and 343-44.

Riel was not charged under this Canadian *Treason-Felony Statute* because the government knew he could not have been executed under it.

- Those parts of the charges against Riel referred to in paragraph (ii) of section 2 of this Chapter related to subverting etc. the constitution and government did not appear in the *1351 Statute of Treasons* or either of the *Treason-Felony Statutes* of 1848 and 1868. The latter statutes did make it a non-capital felony to use force to intimidate Parliament, but Riel was not charged under these statutes or with this offence. However, judicial construction likely extended the meaning of levying war to the matter referred to in section 2(ii) of this Chapter, but it was limited to the Realm.

- The *1351 Statute of Treasons* was a severe penal statute carrying the death penalty. As such, statutory interpretation required that it be strictly construed. Arguments that even if the "Realm" is restricted to England the statute nevertheless applies to levying war in Canada cannot be sustained. The words of a severe penal statute cannot be construed to extend to Canada if the words of the statute are not (as Chief Justice Maxwell wrote) "sufficiently comprehensive" to do so. Matters, which do not come within the words of the statute, must not be brought within it.

The result is decisive. The *1351 Statute of Treasons* with respect to the charges against Riel had no application outside the Realm, outside the *quatuor maria*, outside England, Wales, and the adjacent narrow four seas. That statute had no application to a charge of levying war against the Queen in the North-West Territories or anywhere else in Canada. Serious injustices suffered by Riel have been discussed in other Chapters. Riel's conviction and execution under the *1351 Statute of Treasons* for levying war against the Queen in the North-West Territories of Canada was contrary to law and a further serious injustice.

Chapter XVII

APPEAL COURT JUDGES

Under section 77 of the *North-West Territories Act of 1880*, a person convicted of an offence punishable by death had a right of appeal to the Court of Queen's Bench of Manitoba. That court had no jurisdiction to reverse a conviction. Its authority was either to confirm the conviction or order a new trial.

Riel's life was now in the hands of three appellate judges in Winnipeg, namely Lewis Wallbridge, Thomas Wardlaw Taylor and Albert Clements Killam. All three judges had been appointed under the government of which John A. Macdonald was Prime Minister and Alexander Campbell was Minister of Justice. Another judge, Joseph Dubuc who had come to Manitoba in 1870 at the request of and who had been a friend of Riel, conveniently absented himself in Montreal during Riel's appeal. The following is a short profile of the three judges who heard Riel's appeal.

1. Chief Justice Lewis Wallbridge

Wallbridge was born in Belleville, Upper Canada on November 27, 1816. His paternal grandfather, Elijah, was a United Empire loyalist who settled in the Bay of Quinte area, Upper Canada, shortly after the War of American Independence. Wallbridge's ancestors came from Dorsetshire in England. They fled England after taking sides with the Duke of Monmouth in the Rebellion against the Catholic King, James II. The Duke of Monmouth was the illegitimate son of Charles II. On the death of Charles in 1685, his brother succeeded to the throne as James II. James' royalist troops quashed Monmouth's unruly rabble of whom many fled from England. However a number of Monmouth's supporters who were captured were tried and executed in the "Bloody Assizes" of 1685. It was fortunate for Chief Justice Wallbridge that his ancestors were not executed under the *1351 Statute of Treasons*.

Lewis Wallbridge received his early education at Dr. Benjamin Workman's school in Montreal and at Upper Canada College in Toronto (York). He was an Anglican. After articling in the Toronto law firm of Robert Baldwin, he was called to the bar in Hilary Term, 1839. He practised law in Belleville and became a Queen's Counsel in 1856.

Wallbridge was elected to the Legislative Assembly of Canada in 1858. In 1863 he was appointed Solicitor General for Canada West in the Macdonald-Dorion Government. In August of that same year he was elected Speaker of the Assembly. According to the *Dictionary of Canadian Biography* (Volume XI, page 908), his nomination caused a noisy outburst, led by a previous speaker, J. E. Turcotte, alleging that Wallbridge was anti-Catholic and anti-French. It is interesting to observe that another Speaker who preceded Wallbridge in 1863 was none other than Alexander Campbell. Alexander Campbell, of course, was later appointed Minister of Justice by John A. Macdonald and, as noted hereafter, received startling correspondence in that capacity from his old fellow Parliamentarian, then Chief Justice Wallbridge (another Macdonald appointee) prior, and relevant, to the Riel trial.

In 1864 John A. Macdonald and Étienne-Paschal Taché approved the continuation of Wallbridge as Speaker in the Government they formed in that year and in the "Great Coalition" which ensued. Wallbridge presided during the debates on Confederation. He had John A. Macdonald's ear on matters of local patronage. He did not seek re-election in 1867, but continued to back the Coalition headed by Macdonald and Taché. After retiring from politics Wallbridge practised law in Belleville. In 1878 he attempted to re-enter politics by seeking nomination for John A. Macdonald's Conservative party, but lost the election due in part to the hostile Catholic vote.

In 1882 the Chief Justice of Manitoba, Edmund Burke Wood, died. Latterly, Wood's intemperance and indiscretions had been an embarrassment. In 1881 a censorious petition against him had been presented to the House of Commons.

After Wood's death a number of Manitoba lawyers met and pressed for the appointment as Chief Justice of one of the local sitting judges. James Andrews Miller, whom Macdonald had appointed a puisne judge of the Court of Queen's Bench of Manitoba in 1880 with the promise that Miller would succeed Wood as Chief Justice, threatened to quit the bench if he was not elevated to the position of Chief Justice.

Macdonald paid no attention to the pleas of Miller or the Manitoba lawyers. In December 1882 he parachuted the Belleville bachelor Wallbridge, then of the relatively advanced age (for the time) of 66 years, and who had never held judicial office, into Winnipeg as Chief Justice of

Manitoba. Miller immediately resigned from the Court of Queen's Bench in protest and in his place, Macdonald appointed Thomas Wardlaw Taylor. Alexander Campbell was then Minister of Justice in John A. Macdonald's government. Campbell, the former Speaker, defended the former Speaker Wallbridge's appointment as Chief Justice stating that Wallbridge was acquainted with many Manitoba lawyers.

According to the *Dictionary of Canadian Biography*, Wallbridge was a "local informant" for John A. Macdonald, this at a time when he was Chief Justice of Manitoba. While in Winnipeg, Wallbridge lived in a hotel. While Chief Justice of Manitoba, Wallbridge died unmarried at Winnipeg on October 20, 1887. His remains were taken to Belleville, Ontario for burial.

2.   Thomas Wardlaw Taylor

Taylor was born in Scotland on March 23, 1833. In 1852 he graduated with a Bachelor of Arts degree from Edinburgh University. Shortly after, he moved to Canada West (Ontario) and obtained a Master of Arts degree from the University of Toronto in 1856. He was called to the bar in Canada West in 1858. In 1869 he became a referee for quieting titles in Upper Canada. He was a Master of Chancery from 1872 to 1883.

Taylor became a Queen's Counsel in 1881. On January 5, 1883, under the government of the time of which John A. Macdonald was Prime Minister and Alexander Campbell was Minister of Justice, Taylor was appointed a puisne judge of the Court of Queen's Bench of Manitoba. This was the same government, Prime Minister and Minister of Justice as at the time of Riel's trial in 1885. On the death of Chief Justice Wallbridge in 1887, John A. Macdonald had Taylor appointed Chief Justice of Manitoba, a position he held until 1899. In 1892 he and Justice Bain, with Justice Dubuc dissenting, upheld the abolition of separate schools in Manitoba. The right for separate schools was part of the terms pursuant to which Manitoba had entered into Confederation under the leadership of Louis Riel. In 1897, the year of her Diamond Jubilee, Queen Victoria knighted Taylor. He wrote several legal books including one entitled *Investigation of Titles*. Perhaps he initially wrote it in shorthand since he stated in his judgment on the Riel appeal "I am myself a stenographer."

Taylor retired to Toronto in 1899 and moved to Hamilton in 1906. Taylor, a Presbyterian elder in the early 1900s, was considered an expert on church law in Canada. He died in Ontario on March 2, 1917.

3.   Albert Clements Killam

Killam was born at Yarmouth, Nova Scotia on September 18, 1849. After taking his early education in Yarmouth he attended the University of Toronto and obtained a Bachelor of Arts degree in 1872. After being called to the Ontario Bar in 1877, he practised law in Windsor, Ontario until 1879. In that year he moved to Winnipeg to practise law. In 1883 he was elected as a Liberal member for Winnipeg South to the House of Commons. In 1884 Killam was made a Queen's counsel.

On February 3, 1885, when John A. Macdonald was Prime Minister and Alexander Campbell was Minister of Justice, Killam was appointed by them as a puisne judge of the Court of Queen's Bench of Manitoba. In 1899 Killam succeeded Thomas Wardlaw Taylor as Chief Justice of Manitoba, and in 1903 he was appointed to the Supreme Court of Canada. He left that position two years later to accept an appointment as Chief Commissioner of the Board of Railway Commissioners. Killam died at Ottawa in March 1908.

These brief outlines of the three judges of the Court of Queen's Bench of Manitoba indicate that all three of them were appointed to the Manitoba judiciary by a government of which John A. Macdonald was Prime Minister and Alexander Campbell was Minister of Justice. Later Macdonald and Campbell, of course, were the two top government ministers who were determined to see Riel tried, convicted and executed. None of the three judges was a native (in two senses of that word) of Manitoba or of Western Canada (Rupert's Land). None was of French or Metis extraction. Two of them eventually left Winnipeg for Eastern Canada and the third's body was returned after his death to Ontario for burial. These three judges, as noted hereafter, were unanimous in deciding that there was no merit in the appeal and in confirming Riel's conviction. Riel himself was not permitted to be present while the Court determined his fate.

Chapter XVIII

RIEL'S APPEAL OF HIS CONVICTION

After Riel's conviction on August 1, 1885, his lawyers appealed to the Court of Queen's Bench of Manitoba, the appellate court for the North-West Territories with respect to offences punishable by death.

1. Riel's Application to Appear at the Appeal Hearing

Prior to the appeal itself, Riel's lawyers (Lemieux, Fitzpatrick and John S. Ewart) made an application to the Court of Queen's Bench with respect to Riel being personally present in Winnipeg at the appeal in the Court of Queen's Bench of Manitoba and concerning the production of the original trial papers. With respect to the original trial papers, the Court stated if they could not be had it would accept verified copies.

As for Riel's personal attendance at his own appeal hearing, Chief Justice Wallbridge on behalf of the Court ruled that the Court had authority to hear Riel's appeal from the North-West Territories (which was outside the limits of Manitoba). It further ruled that it had no legal authority to bring Riel before the Court, that it could not send a *habeas corpus* to Regina to bring Riel to Winnipeg for this purpose. This astonishing ruling, that the Court had power to adjudge the appeal but was powerless to order Riel to be present in Winnipeg, meant that Riel languished in the Regina jail hundreds of miles away, with a twenty pound ball and chain on his leg. In his absence the appeal affecting his life or death was being argued in Winnipeg by lawyers who had disobeyed his instructions with respect to his trial.

The Report and Wallbridge's ruling (made on September 2, 1885) appear at (1885) 2 *Manitoba Law Reports*, pages 302 to 304.

2. Riel's Appeal of His Conviction

The three judges of the Court of Queen's Bench who heard the appeal launched by Riel's lawyers, in addition to all being appointees of Prime Minister John A. Macdonald (when Alexander Campbell was Minister of Justice), shared several common themes in their reasons for judgment.[238] The page numbers in the text correspond to the page numbers in their judgments. Each of the appeal judges:

---

[238]   *The Queen v. Louis Riel*, (1885) 2, *Manitoba Law Reports*, p. 321.

(i)   stated he had carefully read the evidence (pages 328, 343 and 359);

(ii)   praised the abilities of defence counsel (pages 323, 330, 343 and 359); and

(iii)   dismissed each of the four grounds of appeal.

On analysis, this judicial united front could not conceal certain startling deficiencies or outright misstatements in their judgments.

Notwithstanding the assertion of Chief Justice Wallbridge that he had carefully read the evidence, he made the blatantly false statement that "all evidence [was] called which [Riel] desired" (page 323). As discussed in Chapter IX, Riel made an application to Magistrate Richardson to have the Deputy Minister of Indian Affairs, Lawrence Vankoughnet, the Deputy Minister of Indian Affairs A. M. Burgess, Gabriel Dumont, Napoléon Nault, and Michel Dumas called as witnesses. As well he applied to have certain documents and papers in the possession of the government produced at his trial. Not one of these persons (whom Riel had sworn were "essential and material witnesses to my defence") nor the documents and papers, all of whom and which Riel "desired", was made available at his trial. Wallbridge was being deceptive either when he said that he had carefully read the evidence, or alternatively when he stated that "all evidence [was] called which [Riel] desired."

Justice Taylor made several far-fetched comments. He categorized Riel's conduct, his claims to divine inspiration and "the prophetic character" as part of

> a cunningly devised scheme ... to secure personal immunity
> in the event of his ever being called to account for his
> actions. (page 343)

Notwithstanding Taylor's statement that he had made a critical examination of the evidence, there was nothing in the evidence to indicate Riel was attempting to secure personal immunity. To the contrary, personal immunity for Riel would have resulted if he had fled to the United States with Dumont. Personal immunity would also have resulted from a successful plea of insanity, but the transcript of the trial clearly shows that Riel vigorously rejected this plea and fought with his own lawyers against it. If he had convincingly feigned insanity he would have been acquitted and thereby immunized himself from execution. Taylor also stated at page 345 that Riel's thought of taking Major

Crozier and the police as hostages was to compel the government to accede to his demands. He then characterized these demands of Riel as money for himself. In doing so he prejudicially and completely ignored Riel's purpose, expressed openly to General Middleton and Major Crozier, that he wished to take hostages so that the government would consider the situation and so that better terms could be obtained.

Taylor wrote, at page 332, to the effect that, notwithstanding the inhabitants of the North-West Territories were not represented in the Dominion Parliament by members elected by them, it could not be "successfully disputed" that the "Dominion Parliament represents the people of the North West Territories." He conveniently ignored the fact that because they had no representation they sought out Riel to assist them.

Taylor is the same judge who made a preposterous statement in the Connor case. At page 243 of that case he wrote that

> at the time of its occupation by English subjects the country
> now known as the North West Territories would fall within
> the description of an uninhabited country

So much for the aboriginals who had lived there for centuries.

Each of the three appellate judges made a point of praising Riel's lawyers. At page 330 Taylor said that Riel was defended by "three gentlemen of high standing at the bar of the Province of Quebec" (making no mention of the Regina lawyer Thomas Cooke Johnstone). Taylor added that they were "learned, able and zealous" and fully competent to render to Riel "all the assistance in the power of counsel to afford him." For good measure, some thirteen pages later (page 343), Taylor referred to Riel's counsel having argued "with great force and ability." Wallbridge stated at page 323 that Riel was defended by "able counsel", and that no complaint

> is now made as to unfairness, haste, or want of opportunity
> of having all of the evidence heard which [Riel] desired to
> have heard.

At page 359, Killam wrote that Riel had been

> ably and zealously defended, and that nothing that could
> assist his case appears to have been left untouched.

Some judges effusively laud counsel for an accused as an implicit means of emphasizing that notwithstanding the ability, zeal and competence exhibited by his lawyers who had done all they could to assist the accused, there was no doubt of the accused's guilt. However, in praising Riel's lawyers, none of the appellate judges referred to the deep disagreements Riel had with his lawyers in relation to the plea of insanity (disagreements vividly reflected in the evidence which each stated he had carefully read). These judges also did not note that his lawyers had taken instructions on this defence not from Riel (who bitterly opposed it) but from some mysterious "others", nor were a number of matters (discussed in Chapter XXII) relating to the shortcoming of Riel's lawyers referred to.

On the appeal the defence lawyers (Lemieux and Fitzpatrick, led by John S. Ewart) presented four grounds to the appellate judges. Two of the grounds were of a procedural or technical nature and the other two were more substantive.

The first technical ground of appeal was that the information or charge was invalid because it was taken before a stipendiary magistrate only when it should also have been taken before a justice of the peace. The three judges were unanimous in disagreeing with this argument. Wallbridge stated that in the North-West Territories a magistrate, a justice of the peace and a six man jury constituted a "superior court", not an inferior one, and as such the Court need not show jurisdiction on the face of its proceedings.

The second technical ground of appeal, also a weak one, was that at the trial full notes of the evidence and other proceedings were not taken in writing as required by subsection 76(7) of the *North-West Territories Act of 1880*. The evidence and notes were taken by short-hand reporters (appointed by Magistrate Richardson) who afterwards extended their notes. The appellate judges were unanimous in agreeing that in these circumstances Magistrate Richardson had caused full notes of the evidence to be taken in writing. Justice Taylor stated that in considering the matter he was not prejudiced by the fact that he himself was a stenographer. With Louis Riel's neck on the line, the judges discussed the meaning of "writing" and "stenography" and concurred in the conclusion that short-hand writing extended into full notes by a stenographer complied with legal requirements.

A more substantive basis of appeal, but the success of which (given the circumstances) was highly implausible was that relating to the jurisdiction of the North-West Territories Court which tried Riel. This Court (as discussed in Chapter IV, section 2 and in Chapter V) consisted of a stipendiary magistrate, a justice of the peace and a jury of six men.

The defence argument was that this Court was not constitutionally valid
and had no authority to try a treason charge. As noted in Chapter VII,
before any witness were called at the trial Riel's lawyers presented a
lengthy argument against the jurisdiction of the North-West Territories
Court. Fitzpatrick had stated at the trial in Regina

> My contention is that the Act of 1880, in so far as it relates
> to the trial of capital cases is *ultra vires.*

"*Ultra vires*" is a legal expression meaning in excess of authority
conferred by law, and therefore invalid. Magistrate Richardson curtly
dismissed the lengthy defence presentation in less than a dozen words.

Riel's lawyers now attempted to have the appeal court in Manitoba
agree that the North-West Territories court had no jurisdiction in
relation to the charges against Riel.

Two of the three judges (Wallbridge and Taylor) who were sitting
on Riel's appeal were two of the three judges who gave judgment in the
Connor case discussed in Chapter XX. Accordingly it was scarcely to be
expected that they would find the North-West Territories Court was
incompetent to hear the charges against Riel. In the Connor appeal, the
judges were Justices Wallbridge, Taylor and Dubuc (Riel's former friend
who left town when Riel's appeal was being heard). In ruling that an
indictment by a grand jury was not required, the judges upheld the
power of a North-West Territories court (constituted exactly the same
as in Riel's case) to try a person for the capital offence of murder. It
was a forlorn hope to anticipate that in the Riel case these same two
judges (Wallbridge and Taylor) would hold that the North-West
Territories Court had no jurisdiction over the capital offence of treason.
This result was hardly to be expected when they had upheld the
jurisdiction of the same court (also presided over by Magistrate
Richardson) in respect of the capital offence of murder in the Connor
case. A ruling against the jurisdiction of the trial Court in Riel's case
would have been tantamount to finding that they had made an egregious
mistake in confirming Connor's conviction by that Court, an error fatal
to Connor's life. Wallbridge and Taylor, of course, both ruled that the
North-West Territories court was constitutionally valid and empowered
to try Riel for the capital crime of treason.

In the Riel appeal the third judge Killam (who had not participated
in the Connor case) did state that the question with respect to
Parliament's power to establish the North-West Territories Court to try

Riel for treason seemed to be open to Riel. However, he then ruled Parliament had the power to legislate regarding treason and had full power to establish the North-West Territories Court that tried Riel. Thus all three appellate judges shot down in flames this constitutional, jurisdictional attack.

With respect to the final ground of appeal, that Riel was insane, one or more of the appellate judges found that the defence evidence of Dr. Roy was "unsatisfactory"; and that Dr. Clark was not sufficiently positive and had assumed Riel was not a malingerer. The Court confirmed that the burden of proof of insanity was on the defence and that on appeal the evidence must be "overwhelming" in favour of insanity. Based on the evidence of Dr. Wallace, Dr. Jukes, General Middleton and Captain Young for the Crown, who all failed to find insanity in Riel's conduct or conversation, Wallbridge stated that evidence against insanity "very greatly preponderates". The other two judges agreed that Riel was not insane.

Killam held that Riel's actions were based on reason and not an insane delusion. Taylor proclaimed that "heresy is not insanity". Wallbridge stated Riel knew he was acting illegally and that he was responsible for his acts. All these appellate judges applied the McNaghten Rules (discussed at Chapter XII, section 1) in finding Riel was responsible for his acts. In so doing they effectively destroyed the evidence of Dr. Clark who had testified that Riel knew the nature and quality of his acts and that they were wrong. His qualification, "subject to his delusions", was not referred to by the appellate judges.

The appellate judges unanimously rejected the insanity plea. However in doing so some statements were made by them which were not supported by the trial testimony. Wallbridge stated at page 329 that after Riel's arrest he spoke to General Middleton "of his desire to negotiate for a money consideration." There was nothing whatsoever in General Middleton's testimony to this effect. Taylor stated at page 345 that Riel told Captain Young that his plan was to capture Major Crozier and his force of police and, holding them as hostages, "compel the government to accede to his demands." Taylor then said that those demands, as told to Father André, were "$100,000, or $35,000 in cash." Taylor also stated that Riel hoped to snare and hold General Middleton and a small force "to hold them as hostages for a like purpose." The statements by Wallbridge and Taylor are nowhere supported by the evidence of the witnesses they refer to, i.e. Middleton, André and Young. Their testimony belies the statements of these judges, and belies their assertions that they had carefully read the evidence. General Middleton at no time testified that Riel mentioned to him his desire to negotiate for a money consideration. Taylor's conclusion that Riel's desire to take hostages was for the purpose of having the government pay Riel $100,000 or $35,000 was an implausible stretch of the evidence. André, who Taylor quoted about the money, mentioned Riel's request was made in December 1884, months before talk of hostages.

Middleton and Young gave evidence about what Riel told them concerning his plan to take hostages. Neither one at any time made any mention of Riel stating that he wished to do so for money. Money was never mentioned in their conversations. According to Young, Riel stated that his purpose was to compel the government to consider the situation, or accede to his demands. Young also testified that Riel told him that his "mission was to accomplish practical results" and Riel explained this to Young as wanting "to save the people of the North-West from annihilation." See Young's testimony in Chapter X. Middleton said Riel told him Riel's idea was to take prisoners to obtain better terms from the government. Since hostilities did not start until late March 1885, more than three months after Father André said Riel wished to receive money from the Canadian Government, Taylor's linking that request to events a number of months later was a leap unsubstantiated by the evidence.

With respect to Riel's request for money, he had told the Metis delegation who came to him in Montana in June 1884 that he would accept their invitation to petition the government for their rights. He also told them that he had a personal interest – Canada owed him land under the Manitoba Metis land grant and "something else". This "something else" was most likely Riel's belief that he was entitled to compensation:

(i)   for his services in administering Manitoba for a number of months after the 1870 agreement was reached;

(ii)   for helping the Lieutenant-Governor of Manitoba during the 1871 Fenian scare;

(iii)   for permitting George Étienne Cartier to assume the Parliamentary seat that was Riel's for the asking; and

(iv)   for emotional and other hardships he endured as an exile
          when his promised amnesty was not forthcoming.

Riel never raised the question of an indemnity in Canada until
December 1884, the month in which he and the others had finalized and
sent the petition to the Canadian government requesting that it redress
the grievances of the peoples of the North-West – the Indians, the
whites and the half-breeds. The petition asked for representation in
Parliament (something more than Taylor's comment quoted above that
the "Dominion Parliament represents the people of the North-West
Territories"); responsible government; land grants and patents; better
treatment of the Indians; etc. etc.

Riel mentioned the amount of $35,000 in his remarks to the court
after his conviction. He stated that in 1873, while in the woods awaiting
his election to Parliament, Prime Minister John A. Macdonald had

> sent parties to me offering me $35,000 if I would leave the
> country for three years ... At the time I refused it.[239]

In his address to the jury Riel stated that his wife and children were
without means and that he had never had any pay for trying to better the
condition of the people of Saskatchewan. Some commentators have
suggested that Riel wanted the money to purchase a newspaper to
advocate for Metis causes. Dr. Clark's notes of his examination of Riel
state that Riel told Clark that if he had received the $35,000 he would
have established a newspaper to advocate the rights of his kindred.[240]

Father André testified that in relation to the $35,000 Riel said "if I
am satisfied the half-breeds will be." At least two of Riel's biographers,
Joseph Howard and Peter Charlebois,[241] collectively mentioned non-
insidious interpretations of these words, namely that Riel felt that a
payment would indicate a change in attitude toward the Metis and be
part of an over-all settlement of Metis claims. Riel himself in his address
to the jury said that he began to speak of himself after the petitions had
been sent to the Canadian Government, not before. He added "my
particular interests passed after the public interests."[242]

---

[239]   *The Queen v. Louis Riel*, p. 369.
[240]   C.K. Clarke, "A Critical Study of the Case of Louis Riel", *Louis Riel, Selected Readings*, Hartwell Bowsfield ed., p. 203.
[241]   Joseph Howard, *Strange Empire, Louis Riel and the Metis People*, p. 523;
Charlebois, p. 224.
[242]   *The Queen v. Louis Riel*, p. 313.

Although all appellate judges stated they had carefully read the evidence no mention was made by any of them of the biased remarks made by Magistrate Richardson in his charge to the jury (see Chapter XIV, section 1). This is perhaps understandable given the fact that Riel's own lawyers did not raise the matter. At page 323 Wallbridge wrote "No complaint is now made as to unfairness"; and at page 357 Killam wrote "No objection has been made to the charge of the magistrate to the jury." An allegation of bias against Magistrate Richardson played no part in the appeal arguments by Riel's lawyers. One may ask why not?

Based on the weak grounds of appeal that were used by Riel's lawyers, the existing law at the time and the composition of the appellate court, it is not surprising that Riel's conviction was upheld. There were cogent matters that could have been raised but which were not, due either to Riel's lawyers ignorance of them or because of inconsistency with their self-designated line of defence. Some of these matters which were not raised were:

(i)   Magistrate Richardson's bias discussed in Chapter IV, section 4, and his biased charge to the jury discussed in Chapter XIV, section 1;

(ii)   failure to obtain essential and material witnesses such as Gabriel Dumont and the two Deputy Ministers of the federal government, and failure to obtain production of documents requested by Riel (see Chapter IX) contrary to Chief Justice Wallbridge's false statement that all evidence was called which Riel desired;

(iii)   failure (due to understandable lack of knowledge) to challenge the propriety of Chief Justice Wallbridge presiding over the appellate court after Wallbridge had given secret advice to the Minister of Justice and received "private" correspondence from him (see Chapter XX);

(iv)   failure to have the three charges alleging Louis Riel was a British subject thrown out on the basis that there was no evidence whatsoever given by any witness, either for the Crown or for the defence, confirming where Riel was born or that he was a British subject;

(v)   failure to have the three charges alleging Louis Riel was a British subject thrown out on the basis that he was an

American citizen and, as such, not a British subject by virtue of either section 6 of the *British Naturalization Act, 1870* or section 9 of the *Canadian Naturalization Act, 1881*;

(vi)   non-observance of Riel's legal right (under section 76(7) of the *1880 North-West Territories Act*) "to make full answer and defence" since he did not obtain the witnesses that he swore were essential and material to his defence, nor the production of essential documents he asked for, nor a defence on the merits he had instructed his lawyers he wanted;

(vii)   failure to argue that none of Riel's acts were committed in the King's (or Queen's) "Realm" as specifically required by the *1351 Statute of Treasons* (see Chapter XVI); etc.; etc.

If justice requires that one receive that to which he is entitled, the foregoing indicates that in a number of respects Riel did not receive justice.

Chapter XIX

RIEL'S APPLICATION TO THE PRIVY COUNCIL IN ENGLAND

After the Manitoba Court of Queen's Bench confirmed Riel's conviction, his lawyers petitioned the Privy Council for leave to appeal against that order. The hearing before the Lords of the Judicial Committee of the Privy Council on October 21 and 22, 1885 was not in itself an appeal but an application to be permitted to appeal.[243] The petition was heard in the Privy Council courtroom at 1 Downing Street in London, England. Downing Street today is behind a high-gated iron-bar fence guarded by two English bobbies (police officers). On Mid-summer's Day, 1999, Ken W. May (the bearded, pipe-smoking Second Clerk of the Judicial Committee) provided the author with a copy of the Privy Council judgment. He also arranged for a personal tour for the author and his wife of the courtroom in which Riel's application was heard. The ceiling of the richly-panelled court-room, with William IV chairs, appeared to be some four times higher up than the ceiling in the tiny Regina courtroom in which Riel was tried.

In the application to the Privy Council, Riel's counsel (who included Fitzpatrick) contended that leave to appeal ought to be granted because a substantial question of law arose, namely whether the trial court (that of the North-West Territories) had jurisdiction to try Riel in the way it did. They also objected to the evidence having been taken in shorthand. No argument was presented on the insanity issue, a startling situation when that was the plea to which the evidence of every defence witness, and the cross-examination of many Crown witnesses, was directed. Presumably Riel's lawyers had come late to the realization that there was no hope whatsoever of proving that Riel was insane, a stupefying conclusion that calls into question their entire misguided trial strategy before the jury.

There was also no contradiction of Wallbridge's preposterous statement that all evidence had been called at the trial that Riel desired. Nor, understandably due to its surreptitious nature and unknown to them, did they argue the impropriety of the private correspondence between the Minister of Justice Campbell and Chief Justice Wallbridge

---

[243]   *Riel v.The Queen* [1885] 10 *Appeal Cases*, 675 (Privy Council).

(discussed hereafter), indicative of bias on the part of Wallbridge who presided over Riel's appeal.

After the presentation by Riel's counsel, the Privy Council thought it unnecessary to hear representations from Crown counsel. A brief judgment was delivered by Lord Halsbury (the Lord Chancellor) on behalf of himself and Lords Fitzgerald, Monkwell, Hobhouse and Esher, and Sir Barnes Peacock. In accordance with convention the judgment was unanimous. In the judgment the Privy Council stated that there was no denial before the North-West Territories Court, or the Court of Queen's Bench of Manitoba, that the acts attributed to Riel amounted to high treason. There was no such denial, of course, because Riel's lawyers had pursued, not justification but, an insanity plea at the trial, which they had now abandoned.

The judgment stated that there were only two objections in the petition which "seem to be capable of plausible or, indeed, intelligible expression". The first objection was that the *North-West Territories Act 1880* (under which the trial court and its jurisdiction was created) was invalid. The second objection was that there was non-compliance with the requirement to take full notes under the very same Act, due to the trial evidence being taken by a shorthand writer prior to being extended into ordinary writing.

The Privy Council upheld the jurisdiction of the Canadian Parliament to enact the statute under which Riel was tried and to try a case of high treason. It stated that to throw doubt upon the validity of the powers conveyed "would be of widely mischievous consequence". As for the shorthand argument, this was dismissed in one paragraph which included the comment "no complaint is made of inaccuracy or mistake". It is obvious from this remark that Fitzpatrick did not point out to the Privy Council the glaring mistake that was made in the typed transcript of the first charge. The blatant error in the transcript is discussed in Chapter IV, section 3. There were other errors that could have been mentioned to point out inaccuracies and mistakes and to argue that omissions in the transcript constituted a failure to take full notes of the evidence as required by law.

The Privy Council concluded its judgment by stating it would
> humbly advise Her Majesty [against whom Riel was charged with levying war] that leave should not be granted to prosecute this appeal.

Needless to say the cogent matters which could and should have been raised by Riel's lawyers in the appeal of his case to the Manitoba Court of Queen's Bench (as discussed in Chapter XVIII), were not raised by Riel's counsel before the Privy Council.

An interesting question is why an appeal was not first taken from the Court of Queen's Bench of Manitoba to the Supreme Court of Canada rather than to the Privy Council. In the letter of June 16, 1885 from Crown counsel Robinson and Osler (see Chapter IV section 2 and Chapter X), they advised the Minister of Justice Alexander Campbell that it would be "anomalous and inappropriate" to try Riel "for Treason in a Magistrate's Court". In this same letter they mentioned the possibility of an appeal from the Court of Queen's Bench in Manitoba to the Supreme Court of Canada and a petition to the Privy Council. This author has found no explanation as to why the Supreme Court of Canada was bypassed in this respect.

One may also note that before the Privy Council Riel's lawyers based their jurisdiction argument on the invalidity of the *North-West Territories Act of 1880*. However, as the Privy Council judgment stated, their other argument on use of shorthand note-taking "assumes the validity of the [same] Act". The fact that one argument was based on a premise of validity, which was totally inconsistent with the other argument based on invalidity, of the *North-West Territories Act of 1880*, did not prevent Riel's lawyers from making both arguments. This adds further strength to the contention that Riel's lawyers could have insisted on pleading justification or exculpation, as well as insanity, at the trial notwithstanding Crown counsel Osler's objection that "these two defences are inconsistent".[244] See Chapter XXII, section 1 (c).

The jurisdiction of the Judicial Committee of the Privy Council of England as the final court of appeal for Canada (one of the Canada's last colonial vestiges) was abolished in 1949.[245]

---

[244]   *The Queen v. Louis Riel*, p. 229.
[245]   *The Supreme Court Amendment Act, 1949 (Can.)*, Ch.37.

Chapter XX

IMPROPRIETIES OF CHIEF JUSTICE WALLBRIDGE AND JUSTICE MINISTER CAMPBELL

The profile of Chief Justice Wallbridge set forth in Chapter XVII, section 1 points out that he had been speaker of the Legislative Assembly of Canada in 1863 succeeding Alexander Campbell who held that position for several months in the same year. John A. Macdonald supported the continuation of Wallbridge as speaker when the Great Coalition of 1864 was formed with a Taché-Macdonald administration to pursue the federation of British North America.

Prime Minister Macdonald appointed Wallbridge Chief Justice of Manitoba in 1882 when Alexander Campbell was Minister of Justice. Needless to say at the time of the Riel disturbances in the North-West Territories in 1885 Wallbridge was very well known to Macdonald and Campbell. As indicated in the above-noted profile, Wallbridge was "a local informant" for Macdonald and, to some extent in relation to pending proceedings against Riel, Wallbridge acted as an informant for Campbell as discussed below. On April 13, 1885 Minister of Justice Campbell wrote Prime Minister John A. Macdonald stating:

> Wallbridge has been writing to me about the **difficulty** which might be found in Winnipeg, supposing that some of the men in arms against the Government in the North West Territories should be brought there for trial for high treason.[246] [Emphasis added.]

The letter stated that in Winnipeg there would be a jury of twelve and the accused could insist that a "moiety [i.e. one-half] should be half-breeds." The letter further stated that in the North-West Territories the trial would be before a stipendiary magistrate, justice of the peace and a jury of six, and the accused "is not entitled to a mixed jury".

It is interesting to note that an unsympathetic Riel biographer, Thomas Flanagan, made reference to this letter of April 13, 1885 and other correspondence from Justice Minister Campbell to Prime Minister

---

[246] "Macdonald Papers", NAC-MG26 A Volume 197, p. 82791 to 82794. The letter from Wallbridge to Campbell is apparently missing.

John A. Macdonald.[247]   Flanagan opined that the correspondence did
not reveal that Campbell was determined to prevent Riel from having
French jurors but that Campbell was uncertain of the law, seemed to
have no reliable advisers in Ottawa and had to get information from
Wallbridge. This benign interpretation is naïve. There were lawyers in
the Department of Justice to advise Campbell as to the law if he asked
them.   Prior to the trial on a treason-felony charge of William Henry
Jackson (who had acted as Riel's secretary for a time after Riel's arrival
in Saskatchewan), George W. Burbidge the Deputy Minister of Justice
(who was one of the prosecutors in the Riel trial) did precisely that.   In
considering how to proceed against Jackson, Burbidge "telegraphed his
assistants in Ottawa several times" to find out the relevant laws that
were in force before his decision to accept an insanity plea on behalf of
Jackson.[248]   If a Deputy Minister of Justice could obtain legal advice
from lawyers in the Department of Justice, so too could his superior, the
Minister of Justice. The suggestion that Justice Minister Campbell had
no reliable advisers in Ottawa and had to obtain information from Chief
Justice Wallbridge is cockamamie. The normal procedure would be for
the Minister of Justice to seek advice from his staff lawyers in the Justice
Department. This method would minimize the potential danger of a
conflict of interest arising from receiving advice from a potential judge
of a case. In the Riel case that danger became a reality with Wallbridge
adjudicating on the Appeal of the Riel case after giving advice (perhaps
unsolicited) to the Minister of Justice who wanted Riel convicted.

There is other evidence of contact between Campbell and
Wallbridge, which arguably amounted to behind-the-scenes conniving.
As for the above referred to letter of April 13, 1885, why did Wallbridge
write Campbell about "the difficulty" of a high treason trial in
Winnipeg? Was it a "difficulty" that in Winnipeg Riel would have been
tried by a jury of twelve? Was it a "difficulty" that Riel (according to
this letter) would have been entitled to "insist that a moiety [of the jury]
should be half-breeds?" Was it a "difficulty" that a jury so composed
would likely, at the very least, be a hung jury?

Campbell's comment to Macdonald in this April 13th letter about
the "difficulty" of a high treason trial in Winnipeg did not mention that

---

247   Flanagan, *Riel and the Rebellion*, p. 123 and 167, note 39.
248   Bingaman, p. 45.

Wallbridge raised any judicial difficulty. It mentioned only the rights Riel and the others would have in Winnipeg, rights they would not have in the North-West Territories. One may interpret this letter to the effect that Wallbridge had abandoned his judicial independence to side with his old political cohorts in wanting to see Riel convicted.

Campbell knew the significant effect which the decision in the Connor case would have on the Riel proceedings. In his zeal to ensure Riel would be convicted, Campbell did something injudicious and improper. The appeal of the Connor case from the North-West Territories Court, made up the same as the later Riel court, was then pending before the Court of Queen's Bench of Manitoba presided over by the same Chief Justice Wallbridge. Campbell told Macdonald (in his letter of June 17, 1885)[249] that he had arranged for Osler and Burbidge to leave for Winnipeg on Friday (i.e. June 19, 1885) to have the question of the necessity for a grand jury "well argued". He added that the hearing of the appeal "has been postponed, at my request, until their arrival." Campbell then continued:

> I have also, at the suggestion of Mr. Osler, **written privately** to Wallbridge urging that the Court should give as early a decision upon the point as they can.[Emphasis added.]

This Ministerial entreaty was shocking – it was government interference at the highest level in the judicial process in matters in which two lives were involved. Repeating a word attributed to Wallbridge in his April 13th letter, Campbell continued in his June 17th letter

> there is less **difficulty** and danger in trying Riel and his fellows under the N.W.T. Act of 1880 than in any other way. [Emphasis added.]

Campbell was obviously concerned about the necessity for a grand jury in the North-West Territories, a question to be determined by the Court of Queen's Bench of Manitoba headed by Chief Justice Wallbridge. He stated that if a grand jury was required in the North-West Territories

> we must do one or other of the two things [here ink blots cover some words but one word appears to be "legislate"] ... have the trial take place in Quebec or Ontario.

One could interpret this as meaning "stay away from Manitoba".

---

249   "Macdonald Papers", NAC, MG26 A, Vol. 197, p. 82862-67.

Campbell, Robinson and Osler were concerned that if Riel went directly to trial before Magistrate Richardson without an indictment first having been obtained from a grand jury, the entire Riel trial might subsequently be set aside. The purpose of a grand jury was to decide whether a bill of indictment presented to it (with accusations against an accused) contained sufficient grounds to send the accused to trial before a petit jury i.e. a trial jury. If it so decided it endorsed "true bill" on the back of the bill and upon presentment by the grand jury it became an indictment.   If "no true bill" was endorsed thereon, the bill of indictment was rejected. Campbell, understandably, wanted to avoid the grand jury procedure in Riel's case. There was a danger that a grand jury would find "no true bill" and there would be no indictment against Riel. The grand jury system prevails to this day in the United States as evidenced by the recent investigations involving President Bill Clinton.

In an editorial in the February 1998 issue of *Canadian Lawyer* magazine the executive editor Michael Fitz-James wrote "Wallbridge, it seems, was very keen on seeing Riel hanged ...". In commenting on letters between Chief Justice Wallbridge and Justice Minister Campbell, the editorial states that

> The letters reveal a shadowy partnership between the
> politicians and the bench – one which created conditions
> which made certain Riel would be executed.[250]

The exact date when Osler and Burbidge arrived in Winnipeg is not known, but it was sometime during the week of June 21, 1885. On Monday June 29, 1885 the Court of Queen's Bench of Manitoba gave an "early" decision in the Connor case ruling that in the North-West Territories it was not necessary that a trial for a capital offence of murder be based upon an indictment by a grand jury. Campbell need not, after all, consider having Riel's trial in Ontario or Quebec. Exactly one week later, on July 6, 1885, Riel was indicted directly before Magistrate Richardson in Regina in the North-West Territories without the intervention of a grand jury.

There are other examples that point to a conclusion that, contrary to Flanagan's view, Campbell was determined to prevent Riel from having French jurors. In his letter of May 21, 1885 to Prime Minister

---

[250]   Michael Fitz-James, "An Apology for Louis Riel Too?", *Canadian Lawyer* magazine p. 4.

Macdonald,[251] Campbell mentioned that General Middleton was sending Riel and the other prisoners to Winnipeg. Campbell then wrote:

> I have written very urgently to Caron [Minister of Militia and Defence] to send the prisoners to Regina ... if the prisoners go to Manitoba, we have no power to take them out of that province and send them back to the North West Territories ... **should they be tried in Manitoba there will be a miscarriage of justice**...I wish very much that you would tell [Caron] absolutely to send them to Regina. ... Do not, pray, send this letter to Caron, as I have written to him as strongly as I can, but send him a note from yourself. [Emphasis added].

In this letter Campbell referred to the possibility of Riel and the other prisoners being put on trial in Manitoba. He was concerned that this would result in "a miscarriage of justice". The question presents itself – why did Campbell think that a trial in Manitoba would amount to a "miscarriage of justice?" His reason must have been his knowledge of the "difficulty" and the reference to Riel's right to a "moiety" of half-breeds [actually French-speaking] on a Manitoba jury which were referred to by Chief Justice Wallbridge in the April 13, 1885 letter.

Shortly after, in May 1885 a telegram was sent from Caron to General Middleton, to take Riel to Regina rather than Winnipeg.[252] In his letter of April 16, 1885[253] to John A. Macdonald, Campbell repeated to the Prime Minister that the law in Manitoba allowed "half-breeds to claim a mixed jury – English and French." He added that he had told Macdonald in a prior letter (obviously the one of April 13, 1885) "what the law is in the N.W.T." In that letter he had said that in the North-West Territories "the prisoner is not entitled to a mixed jury." In his letter of June 17, 1885 to Macdonald referred to above Campbell said

> there is less difficulty and danger in trying Riel and his
> fellows under the N.W.T. Act of 1880 than in any other way.

This compares with his letter of April 13th in which Campbell told Macdonald that in the North-West Territories a prisoner was "not entitled to a mixed jury."

An interesting aspect of Campbell's letters to Macdonald is that the bibulous Macdonald forgot that he had received a couple of them. In Campbell's letter of April 16, 1885 he refers to Macdonald's letter of

---

251 "Macdonald Papers", NAC, MG26, Vol. 197, p. 82819-24.
252 Morton and Roy, p. 288; 308.
253 "Macdonald Papers", NAC, MG26 A, Vol. 197, p. 82799-801.

April 15th (only two days after Campbell's prior letter of April 13th) in which Macdonald said he was not aware of "any law in Manitoba to allow half-breeds to claim a mixed jury." Campbell reminded him that he had mentioned this law to Macdonald in his prior letter, as well as the law in the North-West Territories.   In his letter of May 20, 1885[254] Campbell told Macdonald that his previous letters to Macdonald, relating to trials for treason in the North-West, were dated April 13 and April 16. Campbell added

> In your note of yesterday you say that you did not get them,
> but I think you must have forgot them – in fact you
> acknowledged the receipt of the first one.

An outstanding situation occurred when Riel's lawyers appealed his Regina conviction to the Court of Queen's Bench of Manitoba in Winnipeg. Chief Justice Wallbridge

(i)   who had been described as a "local informant" for John A. Macdonald (at a time when Wallbridge was Chief Justice);

(ii)   who had advised the Minister of Justice of the "difficulty" of having a high treason trial in Winnipeg;

(iii)   who had received a "private" letter from the Minister of Justice urging the Manitoba court to expedite the Connor appeal, the result of which would have a material effect on Riel's trial proceedings; and

(iv)   who and whose judicial brethren gave an early decision on the Connor appeal;

did not disqualify himself, but presided over Riel's appeals, including the appeal in which he said that Riel could not be present on his own appeal because the Court had no power to bring Riel before it, although they had the right to adjudicate on his appeal. Wallbridge's participation in Riel's appeal was stupefying and improper. If the above facts had been publicly known at the time of the appeal there would have been a hue and cry and allegations of bias.   If these facts had been known to the Privy Council, on the application to it for leave to appeal, the Privy Council might well have permitted Riel to appeal.

The conduct of Minister of Justice Campbell and Chief Justice Wallbridge in relation to Riel left much to be desired. Some may say it was unjust and shameful. The ideal of justice consists of formal as well as substantive components. The formal element requires impartiality,

---

254   "Macdonald Papers", NAC, MG26 A, Vol. 197, p. 82817-18.

and a lack of bias. Procedural justice requires judicial neutrality, fairness, impartial administration of the laws and abstention from efforts to secretly influence a court in its proceedings.[255]

In the February 1998 edition of *Canadian Lawyer* magazine, the cover-page article on Louis Riel features photos of Riel and Chief Justice Wallbridge. On page 3 of this edition of *Canadian Lawyer*, the following statement appears:

> A senior judge interfered with the venue of Louis Riel's trial and prosecution witnesses suppressed evidence or told outright lies on the stand. The treason trial of Canada's most famous Metis revolutionary was perhaps the most unfair legal proceeding in Canadian history, at least until his appearance before the Manitoba Court of Appeal came along.

At page 13 of the article itself, the author (Winnipeg lawyer Ronald L. Olesky) in referring to Campbell's private letter to Wallbridge (i.e. the June 17, 1885 letter) wrote that this communication "materially affected the administration of justice in both the *Connor* and *Riel* cases."

Judicial and political skulduggery at the highest level, and lack of justice, may be inferred from

(i)   the correspondence involving Chief Justice Wallbridge, Minister of Justice Campbell and Prime Minister Macdonald, particularly the letters of April 13, May 21 and June 17, 1885;

(ii)   the telegram of May 1885 from Minister of Militia Caron to General Middleton to redirect Riel to Regina from Winnipeg;

(iii)   the early decision which the Court of Queen's Bench of Manitoba gave in the Connor case after the private letter from Campbell to Wallbridge; and

(iv)   the fact that Wallbridge subsequently presided over the appellate court hearing Riel's appeal.

---

[255]   Professor Martin P. Golding, *Philosophy of Law*, discusses formal and procedural justice in Chapter VI of his text.

Chapter XXI

MERCY DENIED

Political turmoil broke out in anticipation of Riel's execution. Intense, passionate feelings for and against the prospect of the Metis leader's death erupted. Protestant Orange Ontario was ecstatic; French Catholic Quebec was enraged. Quebec demanded that Riel be reprieved. Ontario howled for his neck. It wanted revenge for the death of Thomas Scott in 1870.

Protest meetings in Quebec united the Conservatives, Liberals, Ultramontanes, Radicals and others in that province in clamouring for clemency for Riel. Many Ontarians were equally clamourous in calling for Riel's blood, and threatening political reprisals against John A. Macdonald and the Conservative Party if Riel's life was spared. One example of the political Zeitgeist emanating from Orange Ontario is a seven-page letter of October 29, 1885 from J. C. Gilroy of Clinton, Ontario to Macdonald.[256] Gilroy told Macdonald that in his travels in Ontario he found the question of whether Macdonald would have Riel hanged the important topic wherever he went. In his rambling letter Gilroy wrote that almost every day he spoke to Conservatives and that

> without a dissentient voice they openly declare ... that if Riel
> is not hanged they have given there [sic] last Conservative
> vote and that as long as they live they will never support you
> again ... if Riel is not executed I will never vote for you again
> ... I can furnish you the names of five thousand
> straightforward honest fearless Conservatives who will do
> the same.

Many petitions and telegrams poured into Macdonald's office for and against the execution of Riel. The Prime Minister appointed a medical commission to inquire as to Riel's "present medical condition". He did so not because of the vitriol spewing forth from the likes of Gilroy in Ontario and the fervid Riel supporters in Quebec but because of the need to placate his own cabinet ministers and Conservative supporters in Quebec.

Appointment of two so-called "medical experts" as the commissioners was a smokescreen, a political subterfuge, by John A. Macdonald to conceal his unflinching determination to have Riel

---

[256] "Macdonald Papers", NAC, MG26, Vol. 108, p. 43541-47.

executed. He selected commissioners whom he felt confident would report to him the result which he wanted, a result which would enable him to convince the Cabinet, particularly his Quebec ministers, that Riel should be killed. Macdonald appointed Dr. Michael Lavell of Kingston and Dr. François-Xavier Valade of Ottawa, who had been born in Montreal, as the commission. He also asked Dr. Augustus Jukes to prepare a report on Riel's soundness of mind. Jukes had been a Crown rebuttal witness in the Riel trial and had testified that he had never seen unsoundness of mind in Riel.[257] With these three appointees Macdonald thought he had stacked the commission to meet his objective.

Lavell was no insanity expert. He was then Warden of Kingston Penitentiary and previously an obstetrician. Lavell, a Methodist, was from Macdonald's own riding and a steadfast Conservative. Alexander Campbell told Macdonald on October 23, 1885 that Lavell was "the man in whom I should have the greatest confidence."[258]

Valade was no insanity expert. He was selected because Macdonald knew that a French-Canadian Catholic was needed on the commission to give it an air of credibility in Quebec. Valade was a general practitioner. He was chosen because of his relative youth (a factor which might mean he would be influenced by the views of the older Lavell). He was also chosen because he did work for the federal government and was paid by it, and because Adolphe Caron, the Minister of Militia and Defence, knew and liked him.

Dr. Jukes was no insanity expert. However, evidence he gave at Riel's trial, if repeated, would support Macdonald's desired result.

Macdonald's instructions to Lavell and Valade were set forth in his letter to them of October 31, 1885.[259] Macdonald designed these instructions with a view to foreordaining the conclusion he wanted. He wrote in his letter of instructions that the jury had found Riel sane at the time of the rebellion and at the time of his trial, that the presiding judge had approved the verdict, and the Court of Queen's Bench of Manitoba had refused a new trial. He then added:

> Under these circumstances you are not called upon to go behind the verdict but your enquiry must be limited to his present mental condition.

---

[257] See "The Crown's Rebuttal Witnesses" in Chapter XII, section 2.
[258] "Macdonald Papers", NAC, MG26 Vol. 106 p. 42613.
[259] "Macdonald Papers", NAC, MG26, Vol. 106 p. 42627-29.

Macdonald continued that representations had been made to the government since Riel's conviction that his "mind has lately given way". He added that the enquiry was not as to whether Riel was subject to illusions or delusions but

> whether he is so bereft of reason as not to know right from
> wrong, and as not to be an accountable being.

On that same day Macdonald wrote a second letter marked "private and confidential" to Lavell. He told Lavell that "A. Campbell" (the Minister of Justice) had explained to Lavell the object of his mission to the North-West Territories. Macdonald advised Lavell that his trip and its object should be kept "a profound secret". He mentioned that he had fully impressed Valade with the idea that Lavell was an expert and counseled him "So don't be too modest about it."

Macdonald directed Lavell to talk to Dr. Jukes and others but added rather ungrammatically:

> as few as possible – so soon as you are convinced that Riel
> knows right from wrong and is an accountable being.

In his letter of October 31 Macdonald instructed Lavell that he could not go beyond the jury's verdict. His enquiry was limited to whether at the time of Lavell's report Riel was "sufficiently a reasonable and accountable being to know right from wrong." If he did "the law should be allowed to take effect."

Macdonald added a comment that made clear that there was no way he would grant Riel mercy regardless of the outcome of the commission's enquiry. He wrote

> If a man has raging dementia after conviction the law
> humanely postpones the Execution so that he may have an
> opportunity of preparing for death.

In other words if Riel suffered from "raging dementia" not simply "illusions" the only mercy, if such it was, would be not commutation of his death sentence but merely postponement of it. Public pressure in favour of Riel was, of course, in favour of commutation not simply postponement. Macdonald did not make his true feelings in this respect known generally to the public.

Macdonald ended his letter by telling Lavell that his "compensation will be liberal". He added a post-script that if Lavell wished to inform him of anything separately Governor Dewdney would manage it. Macdonald's directions were quite clear. Lavell and Valade must not reopen the jury's finding that Riel was sane. They were restricted in effect to determining whether Riel had become insane after his conviction. If he had not "the law should be allowed to take effect."

The test to be applied was the McNaghten Rules (discussed in Chapter XII, section 1).

Lavell and Valade made their separate ways to Regina under pseudonyms. On November 6, the day prior to their arrival, Dr. Jukes (the North West Mounted Police senior surgeon in Regina) had written a report to the Prime Minister that Macdonald had requested. In the report, transmitted through Lieutenant-Governor Dewdney, Jukes opined that except upon certain religious and private matters (re Divine mysteries) Riel was "perfectly sane and accountable for his actions." However three days later on November 9 Jukes had second thoughts. He again wrote to Macdonald recommending that Riel's papers be scrutinized to determine his sanity.[260] He also stated he would be happy if "justice and popular clamour could be satisfied without depriving this man of his life." In referring to "popular clamour" Jukes was recognizing the virulent hostility in Ontario and other quarters to sparing Riel's life.

Lavell and Valade interviewed Riel without revealing who they were. Lavell in his report to Macdonald said that he "contested" with Valade the latter's view as to Riel's insanity but felt Father André had influenced Valade. Each penned his own opinion and gave it to Governor Dewdney for transmittal to Macdonald. Lavell expressed the opinion that although Riel had foolish and peculiar views on religion and general government he was "an accountable being and capable of distinguishing right from wrong",[261] almost precisely the words used by Macdonald in his letter of instructions to Lavell and Valade.

Valade turned out to be not the obliging patsy that Macdonald had anticipated. Valade , in his report of November 8, 1885, found that Riel

> is not an accountable being, that he is unable to distinguish between wrong and right on political and religious subjects which I consider well marked typical forms of a kind of insanity under which he undoubtedly suffers, but on other

---

260   "Macdonald Papers", NAC, Vol. 106, p. 42652-70 @ 42668.
261   *Epitome of Parliamentary Documents in Connection with the North-West Rebellion —
1885*, p. 2 .

points I believe him to be quite sensible and can distinguish
right from wrong.[262]

On November 9, 1885 Lieutenant Governor Dewdney sent the
Lavell and Valade reports to Macdonald along with his own absurd view
that the reports basically came to the same conclusion.[263]

The Federal Cabinet (including the Quebec ministers) acted as
Macdonald wished, ignored the unanimous recommendation of the jury
for mercy and permitted Riel to be killed. This decision was made
before Lavell or Valade could prepare more comprehensive reports (as
they had intended to do) and without reviewing the letter of November
9 from Dr. Jukes in which he backtracked to a degree from his first
letter. Macdonald had said that Riel

shall hang, though every dog in Quebec bark in his favour.[264]

He had his way.

The designated government "spin doctor", to use a current
colloquial term, to justify Riel's execution and lack of mercy towards
him, was Alexander Campbell the Minister of Justice at the time of the
proceedings against Riel. Campbell issued a Memorandum dated
November 25, 1885, nine days after Riel's capital punishment.[265]
Campbell proceeded to present what he called "the true facts of the
case, and the considerations which have influenced the government" in
relation to the conviction and execution of Riel for high treason. He
said that he would not deal in the Memorandum with the assertion of
government opponents

that the rebellion was provoked, if not justified, by
[government] maladministration of the affairs of the North
West Territories, and inattention to the just claims of the
half-breeds.

He would not do so, he said, because the question had been made one
of party politics and "it is not thought becoming".

In the Memorandum Campbell made several blatantly false and
misleading statements. With respect to the doctors of the medical

---

262   "Macdonald Papers", NAC Vol. 106, p. 42650-51.
263   "Macdonald Papers", NAC Vol. 106, p. 42645-46.
264   Parkin, p. 244; also Stanley, *Louis Riel,* p. 367.
265   *Epitome of Parliamentary Documents in Connection with the North-West Rebellion –
1885,* p. 2 to 11.

commission he flagrantly and untruthfully described them as "medical experts". He added that nothing was elicited to cast

> any doubt upon his [Riel's] perfect knowledge of his crime,
> or justifying the idea that he had not such mental capacity as
> to know the nature and quality of the act for which he was
> convicted, as to know that the act was wrong and as to be
> able to control his own conduct.

The latter statement (based on the McNaghten Rules) was intended to convey the erroneous impression that Valade and Lavell had gone behind the verdict of the jury, and not restricted the enquiry (as specifically instructed by Macdonald) to Riel's "present mental condition".

On the first and second pages of the Epitome referred to in the previous footnote, the reports of Jukes, Valade and Lavell are reproduced. Valade's telegram of November 8, 1885 was expurgated in a cover-up. The bowdlerized report stated that Riel

> suffers under hallucinations on political and religious
> subjects, but on other points I believe him to be quite
> sensible and can distinguish right from wrong.

Valade's opinion had been gutted. His conclusion that Riel

> is not an accountable being [and] that he is unable to
> distinguish between right and wrong

on political and religious subjects was nowhere to be found.

Donald Creighton, a sympathetic biographer of John A. Macdonald, stated that the abridged version "was not an unfair exercise in condensation."[266] On the other hand Professor Thomas Flanagan called it a "relatively crude forgery". [267]

As for Jukes, passages from his letter of November 6 were expunged and as well the Epitome nowhere referred to his letter of November 9 with his second thoughts and recommendation to review Riel's writings.

In his Memorandum Campbell lapsed into hyperbole when he asserted

> with confidence that there never had been a rebellion more
> completely dependent upon one man.

---

[266]   Donald Creighton, *John A. Macdonald ... The Old Chieftain*, p. 447.
[267]   Flanagan, *Riel and the Rebellion*, p. 142.

This was in keeping with the resolve of Macdonald and Campbell to pin the entire blame for instigation of the uprising on Riel, thereby justifying their actions in allowing the execution to proceed.

Neither Campbell nor Macdonald, of course, called attention to the speech which Macdonald made in the House of Commons on July 6, 1885, shortly after Riel's surrender. In that speech Prime Minister Macdonald blamed the "white speculators in Prince Albert" for bringing Riel into the country. Macdonald continued:

> It is to the white men, it is to the men of our own race and
> lineage, and not to the half-breeds, nor yet to the Indians,
> that we are to attribute the war, the loss of life, the loss of
> money ... [268]

In discussing whether rebellion alone should be punishable with death, Campbell stated that opinions may differ and that a treason conviction must be dealt with by the Executive Government upon its own merits with a full consideration of all the attendant circumstances. The very first circumstance that Campbell then mentioned with respect to the rejection of commutation was that Riel's offence was "a second offence" referring to the events in Manitoba in 1870, the year in which Thomas Scott was executed. There were four problems with that "circumstance" supporting Riel's execution

(i)   Riel had never been convicted of an offence in Manitoba;

(ii)   at the time of the troubles in 1870, Manitoba was not part of Canada;

(iii)   in 1875 Parliament had granted Riel a full amnesty with respect to the troubles in Manitoba conditional on his being exiled for five years (an amnesty is the annulment of an offence generally of a political nature); and

(iv)   John A. Macdonald had effectively recognized Riel's provisional government in Manitoba (which had court-martialled Thomas Scott) as valid (see Chapter II section 2 herein).

These facts did not deter Macdonald and his cohorts. In his letter of August 12, 1884, many months before the North-West uprising, Macdonald wrote in a letter to Lord Lansdowne, the Governor General of Canada, that Riel:

---

[268]   *Debates, House of Commons*, 1885, p. 3117.

committed a cold-blooded murder in 1870 which will never

be forgotten by the whites, either in Manitoba or Ontario [269]

and obviously never forgotten by Macdonald himself.

One of the jurors, Edwin J. Brooks, subsequently stated that while the jury had tried Riel for treason he was hanged for the murder of Scott.[270]

Campbell was not candid in stating that "every opportunity for the fullest defence was afforded" Riel. On page four of the Memorandum, Campbell referred to affidavits by the defence relating to witnesses and said "the witnesses were procured". The discussion at Chapter IX, concerning the non-appearance of witnesses and documents Riel requested as being "essential and material" to his defence, and the failure of his counsel to follow his instructions, give the lie to Campbell's assertion that Riel had had the "fullest defence" and that "the witnesses were procured". Many of these "essential and material" witnesses were not procured, nor were any documents.

Campbell also used the technique that had been used by the Manitoba appellate judges by referring to the "zeal and ability" of Riel's counsel and that his defence could not "have been more carefully or more ably conducted." He then contrarily said that defence counsel's plea to the jurisdiction (discussed in Chapter VII) had been decided against their position in the Connor case (without specifically naming it) and consequently Magistrate Richardson could not give effect to this defence plea. The "zeal and ability" and able conduct of defence counsel (referred to by Campbell) was devoted to a significant extent in arguing a question of jurisdiction, which as Campbell said had already been decided against their position by the Connor case. This jurisdiction argument in Riel's trial was subsequently rejected by the trial magistrate, the appellate court and the Privy Council, with the Privy Council even stating that it was not necessary to hear Crown counsel's argument in favour of jurisdiction. The other main defence argued by Riel's counsel, namely insanity, was rejected by Riel, by the jury and by the appellate court, and jettisoned by Riel's lawyers before the Privy Council application.

Macdonald had no intention to grant mercy to Riel, as unanimously recommended by the jury. He was adamant in his own mind that the

---

[269]   Pope, p. 317-19 .
[270]   Howard, p. 542; and Charlebois, p. 227.

Metis leader should hang. Macdonald was governed in his rigidity on the question of mercy by two principle factors: one was his personal animosity towards Riel, the other was political considerations.

Riel had caused Macdonald great aggravations not only in the North-West Territories, but also in 1869 and the early 1870s in Manitoba. Macdonald had not forgotten this. Macdonald had once called Riel "a gone coon".[271] On another occasion, in 1884, he stated that Riel had "committed a cold-blooded murder".[272] These statements were made before any uprising in Saskatchewan.

As for the political aspect, Macdonald weighed the views of his anti-Riel Ontario and other supporters against those of his pro-Riel backers. Macdonald considered the former were more numerous and politically favourable to him. Macdonald thought the commotion in Quebec would wither away. He also did not want the imperial authorities to intervene in support of commutation. In a letter of August 28, 1885 to the Governor General, Lord Lansdowne, Macdonald said:

> this Northwest outbreak was **a mere domestic trouble**, and ought not to be elevated to the rank of a rebellion. The offences of Riel were riot and murder of such an extensive nature as to make them technically amount to treason. [Emphasis added.]

Lansdowne replied to Macdonald's letter of August 28 on August 31 and stated that

> we have all of us been doing what we could to elevate it to the rank of a rebellion, and with so much success that we cannot now reduce it to the rank of a common riot.

Macdonald wrote back to Lansdowne on September 3, 1885 that the rising was in a limited area, was confined to a small number of persons and "never endangered the safety of the State."[273] If Macdonald considered that the Saskatchewan Uprising did not endanger the safety of the State, the question is raised as to why Riel was charged with endeavouring to subvert and destroy the constitution and government of Canada. In any event the thought that a few hundred ill-equipped, ill-trained Metis could destroy the Canadian Government

---

[271] Pope, p. 127-28.
[272] Pope, p. 317-19.
[273] Pope, p. 354-58.

with, as Commanding Officer General Middleton said, "England at its back" is ludicrous. Contrast Macdonald's September 3 letter to Lansdowne with his telegram to Lieutenant Governor Dewdney on June 1, 1885, several days after Riel's capture:

> Consider Riel **a prisoner of war** – surrender him to no one without my orders. [274] [Emphasis added.]

What Macdonald classified as a "war" in June, before Riel's conviction, had become "a mere domestic trouble" in August after his conviction. The telegram is also corroborative of Macdonald's keen involvement in Riel's fate.

In his letter of August 28, 1885 Macdonald stated to Governor General Lansdowne that Riel's offences included murder. There was no evidence whatsoever (either then, later or now) that Riel had murdered anyone. Macdonald also did not think that the "Northwest outbreak ... [should] be elevated to the rank of a rebellion." He further wrote that Riel's acts "technically amount to treason".[275] Based on Macdonald's view in his letter to Lord Lansdowne, there was no rebellion in the North-West Territories and Riel was only **technically** guilty of treason. Based on Macdonald's view Riel was executed for a technical treason.

There is another factor which likely motivated Macdonald to repudiate the unanimous recommendation of the jury to grant mercy to Riel. He likely felt that granting mercy to Riel might give credence to the sentiment of many, including a number of members of Parliament, that the uprising in the North-West Territories was due to the Government's maladministration and neglect relating to the North-West.

Edward Blake, leader of the Liberal Party and of the Opposition, in a debate on a proposed motion deeply regretting that the death sentence was allowed to be carried into execution, read a letter from one of Riel's jurors. The letter read in part that the jury found Riel guilty and sane but continued:

> In recommending [Riel] to the mercy of the court ... we felt that had the government done their duty and redressed the grievances of the half-breeds of the Saskatchewan, as they had been requested time and again to do, there never would have been a second Riel rebellion, and consequently no

---

[274] "Macdonald Papers", NAC MG26A Vol. 107 p. 43099.
[275] Pope, p. 355.

prisoner to try and condemn. We could not but condemn in
the strongest terms possible the extraordinary dilatoriness of
Sir John Macdonald, Sir David McPherson and Lieutenant-
Governor Dewdney ... [276]

In that same debate Sir Hector Langevin, senior Quebec minister
in Macdonald's cabinet, exposed his ignorance of the statute under
which Riel was prosecuted and condemned to death. Langevin
mistakenly thought it was the *1868 Canadian Treason-Felony Act.*
Langevin stated that Magistrate Richardson's sentence of death imposed
upon Riel "was the sentence provided for by the Act of 1868, passed in
this House." He did not realize that Riel was convicted under the
English *1351 Statute of Treasons* nor did he realize that if Riel had been
tried under the 1868 treason-felony *Act of Canada* he could not have
been sentenced to death.

In his speech Langevin stated that the Jukes, Valade and Lavell
reports were laid before the "Privy Council" (i.e. the federal cabinet) and
"after weighing all the circumstances" they allowed the law to take its
course. He read the reports to the House of Commons, but in the case
of Valade and Jukes what he read were their expurgated reports, reports
which Edward Blake, leader of the opposition called "cooked-up
documents".[277] Consequently he was either part of the cover-up relating
to the purged reports, or he allowed Riel to be killed without knowing
"all the circumstances". On this point he was either deceitful or dumb.
Since he was a senior Minister most of the other members of
Macdonald's cabinet must have shared one or other of these mental
circumstances. Langevin also referred to the death of Thomas Scott
fifteen years earlier. In doing so he effectively contradicted Minister
Campbell (who had said that the North-West Uprising was a second
offence for Riel) by stating that Riel "was not brought before a tribunal
to be tried and punished or absolved, for the death of Thomas Scott."[278]

One of the jurors, Edwin J. Brooks, gave an interview to William
M. Davidson, one of Riel's biographers, many years after the trial.
Brooks stated that Riel was more interesting and effective than the
lawyers who addressed the jury and that he was not insane. He added
that the jurors would have liked the Minister of Interior on trial, for his

---

[276] *House of Commons Debates,* March 19, 1886, p. 255.
[277] *House of Commons Debates,* 1886, p. 122.
[278] *House of Commons Debates,* 1886, p. 74; 76; 77.

"gross neglect and callous indifference", which incited the Metis to revolt. Riel, as previously noted, had asked for the presence at his trial of A. M. Burgess (Deputy Minister of the Interior) but neither his lawyers, nor Crown counsel nor the Magistrate did anything to have Burgess appear.

With respect to the jury's unanimous recommendation of mercy, Brooks stated that

> ... it was not an empty formal expression and it revealed the serious desire of every one of the six [the jury].[279]

Brook's statement that the jury found Riel not insane and that the recommendation of mercy "was not an empty formal expression", contradicts the suggestion put forward by some commentators in certain circles. These commentators, including some in Parliament and the press, insinuated that the jury recommended mercy because they were unsure of Riel's soundness of mind.

In May 1999 the author of this text spoke to Mrs. Betty Hughes of Calgary, the granddaughter of Edwin J. Brooks, the same juror that had been interviewed by Davidson. She stated that her grandfather (who ran a general store in Indian Head, Saskatchewan in the 1880s and who died in 1939) was very sympathetic to Native people. Her grandfather told her that when it was stormy he would invite the Indians to come into his store to escape the inclement weather. Mrs. Hughes stated that "he was ahead of his time in his tolerant attitude towards aboriginal people."

In a newspaper report from Medicine Hat, Alberta in 1955, Rhoda Sivell (the daughter of Francis Cosgrove the foreman of the jury, who cried like a child when announcing the jury's mercy recommendation as discussed in Chapter XIV, section 2), said that her father had

> always maintained that Riel should have been set free and allowed to go somewhere in the Northwest Territories and have a place of his own with other Metis.[280]

After Prime Minister Macdonald and his cabinet had considered the reports of Jukes, Lavell and Valade (all of whom had been impressed by Riel's personality) and other matters (obviously including the execution of Thomas Scott in 1870) they made a decision to allow Riel's life to be taken. The Biblical beatitude of mercy preached by Jesus[281]

---

279   Davidson, p. 200.
280   *The Globe and Mail,* July 22, 1955, p. 8.
281   *The Bible, New Testament,* Matthew, Chapter 5, Verse 7.

and recommended by the jury was shunted aside. Portia's plea to Shylock that:

> The quality of mercy is not strain'd, it droppeth as the gentle
> rain from heaven upon the place beneath[282]

was not to be heeded in Macdonald's, Campbell's and the cabinet's hard-hearted firmness of mind. The only thing that "droppeth ... upon the place beneath" was not mercy from heaven but Riel's body from the gallows.

It was around this time that the Canadian Pacific Railway was completed, and that John A. Macdonald's Government imposed a head tax on Chinese immigrants. Low-paid coolies from China were no longer required to build the railway, and new ones were not welcome.

Prior to his execution, Riel was reconciled with the Roman Catholic Church. In keeping with the words of Jesus on the cross "Father, forgive them for they do know not what they are doing",[283] Riel prayed for and pardoned those he felt had wronged him, including Prime Minister John A. Macdonald. However, Macdonald, Campbell and the cabinet knew exactly what they were doing. Riel's sentiments were similar to the Christian attitude of Helene Jerome Goulet, the widow of Riel's friend Elzéar Goulet. Elzéar Goulet was murdered in 1870. His murder was in retaliation for the execution of Thomas Scott as Goulet had been a member of the court martial that had tried Scott and condemned him to death. His murderers included troops under Colonel Wolseley. Macdonald had sent these troops to Manitoba ostensibly to keep the peace, but some of them had a mindset that they had the right to mete out "justice" to Riel's associates. When Goulet's body was laid to rest on the bed in the Goulet home, his widow had their children pray not only for their father's soul but also for the men who had killed their father.[284]. Such was the strength of Christian belief of many of the Metis and the early settlers in Western Canada.

Riel was calm, cool and collected when he was summoned to take his last walk on the morning of November 16, 1885. On Father André's instructions he declined to make a final statement. With a noose around his neck and a mask over his head, Riel recited the Lord's Prayer on the scaffold; before he finished it the trap door was sprung, his body

---

[282]   William Shakespeare, *The Merchant of Venice*, Act IV, Scene 1.
[283]   *The Bible, New Testament*, Luke, Chapter 23, Verse 34.
[284]   Davidson, p. 95.

plummeted, his neck was yanked, his corpse swayed, his breath ceased and his life expired. Macdonald had had his way. Riel, the vanquished Metis hero, went to his death in a dignified and quiet manner. He was 41 years old. After a few days Riel's body was secretly taken to Manitoba where, after a requiem Mass, he was buried in the grounds of St. Boniface Cathedral. A monument marks his gravesite to this day.

The political fallout from Riel's execution affected not only political events of the day, but political events for many generations to come. Quebecers were infuriated and offended by the execution. Many realized that the only two persons of English extraction who were charged in the North-West Uprising, Jackson and the Saskatchewan Thomas Scott, had both been charged with the non-capital offence of treason-felony under the "made-in Canada" 1868 statute. This statute did not carry the death penalty, while Riel had been charged with the capital offence of high treason under the timeworn *1351 Statute of Treasons* of England, which did carry the death penalty. Quebec perceived Riel as a martyr to Ontario and the Orange Order, whose most prominent member was Prime Minister John A. Macdonald. The Orangemen at the time were as militant as today's marching Orangemen of Ulster. They were generally anti-Catholic and conservative. One historian called them "the bully boys of Toryism".[285] Flags in Quebec were flown at half-mast, John A. Macdonald was burned in effigy, meetings were held denouncing the government (and particularly the Quebec cabinet ministers).

On November 22, 1885 (six days after the execution) a mass protest rally of fifty thousand people was held in Montreal's Champ de Mars. The future Liberal Prime Minister Wilfrid Laurier proclaimed to the assemblage:

> Had I been born on the banks of the Saskatchewan I myself
> would have shouldered a musket.

John W. Dafoe who wrote a biography of Laurier stated the "Riel rebellion of 1885" opened up for Laurier "an extraordinary career". [286]

Riel's execution was the beginning of the end for the influence of the Conservative Party in Quebec. Honoré Mercier, the most-fiery orator at the Champ de Mars meeting, shortly after forged provincial

---

[285]   Edgar McInnis, *Canada, a Political and Social History*, p. 221. The comment was in relation to the 1837 rebellion in Upper Canada.

[286]   John W. Dafoe, *Laurier, A Study in Canadian Politics*, p. 21 and 17.

Liberals and Conservatives into a nationalistic French-Canadian party. Mercier led the party to victory in the ensuing provincial election and became Premier of Quebec fourteen months after Riel's death. Provincial nationalism exists in Quebec to this day and plays a significant role in the policies and workings of the Canadian federation. With the odd exception, the federal Conservative Party has had no effective presence in Quebec for over one hundred years and looks to remain moribund there for the foreseeable future.

Execution for a political offence in peacetime was not a habit of the times in civilized nations. There were ample precedents which Macdonald and the government could have followed in granting clemency to Riel. In England executions for treason in peacetime had not been exercised in years. In the United Kingdom William Smith O'Brien was sentenced to death for high treason in Ireland on October 9, 1848 (see section 4(a) of Chapter XVI). The death penalty was commuted to transportation to Australia and after a lapse of time he was permitted to return home where he died in 1864. In the United States Jefferson Davis, President of the Confederacy from 1861 to 1865, was charged with treason with respect to the civil war but he was not only not executed, he was not tried. In Canada the 1837 Rebellion witnessed Louis-Joseph Papineau, George Étienne Cartier and William Lyon Mackenzie (among others) charged with high treason for leading rebellions. They fled to the United States. None of the three leaders was executed. All three fugitives later returned to Canada. Notwithstanding that Governor General Lord Durham issued an ordinance naming seventeen persons (including Papineau and Cartier) against whom warrants for high treason had been issued and proclaiming that if they entered the Province without permission "they shall be deemed guilty of high treason and suffer death"[287] they were eventually pardoned. Cartier later became John A. Macdonald's Quebec leader. The foregoing matters strongly support the conclusion that Riel was denied justice and mercy.

---

[287]   *House of Commons Debates*, 1886, p. 258, quoted by Edward Blake.

Chapter XXII

SHORTCOMINGS OF RIEL'S LAWYERS

In each of their judgments, all three judges of the Court of Queen's Bench of Manitoba who heard Riel's appeal, and in his Memorandum of November 25, 1885 the Minister of Justice Alexander Campbell, made a point of praising the zeal and ability of Riel's lawyers in defending him. Commendation of this sort is sometimes an indirect way of providing further validation of one's own opinion by conveying the message that not even the vigour, competence and skill of his capable counsel could cast any doubt on the accused's guilt. In such a situation the commenders or flatterers will not, of course, refer to any defects or insufficiencies in defence counsel or their methods but only to the force and vitality with which they advanced their arguments. In this Chapter the author gives a number of instances where, in his opinion, Riel's lawyers patently fell short in their methods and manner of defending and representing Riel and in their duty to and treatment of him. In retrospect these failures cumulatively afforded Riel little opportunity of avoiding conviction and the death penalty.

There has been criticism of Riel's lawyers from others. During the trial Matthew Ryan, a past magistrate, said in a letter to Archbishop Taché that Riel's lawyers were not to his taste "and they did not compare at all favourably with those of the Crown."[288] In the *Dictionary of Canadian Biography* there is a statement

> In retrospect, the defence lawyers' handling of Riel's case left much to be desired. ... a serious invasion of the prisoner's rights by his counsel.[289]

Professor J. M. Bumsted, of the University of Manitoba, and author of a number of books on Manitoba history including *The Red River Rebellion*, has written:

> The trial of Riel was an entirely political one. Riel's defence lawyers left so much to be desired that the suspicion would

---

[288] Stanley, *Louis Riel*, p. 352 referring to a "letter from Ryan to Taché", St. Boniface Archdiocese Archives, July 29, 1885.

[289] Lewis H. Thomas, "Louis Riel", *Dictionary of Canadian Biography*, Vol. XI 1881-1890, p. 748.

forever persist that they were somehow in collusion with the Canadian government.[290]

The principal shortcomings of Riel's lawyers, collectively, in relation to his trial were:

(i)   their unauthorized, faulty and doomed strategy and failure to provide Riel with a "full answer and defence" that the law entitled him to;

(ii)   their unseemly mistreatment and defiance of Riel when his life was at stake;

(iii)   the conflict of interest of his lead counsel; and

(iv)   their errors and omissions in the trial, in the court of appeal and before the Privy Council.

1.   DOOMED STRATEGY

The doomed strategy of Riel's lawyers centred around attempting to prove that Riel was insane, the challenge to the jurisdiction of the trial court, and the lack of a justification plea.

(a) Insanity Plea

On June 16, 1885 Riel wrote a letter to Fitzpatrick and Lemieux (the two Quebec City lawyers) and to Romuald Fiset, in response to a prior letter from Fiset, his former schoolmate. Fiset was on the committee that obtained these lawyers and Greenshields to defend him. Riel had not previously known or talked to these lawyers and being a pauper he was in no position to personally pay them or any other lawyers. In his letter of June 16 Riel unequivocally told them that he wanted his trial to "turn on the merit of my actions" (see also section 2(a) of Chapter VIII). Some time after receiving Riel's letter (and knowing his specific instructions) Fitzpatrick, Lemieux and Greenshields headed for Regina to act for Riel. After interviewing Riel, and discussions with some mysterious "others", these defence lawyers (without Riel's knowledge) decided to embark on a plea which went contrary to his specific directive to them at the outset, a plea which Riel not only did not authorize but which he vehemently rejected. This was the plea of insanity. Chronologically this plea came after defence counsel's challenge to the jurisdiction of the North-West Territories court, discussed later in this Chapter, was dismissed.

---

[290] *Winnipeg Real Estate News*, January 16, 1998, p. 3.

Riel's very public, open-court uproar with his own counsel when he realized what his lawyers were doing to him and his defence, is discussed in Chapter XI "Open Court Dissension Between Riel and his Counsel". It and section 2 of this Chapter "Defence Counsel's Mistreatment and Defiance of Riel", depict their offensive behaviour toward Riel for his insolently interfering in their strategy. Fitzpatrick, in open court before the jurors and the audience, proclaimed to Magistrate Richardson that Riel "must not be allowed to interfere" in his own case in which Riel's life, not Fitzpatrick's or Lemieux's, was in jeopardy. They dealt with him as though he was their adversary, not their client.

The plea of insanity certainly did not originate with Riel nor did he want it or authorize his lawyers to use it. Fitzpatrick and Greenshields indicated that some clandestine 'others' concocted this plea. These "others" were faceless persons whose names were not disclosed by Fitzpatrick or Greenshields. Greenshields first referred obliquely to this plea in arguing for an adjournment when he told Magistrate Richardson that

> ... there is the evidence of the doctors from Quebec. This defence, we are instructed by **others than the prisoner** to make.[291] [Emphasis added.]

In his address to the jury, Fitzpatrick said:

> we were bound **in our instructions** as representing this man to say that he is **entirely insane** and irresponsible for his acts.[292] [Emphasis added.]

Who gave Fitzpatrick, Greenshields, Lemieux and Johnstone these "instructions"? Who "bound" them to say that Riel was "entirely insane"? In cross-examining Dr. Jukes, Fitzpatrick (Riel's own lawyer) told Jukes that Riel's delusions were "On religion, and on his mission with reference to the North-West Territories."[293] These comments affirm defence counsel's view that a basic element of Riel's (supposed) insanity was his heretical religious views. One may fairly speculate that the clergy and others who were vexed by Riel's acts and heresies may have attributed them to a mind which had strayed from reason, and may have been the mysterious others who were instructing Riel's counsel as to Riel's defence. One may, for example, query why on the day they

---

[291]   *The Queen v. Louis Riel*, p. 48.
[292]   *The Queen v. Louis Riel*, p. 295.
[293]   *The Queen v. Louis Riel*, p. 274.

first interviewed Riel, Fitzpatrick, Lemieux and Greenshields immed-iatcly after wrote to Archbishop Taché stating that Riel was not of sound mind.[294] What did Archbishop Taché have to do with the case?

Fitzpatrick in addressing Magistrate Richardson on the application for an adjournment made a statement indicating that some persons and not Riel were his real clients when he said

> we had to go to the parties ... who were really our clients in
> this case.[295]

It was clear that the defence lawyers were acting on the instructions of parties other than Riel.

In his address to the jury Fitzpatrick also made it clear beyond doubt that Riel had not contrived this trumped-up plea, so perfidious to Riel. Fitzpatrick told the jury

> we his counsel endeavouring, despite his orders, despite his
> desire, despite his instructions, to make him out a fool.[296]

In zealously presenting the insanity plea as a defence, Riel's lawyers made at least one monumental error in pursuing their unauthorized strategy. They called as their own witness a medical expert, Dr. Clark, whose testimony contributed significantly (i) to the Crown's case that Riel was legally sane; and (ii) to the destruction of their own insanity defence. Fitzpatrick and his defence associates either did not brief Dr. Clark prior to his giving evidence or, if they did so and knew how he would testify, they should not have called him as a witness. In either event they called a witness who drove a stake into the heart of the whole defence strategy once their challenge to the court's jurisdiction had been summarily dismissed. In testifying to the effect that Riel knew the nature of his acts and right from wrong Dr. Clark's testimony effectively amounted to a declaration of Riel's sanity under the McNaghten Rules (the law on insanity applied by Magistrate Richardson and the Appeal Court in Manitoba). Clark did not, of course, directly say that Riel was sane, but his testimony legally amounted to the same thing.

As for the testimony of Dr. Roy, he did not come across with authority. He also stated that he was "not an expert in insanity". The appeal court found his evidence "unsatisfactory".

---

[294] "Taché Papers", *St. Boniface Historical Society Archives.* Letter from Lemieux, Fitzpatrick & Greenshields to Taché, July 15, 1885.
[295] *The Queen v. Louis Riel,* p. 50.
[296] *The Queen v. Louis Riel,* p. 294.

The defence case on this insanity plea, in which the onus of proof was on the defence, was more than unsatisfactory, so much so that his lawyers totally abandoned it in their grounds of appeal to the Privy Council.

For a more detailed discussion of the unsatisfactory evidence of Dr. Clark and Dr. Roy see Chapter XII, section 1 "The Defence Witnesses".

Riel took great satisfaction in seeing this fundamental aspect of his lawyers' case demolished by the Crown. He was elated by its miserable failure. He told the jury when he addressed them that he felt blessed by God in hearing the evidence of General Middleton and Captain Young that he was not insane, and he thanked the "lawyers for the Crown who destroyed the testimony" of Dr. Roy.[297]

The defence approach in cross-examining the Crown witnesses and in direct examination of every one of its own witnesses was directed almost exclusively to endeavouring "to make him [i.e. Riel] out a fool" as Fitzpatrick put it. This parlous strategy (which shifted the burden of proof from the Crown to the defence) foundered because of:

(i)   an uncooperative, unappreciative and very sane Riel;

(ii)   the unconvincing evidence of insanity in the testimony of Drs. Roy and Clark; and

(iii)   the cumulative evidence of the Crown rebuttal witnesses.

However, this strategy willfully implemented by defence counsel left them in the foolish position of having no other points to argue to the jury. Defence counsel, without Riel's approval, had thrust the burden of proof of a plea he rejected onto him and they were unable to convince even one juror to accept it. It was a calculated gamble with Riel's life and it failed, to the detriment of other approaches which could have been pursued, other approaches which might have saved Riel's life.

(b) Challenge to Jurisdiction of the Court

The other principal argument which Riel's lawyers advanced to Magistrate Richardson, eight days before the jury was sworn in or witnesses were called, was that the North-West Territories court convened to try him was unconstitutional and had no jurisdiction. This argument and the opposing one by Crown counsel are discussed at

---

[297]   *The Queen v. Louis Riel*, p. 316.

length in Chapter VII. Fitzpatrick was zealous, able, eloquent and learned in his remarks on the constitutional aspect, and Greenshields was not far behind in pressing the statutory lack of jurisdiction of the court. Crown counsel Robinson and Osler presented strong arguments in favour of the constitutionality and jurisdiction of the court. The detailed arguments were impressive, well-versed and lengthy. However Magistrate Richardson graced the erudite and extensive addresses of counsel for each side by dismissing the challenge to the court's jurisdiction in a pedestrian ruling, without reasons, of less than a dozen words

Notwithstanding the zealous and eloquent pleas of Fitzpatrick and Greenshields, their efforts were misplaced and misguided. Their arguments were doomed to failure as a result of the decision by the Court of Queen's Bench of Manitoba in the Connor case rendered only one week before Riel was charged. Fitzpatrick, Lemieux and Greenshields would have been well aware of this case since Riel's fourth lawyer, Thomas Cooke Johnstone, was one of the counsel for Connor before the Court of Queen's Bench. The Connor case has been discussed more than once elsewhere in this treatise. See for example Chapter XX and the letter of June 17, 1885 from Minister of Justice Campbell to John A. Macdonald as to Campbell writing "privately" to Chief Justice Wallbridge urging him to give an early decision in the Connor case.

In the Connor case the Court of Queen's bench of Manitoba gave a decision soon after Campbell's private letter to Chief Justice Wallbridge. The ruling of the Queen's Bench judges in the Connor case had the effect of upholding the power of the North-West Territories court (constituted precisely as the North-West Territories Court which was to try Riel) to try a person for a capital offence. Crown counsel Robinson pointed this out to Magistrate Richardson in the Riel trial and defence counsel Johnstone referred to the case by that name.[298]

Richardson, of course, was well aware of the Connor case. He was the presiding Magistrate at the Connor trial. Richardson summarily dismissed Fitzpatrick's contention that the *North-West Territories Act of 1880* which established the court was *ultra vires* (beyond the powers of Parliament) as it related to the trial of capital cases. See Chapter XVIII,

---

[298]   *The Queen v. Louis Riel*, p. 30 and 41.

Section 2 for further comments, related to Riel's appeal, with respect to this fruitless attempt to tell the trial court to its face that it was unconstitutional and lacked jurisdiction to try Riel.

(c) Lack of Justification Plea

The defence lawyers were feckless in the manner in which they dealt with the reasons behind the North-West Uprising and in conveying to the jury the deep anger which the settlers of the North-West had towards the federal government. The government had grossly neglected dealing with their grievances and the numerous petitions they had sent to the government and government representatives. John A. Macdonald lied to the House of Commons on March 26, 1885 when he stated:

> Well, Sir, before Riel came in these settlers had never sent in
> a Bill of Rights to us, never sent any complaints to the
> Government.[299]

A more zealous, able and confrontational approach by Riel's lawyers may have resulted in a different final outcome of the trial as discussed hereafter. Riel's lawyers should have used their zeal and ability in a manner which would have fearlessly and vigorously:

(i)   drawn forth in their examination and cross-examination of witnesses the atmosphere of resentment towards the federal government with which both the whites and half-breeds were seething, and to show that this abscess of discontent led the settlers (in the absence of the right to their own elected representatives to speak for them) to seek out Riel to assist them in their dealings with the Government of Canada;

(ii)   demanded that A. M. Burgess the Deputy Minister of the Interior, and Lawrence Vankoughnet the Deputy Superintendent of Indian Affairs, (whom Riel swore in his affidavit were witnesses "essential and material" to his defence) be brought to Regina with the papers, petitions and documents requested by Riel;

(iii)   since they were hard-headed about pushing the insanity plea, also insisted upon the right to pursue a defence of exculpation and justification of Riel and his acts in conjunction with this plea (see the text after paragraph

---

[299]   *House of Commons Debates*, 1885, p. 764.

(viii) below for examples of matters which should have been raised);

(iv)   insisted upon the issuance of a commission authorizing Gabriel Dumont, Michel Dumas and Napoléon Nault, whom Riel swore were essential and material witnesses for his defence, to be examined in Montana (to which they had fled) and their evidence to be read at Riel's trial;

(v)   elicited from trial witnesses the blatant disregard, neglect and mismanagement of the federal government in relation to the petitions and grievances of those in the North-West;

(vi)   stood up to the blustery objections of Crown counsel Osler and not be cowed into accepting his assertion that insanity and justification could not both be argued because of inconsistency. Riel's lawyers used unrelated inconsistent arguments before the Privy Council as noted in Chapter XIX;

(vii)   held firm in the request for a one-month adjournment of the trial to give adequate time to obtain witnesses and documents and properly brief the witnesses; and

(viii) assailed the Crown and the Government for discrimination in charging Riel with high treason, a capital offence, under the ancient *1351 Statute of Treasons* of England while charging seventy-one other participants in the North-West Uprising with the non-capital offence of treason-felony under the *Canadian Statute of 1868*.

Some of the matters which should have been pursued, under paragraph (iii) above, include calling witnesses to testify:

(i)   to the matters Fitzpatrick mentioned to Magistrate Richardson (before a jury was empanelled) that (A) if Riel "had been listened to not one drop of blood would have been shed"; (B) "that the alleged rebellion was commenced and conducted under the direction of a council of fourteen persons" of which Riel was not a member; and (C) that Riel "did not participate in any engagement or permit or countenance any act of overt treason." Fitzpatrick also

referred to items (i), (B) and (C) in his affidavit filed in
support of an application for a trial adjournment;[300]

(ii)   that Riel murdered no one and, in fact, at Duck Lake saved
the lives of many retreating members of the NWMP; and

(iii)   that the Metis acted in self-defence at Duck Lake after the
unilateral killing by NWMP Major Crozier's assistant of
Isadore Dumont and the Cree Assywin and the
commencement of gunfire by Major Crozier's troops.

In cross-examining Major Crozier of the NWMP, Fitzpatrick
utterly failed to elicit information that the commencement of the North-
West Uprising was triggered by the actions of the NWMP. Fitzpatrick
never extracted evidence that the initial bloodshed was caused by Special
Constable Gentleman Joe McKay of the NWMP. This would have
permitted him to subpoena McKay to testify as to what actually
happened at the parley and immediately after, rather than accepting
Crozier's evasive answers. See Chapter X re Gentleman Joe McKay.

Arguments such as the foregoing would have gone a long way
towards giving Riel his right under the law "to make full answer and
defence", a right which he had asked for and which he did not receive.

Chief Justice R. G. Brian Dickson (who was born and raised in
Saskatchewan) was on the Supreme Court of Canada for seventeen years
between 1973 and 1990. He is considered by some to have been the
finest Chief Justice that ever graced that Court.[301]   He wrote many
landmark judgments. In a case involving an abortionist, Chief Justice
Dickson wrote that in a criminal trial before judge and jury, the judge's
role is to state the law and the jury's role is to apply that law to the facts
of the case. He wrote that counsel is wrong to tell a jury that if they did
not like the law they need not enforce it, but added some interesting
observations on juries generally. Chief Justice Dickson wrote:

> The jury is one of the great protectors of the citizen because
> it is composed of 12 persons who collectively express the
> common sense of the community ... It is no doubt true that
> juries have a *de facto* power to disregard the law as stated to
> the jury by the judge ... It may even be true that in some

---

[300]   *The Queen v. Louis Riel*, p. 52.

[301]   Prior to Dickson's appointment as a judge, the author of this text (when
an articled law student) worked for Dickson in the Winnipeg law firm founded
by J. A. M. Aikins (see Chapter VIII, subsection (a) of section 3).

limited circumstances the private decision of a jury to refuse
to apply the law will constitute, in the words of a Law
Reform Commission of Canada working paper, "the citizen's
ultimate protection against oppressive laws and the
oppressive enforcement of the law."[302]

Chief Justice Dickson cited a passage from a United States Court
of Appeals judgment of which one sentence read:

An equilibrium has evolved – **an often marvelous balance
– with the jury acting as a "safety valve" for exceptional
cases** without being a wildcat or runaway institution.[303]
[Emphasis added.]

If Riel's lawyers had tenaciously pursued a defence embracing at
least some of the matters set forth above, possibilities favourable to Riel
would have arisen that could not arise when the only defence plea to the
jury was insanity and each juror was satisfied that Riel was sane.

Possibilities, which might have emerged (in terms referred to by
Chief Justice Dickson), were one or more of the jurors deciding:

(i)   to act as a "safety valve" for an "exceptional case"; or

(ii)   to "collectively express the common sense of the
         community" bearing in mind their awareness of
         government neglect and maladministration relating to
         petitions and grievances in the North-West;[304] or

(iii)   to exercise "a *de facto* power to disregard the law" in the
         face of any charge (biased or otherwise) which might be
         made to the jury legally unfavourable to Riel, particularly if
         they felt it was an "oppressive enforcement of the law" by
         the government's use of a five hundred and thirty-four
         year old English treason statute resulting in the death
         penalty, rather than use of a seventeen year old Canadian
         treason-felony statute without the death penalty.

Two jurors, Francis Cosgrove (foreman of the jury) and Edwin J.
Brooks, as well as the anonymous juror (referred to in Chapter XXI
from whose letter Liberal Leader Blake read to the House of Commons

---

[302]   *Morgentaler et al versus the Queen*, [1988], 44 *Dominion Law Reports*, 4th edition p. 385 @ 417; 418 and 419.
[303]   *U.S. v. Dougherty*, 473 F. 2d 1113 (1972) per Leventhal, J. at p. 1134.
[304]   See, for example, the letter quoted by Liberal Leader Edward Blake and
the comments of juror Edwin J. Brooks in Chapter XXI.

— who may or may not have been Cosgrove or Brooks), were sympathetic to Riel. Further, since each juror recommended mercy, one may surmise that all jurors were sympathetic to Riel. Consequently it does not stretch credibility to the bounds of disbelief to hypothesize that one or more of the jurors may have voted for Riel's acquittal if the defence plea to the jury had not been based solely on insanity. This is so particularly since Brooks and the juror who wrote the letter read by Liberal Leader Blake condemned the gross neglect, indifference and dilatoriness of the federal government representatives.

However since an alternative plea to insanity was never presented by Riel's lawyers as evidence to the jury, none of the jurors was given the option (in the words used by Chief Justice Dickson):

(i)   to act as a safety valve in an exceptional case, or

(ii)   to collectively express the common sense of the community against an oppressive enforcement of the law, or

(iii)   to exercise a *de facto* power to disregard the law,

if one or more jurors thought it just to do so.

If any one of the possibilities referred to above had come to pass there would not have been a unanimous vote in favour of Riel's guilt. **The outcome, at the very least, would have been that the jury was hung, not Riel.** Perhaps the jury might even have acquitted him as a means of sending a censorious message to the federal government or on the basis that, legalities aside, they felt it was right and just to do so. While these are speculative assumptions, their occurrence would not have been inconceivable if Riel had been given the opportunity to "make full answer and defence" as he was entitled to under the law.

Riel's counsel basically restricted themselves to attacking the court's jurisdiction and to endeavouring to prove that Riel was insane, instead of providing Riel with a defence on the merits and with a full defence. Initially, it appeared as though Riel's lawyers would follow a strategy adopting some of the approaches suggested above. In the application for adjournment of Riel's trial (discussed in Chapter IX), before a jury was empanelled, Greenshields seemed to indicate defence counsel wanted witnesses and documents produced tending to exculpate

Riel and attack the government for its neglect of Metis petitions and grievances.[305] Fitzpatrick referred to the desire that

> every possible means should be afforded to [Riel] to make a full and complete defence, that after he had made his defence and **had a fair chance of exculpating himself** or explaining his position then…the law should take its course.[306] [Emphasis added.]

In addressing the jury Riel himself made clear that the North-West Uprising was not initiated by the Metis.

> The agitation in the North-West Territories would have been constitutional, and would certainly be constitutional today if, in my opinion, we had not been attacked.[307]

However Riel's lawyers advanced no evidence in this respect. Fitzpatrick's cross-examination of Superintendent Crozier of the NWMP (whose assistant, Gentleman Joe McKay, started the shooting at Duck Lake) was innocuous and mild-mannered.

Both Greenshields and Fitzpatrick stated that they were instructed that Dumont and Dumas (who were in Montana) could give evidence beneficial to Riel, such as confirming many of the matters listed after paragraph (viii) above.

Greenshields told Magistrate Richardson:

> We are charged with this defence, and if the defence is not properly made, and a verdict of guilty should follow and then execution, as counsel for the defence we cannot help but feel the responsibility that rests upon us in making an application of this kind…[308]

The application, as noted previously, was supported by affidavits calling for an adjournment to provide time to call Dumont, Dumas and Nault in Montana, and Deputy Ministers Burgess and Vankoughnet in Ottawa (accompanied by relevant documents) as witnesses. However when the trial commenced on July 28, 1885 none of these witnesses or documents was present, nor would they be later, notwithstanding that Riel swore in his affidavit:

---

[305]   *The Queen v. Louis Riel,* p. 47.
[306]   *The Queen v. Louis Riel,* p. 50.
[307]   *The Queen v. Louis Riel,* p. 317.
[308]   *The Queen v. Louis Riel,* p. 58.

> That without the said witnesses being heard in court, I
> cannot make a proper defence to the present charges, **and
> will be deprived of justice.**[309] [Emphasis added.]

Fitzpatrick, Lemieux and Greenshields made no application at this,
or any other time, for a commission to have the evidence of Dumont,
Dumas and Nault taken in Montana.

The trial transcript on the first day of the trial (July 28, 1885) makes
no reference to Riel's lawyers objecting to the fact that not one of these
witnesses or documents was present.   In their minds there was
apparently no need to do so.   Riel had wanted these witnesses called
with a view to his exculpation and justification of his and the Metis
activities including their constitutional agitation.   Riel's lawyers knew
these witnesses and documents were irrelevant and unnecessary to the
insanity plea they had been instructed to make by mysterious "others".
These secret "others" undoubtedly were (as Fitzpatrick said) "the parties
... who were really our clients in this case."[310]   As well, to provide Riel
with the defence he wanted would have required an attack on the federal
government for its gross neglect, indifference and dilatoriness referred
to by two of the jurors.   As discussed under "Conflict of Interest"
hereafter, Fitzpatrick would have been in a most awkward and
undesirable position if a defence strategy included upbraiding the federal
government.

Instead of energetically eliciting evidence which would have tended
to vindication or justification, Riel's lawyers made a point of proclaiming
on more than one occasion that they were not justifying the rebellion.
In Lemieux's examination of Father André he did have André refer to
half-breed agitation, unanswered petitions to the government, and
dissatisfaction.   However when Osler objected that they could not lead
evidence of justification because it was inconsistent with insanity and
because it would amount to trying the politics of the government,
Lemieux stated:

> I do not want to justify the rebellion...I want to get further
> facts, not in justification of the rebellion, but to explain the
> circumstances under which the accused came into the
> country.[311]

---

309   *The Queen v. Louis Riel,* p. 61.
310   *The Queen v. Louis Riel,* p. 50.
311   *The Queen v. Louis Riel,* p. 229-30.

Lemieux did not contest Osler's opinion that insanity and justification could not both be argued. There was no law against both an insanity plea and an attempt to justify Riel's acts. In fact, inconsistent arguments (on different points) were later argued by Riel's lawyers before the Privy Council. (See Chapter XIX). If defence counsel insisted on pressing the insanity plea they could have also argued that if the jury found Riel sane they could still have determined that his actions were justified. For example, they could have argued self-defence based on the first shooting having been commenced by the assistant to Superintendent Crozier of the NWMP. They could have argued that self-defence was being presented as an alternative plea. They did not so argue, and Osler won the day on this essential point.

Fitzpatrick in addressing the jury stated that no one "can justify the rebellion".[312]

It is apparent that during the one-week adjournment Fitzpatrick, Lemieux and Greenshields abandoned any idea of attempting to justify Riel's participation in events. This was notwithstanding statements by Greenshields and Fitzpatrick in the application for adjournment of the trial and in Fitzpatrick's affidavit that witnesses sought would establish Riel's "pure and good motives", and that he did not "commit or countenance any overt act of treason."

There is no explanation for this about-face which, when the jurors determined that Riel was sane, proved so prejudicial to the possibilities of a hung jury or acquittal mentioned earlier in this Chapter.

2. DEFENCE COUNSEL'S MISTREAT-MENT AND DEFIANCE OF RIEL

The manner in which Riel's lawyers behaved towards him was overbearing and deplorable. Prior to the trial they received a letter from him dated June 16, 1885 in which he told them specifically that he wanted a trial "on the merit of my actions". Initially in the application for adjournment of the trial they gave some indication that they might be complying with Riel's mandate. However, without Riel's approval and in direct defiance of his authorization, they dispensed with any defence based on the merit of Riel's actions. Instead, acting on instructions from some anonymous "others" and "parties ... who were

---

[312] *The Queen v. Louis Riel,* p. 287.

really our clients in this case", they usurped Riel's legal right to a "full defence" and limited it to a futile attack on the jurisdiction of the court and the fruitless attempt to prove insanity. Since Riel had told them what defence he wanted and since it was Riel's life at risk and not theirs, these lawyers should not have agreed to act if they were not willing to accept Riel's instructions. They should not have acted on the instructions of "others", who were incognito and whose lives were not on the line, in endeavouring as Fitzpatrick told the jury

> to make [Riel] out a fool ... that he is entirely insane and irresponsible in his acts.

Their undivided loyalties should have been to Riel only, not to "parties ... who were really our clients in this case." Disobeying Riel's wishes and acting on the clandestine instructions of some secret "others" (their "real" not "Riel" client) was discreditable enough. However, the behaviour of Fitzpatrick and Lemieux towards Riel during the cross-examination of Charles Nolin was downright shabby and non-professional. Riel attempted to intervene because his lawyers, to use his words were losing "more than three-quarters of the good opportunities" because

> They have to put questions to men with whom they are not acquainted, on circumstances which they don't know ... they cannot follow the thread of all the questions that could be put to the witnesses ... The witnesses are passing and the opportunities.

> Fitzpatrick, after Riel's first interruption, stated in open court that:
> the prisoner in the box [not "Mr. Riel" or "our client"] ... should be given to understand that he should give any instructions to us, and **he must be not be allowed to interfere.** [Emphasis added.]

He said this notwithstanding their refusal to accept his instructions. They were treating Riel like a thrall. Riel said to Magistrate Richardson "my counsellors ... are trying to show that I am insane." Fitzpatrick said:

> this man is actually obstructing the proper management of this case ... and he must be given to understand immediately that he won't be allowed to interfere in it ...

If, as Fitzpatrick claimed, Riel was insane, why did Fitzpatrick state that Riel "must be given to understand"? Could an insane man "understand" that he must shut up when his life was at stake? Fitzpatrick added

> so long as the prisoner is represented by counsel it is his duty
> to give such instructions to his counsel as to enable him to
> do duty to his case.

The problem, of course, from Riel's point of view was that his counsel had disobeyed previous instructions he gave them.

Fitzpatrick stated that defence counsel were entirely free to throw up their brief "if the prisoner is allowed to interfere."

Riel told Richardson:

> I want my cause to be, your Honor, to be defended to the
> best which circumstances allow.

After a brief recess Lemieux told the court that if Riel insisted upon putting questions to the witnesses

> we will not continue to act in this case as counsel. We think,
> however it is too late for him to disavow or refuse.

In other words, Riel's own lawyers were stating that they could unilaterally desert him but he could not terminate their services. The effect of this astonishing assertion (made in a public courtroom in the presence of the jury, the press and the audience) was that his lawyers (according to themselves) had the right to endeavour to prove Riel a "fool" and Riel had no right to interfere. His lawyers brazenly advanced this position notwithstanding Riel's objections and notwithstanding that his life, not theirs, was in jeopardy. This was an injustice to Riel.

Both Magistrate Richardson and Crown counsel stated in open court that they had no objection to Riel putting questions to the witness. However Riel's lawyers were adamantly opposed as it would mean Riel was "allowed to interfere" in their attempts to prove he was a madman. Riel said very reasonably that while the case concerned his lawyers

> in the first place it concerns me ... I have to defend myself
> against the accusation of high treason, or I have to consent
> to the animal life of an asylum.[313]

It remains a mystery as to why his lawyers so adamantly refused to have Riel pose questions to the witnesses. One may speculate that they feared that by doing so Riel would display his rationality and intelligence to such an extent it would, in the eyes of the jury, deal a deathblow to

---

[313] *The Queen v. Louis Riel,* p. 205-15 is the source for the exchanges and quotations herein.

the insanity plea they were so zealously pursuing. This course of action also would displease the unrevealed "others" (the real "clients") from whom they were receiving instructions. They succeeded in preventing the death blow to the insanity plea, but not to Riel.

In the end result the plea of insanity so obstinately pressed by his lawyers at the behest of some covert "others" was an utter and abject failure, so much so that Riel's lawyers totally abandoned this insanity plea prior to making application to the Privy Council for leave to appeal. With the wisdom of hindsight it is apparent that Riel would have suffered no worse fate, and may well have fared better before the jury, if he had summarily dismissed his recalcitrant lawyers.

For a further discussion refer to Chapter XI "Open Court Dissension Between Riel and His Counsel".

3.   FITZPATRICK'S CONFLICT OF INTEREST

Fitzpatrick and Lemieux were the two lead counsel in presenting the defence for Riel, but Fitzpatrick played a more prominent role. Fitzpatrick, not Lemieux,

    (i)   argued (unsuccessfully) that the North-West Territories court was unconstitutional;

    (ii)   examined the majority of witnesses;

    (iii)   cross-examined eleven Crown witnesses (to two by Lemieux);

    (iv)   addressed the jury on behalf of the defence; and

    (v)   appeared as counsel in London, England to make application to the Privy Council for leave to appeal Riel's conviction.

Fitzpatrick was front and center throughout and the driving force in endeavouring

> despite his orders, despite his desire, despite his instructions
> to make him [Riel] out a fool [314]

as Fitzpatrick phrased it in his address to the jury. Of all nine lawyers involved in the trial only Fitzpatrick examined or cross-examined every doctor who was a witness – Roy, Clark, Wallace and Jukes.

Fitzpatrick's conflict of interest arose by virtue of the fact that in 1885 he was the brother-in-law of Adolphe Caron the Quebec Minister

---

[314]   *The Queen v. Louis Riel*, p. 294.

of Militia and Defence in John A. Macdonald's cabinet. It was further compounded by the fact that he was also a law partner of Caron's in the Quebec City law firm of Andrews, Caron, Andrews and Fitzpatrick.[315] To boot, Fitzpatrick was also a partner of Thomas Chase Casgrain, one of the Crown prosecutors in the Riel case, whose appointment his partner (Minister Caron) had pushed for.[316] Consequently, Fitzpatrick for Riel, Casgrain for the Crown, and Caron for the government prosecuting Riel, were all law partners one with the other.

This state of facts involved two aspects:

(i)   members of the same law firm were concurrently representing adverse interests – i.e. two of them wanted Riel convicted and executed, the other wanted him in an insane asylum; and

(ii)   one partner in that same law firm was a Minister in the federal government administration and intimately involved in having Riel and the Metis subdued.

People of the North-West Territories had great resentment against the federal government for its neglect and maladministration with respect to their complaints and petitions and had asked Riel to assist them in this respect. If Fitzpatrick had pursued a case of justification (as discussed in subsection 1(c) of this Chapter), it would have been necessary to assail the very government of which Militia Minister Caron (his law partner and his wife's brother) was an integral part. Caron was in the very forefront of putting down Riel and his adherents.

This raised the question – should Fitzpatrick have put himself in a position where there could be conflict between

(i)   providing Riel with the defence he wanted requiring that the government be excoriated for its neglect; and

(ii)   the objectives of his two partners (one of whom was also his brother-in-law) which were to bring about Riel's conviction and sentence to death?

The answer clearly is that Fitzpatrick should not have exposed himself to this conflict of interest; he should not have represented Riel under these circumstances. In fact the prospect of Riel's lawyers reproaching the government did not arise because they did not follow

---

[315]   *The Globe*, July 11, 1885.
[316]   Morton, intro, *The Queen v. Louis Riel*, p. xii and xiii.

Riel's desire for a trial on the merit of his actions. Instead they followed their own doomed strategy of attacking the Court's jurisdiction and pleading Riel's insanity, neither of which involved an attack on the government's neglect and indifference to the people of the North-West.

One may fairly speculate on the turn the defence's strategy would have taken, and in turn the outcome of the trial, if Fitzpatrick (who pursued an insanity plea on the instructions, not of Riel but of unknown "others") had not been lead counsel or counsel at all. If Riel had had a new lead counsel who had followed his instructions for a trial on the merit of his actions, the result might have been quite different. The end result certainly could not have been any worse.

The author of this text has been unable to locate any information indicating that Riel was aware of the professional relationship (incestuous in the circumstances) among Fitzpatrick, Caron and Casgrain.

4.   ERRORS AND OMISSIONS

There were a number of errors and omissions in Riel's trial, in his appeal to the Court of Queen's Bench of Manitoba, and in his application to the Privy Council for leave to appeal.

Errors and omissions of Riel's counsel, some of which are discussed in detail elsewhere in this text, included the following.

(a)   The Trial

With respect to the trial the following are examples of some of the more significant failures of Riel's lawyers.

(i)   Failure to provide Riel with a "full defence" to which he was legally entitled.

(ii)   Disobeying Riel's instructions for a trial on the "merit of my actions" and acting on the advice of unidentified "others" in pursuing an insanity plea "despite his orders, despite his desire, despite his instructions".

(iii)   Failure to have three of the six charges thrown out on the basis that no evidence whatsoever had been adduced to prove that Riel was a British subject, an essential element of the first three charges. Although that lack of proof was sufficient in itself, Riel's counsel could also have submitted that Riel was not a British subject. They could have pleaded either or both section 6 of *The Naturalization Act*,

260

1870 of the United Kingdom (passed on May 12, 1870 a date
before the North-West Territories became part of
Canada), or section 9 of *The Naturalization Act, Canada,
1881*.

(iv)   Failure to argue that since Canada was not part of the
        "Realm" as required by the charges against him under the
        1351 Statute of Treasons of England (and all of the activities
        alleged in the charges against Riel took place in Canada),
        Riel was not guilty of the offences charged under the *1351
        Statutes of Treasons*. They should have moved for dismissal
        of the charges on the basis that the acts alleged against Riel
        did not fall within the *1351 Statute of Treasons* and that the
        applicable charges were contained in the *1868 Treason-
        Felony Act of Canada*. This Canadian Statute (unlike the
        1351 Statute of Treasons) did not carry the death penalty.
        For a further discussion of this aspect see Chapter XVI.

(v)   Failure to object to the biased remarks made by Magistrate
        Richardson to the jury. These are discussed in Chapter
        XIV, section 1 "Magistrate Richardson's Charge to the
        Jury".

(vi)   Failure to procure the attendance as witnesses of Deputy
        Ministers Burgess and Vankoughnet, or production of
        relevant documents.

(vii)   Failure to apply for a commission to take the evidence of
        Dumont, Nault and Dumas in Montana.

(viii) The immense error of one of Riel's lawyers, T. C.
        Johnstone, in stating in open court that he understood the
        Crown was "proceeding under 31 Victoria" (the *1868
        Treason-Felony Statute of Canada* which did not carry the
        death penalty for the Riel's charges). Crown counsel
        Osler told Johnstone that he was wrong and that "25
        Edward III is the one" (the *1351 Statute of Treasons of
        England* under which one was executed for high treason).

(ix)   On an overall basis, not acting as Riel wished but acting
        for anonymous (to quote Fitzpatrick) "parties ... who
        were really our clients in this case".

(b) Appeal to the Court of Queen's Bench

In the appeal to the Court of Queen's Bench of Manitoba, Riel's lawyers did not ask the court to rule on the matters set forth in paragraphs (iii), (iv) or (v) of section 4 (a) immediately above. They also did not ask this court to rule that because of the failures mentioned in paragraphs (vi) and (vii) of section 4(a) Riel was not given his legal right "to make full answer and defence". In fact Wallbridge wrote that:

> No complaint is now made as to the unfairness, haste or
> want of opportunity of having all of the evidence heard
> which he [Riel] desired to have heard. [317]

Riel's lawyers did argue against the jurisdiction of the North-West Territories Court. It was a forlorn hope to anticipate that this argument would succeed. Three judges unanimously gave judgment in the Connor appeal effectively upholding the jurisdiction of the North-West Territories trial court in that case. The trial court in the Connor case was identical to the North-West Territories court which heard Riel's case. Two of the three judges in the Connor appeal were Wallbridge and Taylor and they were two of the three judges who heard Riel's appeal.

If Wallbridge and Taylor had upheld the challenge to the Riel court they would be effectively ruling that they made a ghastly error in the Connor case, an error which cost Connor his life since Conner had been convicted of murder. The likelihood of such a ruling was remote.

(c) Application to the Privy Council.

In the application to the Privy Council for leave to appeal, no argument was made with respect to the matters set forth in paragraphs (iii), (iv), or (v) of section 4 (a). Neither was an argument made with respect to matters set forth in paragraphs (vi) and (vii) of section 4 (a). Paragraphs (vi) and (vii) refer to the failure of Riel to be accorded his right at law, "to make full answer and defence" and in particular failure to procure the attendance of witnesses (who Riel swore were "material and essential" to his defence) or relevant documents. As well, there is nothing in the Privy Council's judgment which indicates that any mention was made by Riel's counsel of the false statement by Chief Justice Wallbridge that all evidence was called which Riel desired.

---

[317]   *The Queen v. Louis Riel,* (1885) 2 *Manitoba Law Reports,* p. 321 @ 323.

Before the Privy Council, Riel's lawyers abandoned the defence of insanity, the defence that was the *sine qua non*, the very core of the defence's case presented to the jury, the one to which they had directed their examination and cross-examination of witnesses. As for their attack on the jurisdiction of the North-West Territories Court, the Privy Council would not even entertain a right of appeal, stating that there was no validity to the attack on the *North-West Territories Act* under which the Riel court was established.

The other argument, that taking the trial evidence in shorthand was objectionable, was summarily dismissed. As noted in section 3 of Chapter IV, the trial transcript did contain errors. However, Riel's lawyers never raised errors as an issue. As Lord Halsbury stated "no complaint is made of inaccuracy or mistake".

The Privy Council rejected the defence arguments without calling upon Crown counsel to present their case.

This was the denouement to Riel's life-or-death journey through the courts, with death hanging over him like the Sword of Damocles.

Chapter XXIII

CONCLUSION

The trial, conviction and execution of Louis Riel for high treason were unjust and unfair from a number of perspectives. These included

    (a) a presiding magistrate who was not independent and who was biased and whose magisterial acumen left something to be desired;

    (b) improper judicial and political participation and tampering at the highest levels;

    (c) failure of Riel to be provided with a "full answer and defence" (to which the law entitled him) to the charges;

    (d) serious deficiencies in defence counsels' representation of Riel; and

    (e) the illegal application in Canada of the *1351 Statute of Treasons* to the charges against Riel resulting in his illegal conviction and execution.

These points are well canvassed in the body of this treatise. However, the following briefly summarizes them:

(a) Magistrate's Bias and Lack of Independence and Acumen

In the House of Commons, Liberal Leader Edward Blake pointed out Magistrate Richardson's lack of independence. Blake stated that the magistrate in the Riel trial was "the political law officer to the Government in the Territories" answerable to the Attorney-General, appointed and paid a salary during the pleasure of the Government, and the recipient of other "special favours".[318] Blake then cited Richardson's special favours. Richardson's bias was manifested:

    (i)   in his reference to "the evil influence of leading spirits of the Manitoba troubles" (of whom Riel was the chief leading spirit);

    (ii)   by his participation at a meeting with police, government and Hudson's Bay Company officials on March 12, 1885 which concluded that Riel and his supporters should not be permitted to continue their agitation;

---

[318]   *House of Commons Debates*, 1886, p. 241, March 19.

(iii)   by his personal selection of a jury panel made up almost exclusively of persons of Anglo-Saxon extraction; and

(iv)   in the highly prejudicial remarks he made in his charge to the jury.

Richardson held the lowly post of magistrate but presided over a trial for high treason, categorized by Crown counsel Osler in his very first opening remarks to the jury as "the highest crime known to the law". In response to the lengthy arguments of both defence and Crown counsel relating to the question of jurisdiction, which at times ascended to lofty heights of eloquence, Richardson made a ruling in less than a dozen words without giving reasons. Seated beside him Justice of the Peace Henry LeJeune, while warming the bench, said absolutely nothing from the beginning to the end of the trial. In his charge to the jury, Richardson treated the charges against Riel as one. He failed to point out to the jury:

(i)   the difference between local allegiance and natural allegiance;

(ii)   the absence of proof, with respect to the first three charges, that Riel was a British subject and hence these charges hadn't been proven;

(iii)   that the provisions of the *British Naturalization Act, 1870* or the *Canadian Naturalization Act, 1881* each provided that a person ceased to be a British subject on voluntarily becoming naturalized in a foreign state;

(iv)   that the indictment contained six counts and in the circumstances they should consider and bring in a verdict on each count separately;

(v)   that the *1351 Statute of Treasons* required that treasonous acts of levying war must occur "in the Realm", and that this meant "in England, Wales and adjacent narrow seas"; and

(vi)   that liability to execution required a strict interpretation of the penal law, that Canada was not part of the Realm within the meaning of the *1351 Statute of Treasons*, and if they found no acts occurred "in the Realm" all charges must be dismissed.

(b) Judicial and Political Improprieties

The meddling of Chief Justice Wallbridge (the local "informant" in Manitoba for Prime Minister John A. Macdonald, who had appointed Wallbridge to the position of Chief Justice) is evidenced by Minister of Justice Alexander Campbell's letter of April 13, 1885 to Prime Minister John A. Macdonald. This letter also indicated a bias against Riel and the Metis. In this letter Campbell stated that Wallbridge wrote about the "difficulty" of a high treason trial in Winnipeg. However there was no reference to any judicial difficulty, only to the rights which Riel and others would have in Winnipeg, rights which they would not have in the North-West Territories.

Wallbridge was wearing his old political hat, not his judicial robes, when he wrote his former fellow Speaker and fellow Parliamentarian Campbell. The fact that Wallbridge subsequently presided over the appeal court hearing Riel's appeal, after having written to Campbell and having received a "private" letter from Campbell, was improper. Campbell's private letter to Wallbridge to speed-up the Manitoba Court of Queen's Bench decision in the Connor case (a decision which was then to have a direct effect on how matters would proceed in the Riel case) was also improper. Not many days after Campbell informed Macdonald of this "private" letter, the Court of Queen's Bench delivered its judgment in the Connor case. The judgment as to jurisdiction handed down in the Connor case was one that Campbell had hoped for, and a week later Riel was indicted.

Campbell personally intervened to have Riel's trial site changed from Winnipeg to Regina. He did so to ensure Riel would be tried by an Anglo-Saxon jury of six, rather than by a mixed jury of twelve. In correspondence that he wrote to John A. Macdonald on two separate occasions, Campbell referred to the rights of an accused in Manitoba to a mixed jury, something Riel would not be entitled to in the North-West Territories. Campbell wrote "very urgently" to Minister of Militia and Defence Adolphe Caron (law partner and brother-in-law of Riel's lawyer, Charles Fitzpatrick) to divert Riel from Winnipeg to Regina because, as he told Macdonald, a trial in Manitoba would result in "a miscarriage of justice". He didn't say why, in his opinion, a trial in Manitoba would be a miscarriage of justice, but a trial in the North-West Territories would not be. However his view, as just noted, is obvious.

266

The fact that Chief Justice Wallbridge subsequently presided over Riel's appeal was wrong and contrary to procedural justice and natural justice. As well, Wallbridge (who stated he had carefully read the trial evidence) made a blatant misstatement in his judgment that all evidence which Riel desired was called. See Chapter XX for a fuller discussion.

(c) Deprivation of Riel's Right to Full Answer and Defence

Riel was charged with high treason under the ancient *1351 Statute of Treasons* passed in England. However, the make-up of the jury, the presiding magistrate and justice of the peace, and the right to "make full answer and defence by counsel" were provided for in the *North-West Territories Act of 1880*, a Canadian statute.

Riel was deprived of his right to make full answer and defence. The main culprits in depriving Riel of his legal rights in this respect were his own lawyers. There was a failure on the part of Riel's lawyers to provide him with a full defence and answer based on his instructions to them and based on other matters discussed herein and in (d) below.

(i)   Riel specifically instructed his lawyers that he wanted a trial "on the merit of my actions." This would have involved evidence of justification for his actions, e.g. self defence at Duck Lake where the bloodshed was initiated by the assistant to NWMP Superintendent Crozier. This defence would have delved into the reasons which prompted the settlers to seek out Riel in Montana; into Riel's activities in the North-West Territories; and into the maladministration and neglect of the federal government. The latter course would have put Riel's chief defence counsel Fitzpatrick in a most unhappy position. The defence counsel would have had to attack the government in which his law partner and brother-in-law Adolphe Caron (the Minister of Militia in John A. Macdonald's government) was a foremost player in recent events relating to the uprising in the North-West. By not pursuing this defence, Fitzpatrick was saved from this embarrassment.

(ii)   There was a failure on the part of Riel's lawyers to procure the attendance as witnesses of the two federal Deputy Ministers that Riel swore were material and essential to his defence, or to procure relevant documents.

267

(iii)   There was a failure on the part of Riel's lawyers to apply for a commission to take the evidence in Montana of Dumont, Dumas and Nault, further witnesses that Riel swore were essential and material to his defence.

(iv)   There was a failure on the part of Riel's lawyers to forego the insanity plea (which they were pursuing on the instructions of mysterious "others"), a plea vehemently rejected by Riel. This plea was contrary to a full defence and answer, which he wanted, based on his direct instructions to his lawyers. Further failures of the part of Riel's lawyers appear in Chapter XXII "Shortcomings of Riel's Lawyers", including their antagonistic treatment of him in open court.

(v)   Crown counsel and Magistrate Richardson also contributed to the inability of Riel to make full answer and defence. At the outset, the defence made an application for an adjournment of the trial for one month because they were "not in a position to proceed with the trial at the present moment." They had not obtained the presence of any witnesses and certain key documents. Notwithstanding this situation, Crown counsel Robinson initially opposed any adjournment of the trial. After much argument, Robinson agreed to a one-week adjournment. In that one-week interval, the defence failed to obtain the attendance of the "essential and material" witnesses or the documents referred to above. Perhaps if the one-month adjournment had been agreed to they would have done so. As well (as noted in Chapter IX) Robinson stated he opposed production of government documents, and the inspection of correspondence found in Riel's possession at Batoche, on the basis that they were "state documents". None of these items were made available to Riel or his counsel.

(vi)   During the cross-examination of Charles Nolin, Riel specifically referred to making a full defence. Richardson's response was that Riel would be given the opportunity of addressing the court after the examination of witnesses. An accused at the time was not allowed to give evidence.

An address to the court, after all evidence was in, was not in itself evidence and is no part of a full defence.

(d) Unauthorized and Deficient Legal Representation

In addition to their failure to provide Riel with a "full answer and defence" as requested by him, Riel's lawyers pursued a doomed strategy unauthorized by him, and exhibited a number of serious shortcomings. These are discussed in more detail in Chapter XXII "Shortcomings of Riel's Lawyers". However three of them are glaringly conspicuous.

(i)   The doomed strategy of Riel's lawyers in pleading a defence that Riel was insane was done pursuant to the instructions of unknown "others".   This strategy was contrary to Riel's instructions, was unauthorized by Riel, and was wrong.   This wrong was compounded by the abandonment by Riel's lawyers of any other defence before the jury. In any event their medical witnesses, Drs. Roy and Clark, were of little help (from Riel's lawyers point of view) in proving Riel's insanity.   Roy was unsatisfactory and Clark was pig-headed in ignoring the applicable law of insanity. In the latter case, Dr. Clark's evidence was supportive of the legal sanity of Riel argued by the Crown, and against that of the insanity plea argued by the defence lawyers. Not only did Riel not sanction the insanity plea by his lawyers; he vehemently rejected it. He refused "to consent to the animal life of an asylum" as he passionately stated to Magistrate Richardson in interrupting his lawyers cross-examination of Charles Nolin.

(ii)   Another significant deficiency flowed from that just mentioned.   By failing to provide the jury with an additional or alternative defence related to justification, the jurors were not provided with the opportunity, if they were so minded, to take measures described in the judgment of Chief Justice Dickson referred to in section 1 (c) of Chapter XXII. Based on the defence evidence presented to them the jurors were conscientiously unable

• to act as a safety valve in an exceptional case;

- to collectively express the common sense of the community against an oppressive enforcement of the law; or

- to exercise a *de facto* power to disregard the law if they thought it just to do so.

By not presenting to the jury an alternative to the defence of insanity, the prospect of one or more jurors scrupulously following one or more of these courses was not made available. Consequently when the jury decided that Riel was sane the potential for a hung jury or for outright acquittal, which an alternative defence may have provided, was non-existent.

(iii)   The third conspicuous shortcoming of Riel's lawyers is summarized in the following section (e) "Inapplicability of the *1351 Statute of Treasons* to the Riel Charges".

(e) Inapplicability of the *1351 Statute of Treasons* to the Riel Charges

A third and most egregious flaw, in the defence lawyers strategy, was a failure to argue that the law under which Riel was charged (the *1351 Statute of Treasons*) was the wrong statute for acts of levying war **in Canada**, and hence none of the charges were valid. The extensive discussion of the inapplicability of the *1351 Statute of Treasons* to "levying war" outside of the Realm is discussed in Chapter XVI "Riel's Unlawful Conviction and Execution". There was not a whisper of dissent, by Riel's counsel, against the utilization of this primitive enactment from a land far away to occurrences in Canada. There was no challenge to the applicability of this antique law in the North-West Territories. There was no discussion or citation of authorities to prove that the term "Realm" meant England, and not Canada, in the *1351 Statute of Treasons*. There was no stand against the misleading use of the term "realm" (meaning Canada) in the Riel charges which erroneously implied that this was the same "Realm" as that in the *1351 Statute of Treasons*. There was no demand on the magistrate that he rule on the matter, no motion for dismissal of all charges for lack of proof of any alleged activities within the "Realm". Neither were these matters raised on the appeal to the Court of Queen's Bench of Manitoba or before the Privy Council. This attack on the applicability of the *1351 Statute of Treasons*, successfully argued, would have seen every charge against Riel dismissed. In that event there would have been no execution.

After Riel's conviction, Prime Minister Macdonald acted in bad faith and engaged in skulduggery, with respect to the medical commission he appointed to examine Riel. Events surrounding Macdonald's duplicitous activities in this respect are discussed in Chapter XXI "Mercy Denied". Macdonald had not the slightest intention of granting mercy to Riel, notwithstanding the unanimous recommendation of the jury. Some time before the medical commission was appointed, Governor-General Lansdowne, in a letter dated October 7, 1885 to Macdonald, wrote concerning Riel:

> from our conversations … I have no doubt that your mind is fully made up, and that you will advise that the law should take its course.[319]

Macdonald determined that "the gone coon",[320] as he once called Riel, would receive no mercy. His steely determination was motivated by a number of factors. These included

(i)   the troubles Riel had caused him during the Red River Resistance;

(ii)   the consequent incapacitating illness that Macdonald suffered for months;

(iii)   the execution of Thomas Scott in 1870 by Riel's Provisional Government with respect to which Macdonald stated that Riel had "committed a cold-blooded murder … which will never be forgotten by the whites … in … Ontario"[321] (notwithstanding that only a few months earlier Macdonald had stated, in effect, that under the law of nations it was "quite open" for the Red River inhabitants "to form a government *ex necessitate*");

(iv)   the realization that if Riel had not been convicted, Riel's actions and that of the Metis would be a condemnation of his policies, and lack of policies, towards the North-West Territories;

(v)   the frenzied demands of his fellow Orangemen of Ontario; and

---

[319]   Pope, p. 361.
[320]   Pope, p. 128.
[321]   Pope, p. 318.

(vi)   the fact that his supporters clamouring for Riel's execution
            outnumbered those opposing Riel's death.

The sometimes duplicitous, mendacious, unscrupulous and (often)
bibulous Macdonald had decided that the hated Riel

> shall hang though every dog in Quebec bark in his favour.[322]

In sentencing Riel, Magistrate Richardson had asked God to have
Mercy on Riel's soul. John A. Macdonald had no mercy on Riel's body.
This was so not withstanding Macdonald's advice to Governor General
Lansdowne that the

> Northwest outbreak was a mere domestic trouble and ought
> not to be elevated to the rank of a rebellion.

He added that Riel's acts "technically amount to treason."[323]

In the Canada Parks Museum at Batoche in Saskatchewan, there is
an inscription accompanying one of the exhibits reading:

> Execution – To have given him clemency Macdonald's
> government would have in effect accepted responsibility for
> the unrest and many of the unfulfilled promises of the
> North-West. It was much easier to lay the blame on the
> shoulders of one man – Louis Riel.

In the same Batoche Museum there is a cartoon drawing in which
Justice is standing with her back to John A. Macdonald. In the cartoon
Macdonald says "Well Madam, Riel is gone.   I hope you are quite
satisfied" to which Justice responds:

> Not quite – you have hanged the EFFECT of the Rebellion.
>
> Now I want to find and punish the CAUSE.

There is currently a Bill before Parliament to reverse Riel's
conviction for high treason and to recognize him as a Father of
Confederation and the Founder of the Province of Manitoba. In March
1999 a poll found that 65% of those surveyed supported Riel's
exoneration.   As noted throughout this study, there is overwhelming
justification for the reversal of Riel's conviction. Based on the thesis set
forth in this text the weightier demands of the law were overlooked and

- Riel was denied justice;
- Riel was denied mercy;
- Riel died an unjust and unmerciful death.

---

[322]   Parkin, p. 244.
[323]   Pope, p. 355.

BIBLIOGRAPHY

Anson, Sir William R., *The Law and Custom of the Constitution*, (Oxford at the Clarendon Press, 4th ed., 1935) Vol. II.

Archbold's Pleading, Evidence, & Practice, (Sweet & Maxwell, London, 1905) 23 ed.

Beal, Bob and Rod Macleod, *Prairie Fire The 1885 North-West Rebellion* (Hurtig Publishers, Edmonton, 1984).

Berton, Pierre, *The Last Spike: The Great Railway 1881-1885*, (Penguin Group, Markham, Ontario, 1971).

Bingaman, Sandra E., "The Trials of the White Rebels, 1885", *Saskatchewan History* Vol. XXV, Spring, 1972.

Blackstone, William, *Commentaries on the Laws of England, 1795.*

Bliss, Michael, *Right Honourable Men: The Descent of Canadian Politics from Macdonald to Mulroney*, (Harper Collins Publishers, Toronto, 1994).

Bowsfield, Hartwell, ed. *Louis Riel, Selected Readings*, (Copp Clark Pitman Ltd. Mississauga, Ont., 1988).

Brown, D. F., "The Meaning of Treason in 1885" *Saskatchewan History*, Vol. 28 (Spring), 1975.

Bumsted, J. M., "Riel trial complicated by citizenship", *Winnipeg Real Estate News*, January 16, 1998.
—— "The 'Mahdi' of Western Canada? Louis Riel and His Papers", *The Beaver*, August/September 1987.

Canada Sessional Papers, (1871) 34 Victoria (No. 20); (1885), 48 Victoria, (No.116); (1886) (No. 43).

Canadian Charter of Rights and Freedoms, Constitution Act, 1982 of Canada.

Carroll, Lewis, *Through the Looking Glass.*

Charette, Guillaume, *Vanishing Spaces, Memoirs of Louis Goulet*, (Bois-Brules Publishers, Winnipeg, 1976).

Charlebois, Dr. Peter, *The Life of Louis Riel*, (NC Press Ltd., Toronto, 1975).

Clark, Dr. Daniel, "A Psycho-Medical History of Louis Riel, *American Journal of Insanity*, Vol.. 44, No.1 July, 1887.

Clarke, C. K., "A Critical Study of the Case of Louis Riel", *Louis Riel, Selected Readings*, ed. Hartwell Bowsfield, (Copp Clark Pitman Ltd., Mississauga, Ont., 1988).

Creighton, Donald, *John A. Macdonald, The Old Chieftain* (U. of Toronto Press, Toronto, 1998).

—— *The Story of Canada*, (MacMillan Company of Canada Ltd., Toronto, 1975).

Dafoe, John W., *Laurier, A Study in Canadian Politics* (Thomas Allen, Toronto, 1922).

Davidson, William McCartney, *Louis Riel 1844-1885*, (The Albertan Publishing Company Ltd., Calgary, 1955).

Deane, Captain R.B., *Mounted Police Life in Canada; A Record of Thirty-One Years Service*, (Cassell and Company Limited, London 1916).

Debates of House of Commons, Session 1885; and 1886.

Dictionary of Canadian Biography, Vol. XI 1881-1890,(U. of Toronto Press, Toronto).

Dwarris, Sir Fortunatus, *A General Treatise on Statutes: Their Rules of Construction and the Proper Boundaries of Legislation and of Judicial Interpretation*, (William Benning & Co., London, 1848).

Epitome of Parliamentary Documents in Connection with the North-West Rebellion – 1885 (Printed by Order of Parliament, Ottawa, McLean, Roger & Co. 1886) .

Evans, Ivor H. ed., *Brewer's Dictionary of Phrase & Fable*, (Cassell Ltd., London, 2nd Rev. Ed., 1981).

Finlason, W. F., *A Treatise on Martial Law*, (Stevens & Sons, Bell Yard, 1866).

Fischer, David H., *Historians' Fallacies – Toward a Logic of Historical Thought* (Harper & Row, New York, 1970).

Fitz-James, Michael, "An Apology for Louis Riel Too?" *Canadian Lawyer*, February 1998.

Flanagan, Thomas, *Louis 'David' Riel: Prophet of the New World*, (Goodread Biographies, Halifax, 1983).

—— *Riel and the Rebellion* (Western Producer Prairie Books, Saskatoon, 1983).

Forsyth, William, *Cases and Opinions on Constitutional Law*, (Stevens & Haynes, London, 1869).

Foster's *Crown Law*, (Oxford, Clarendon Press, 1762).

Foster, John, "The Metis: The People and the Term", A. S. Lussier, ed. *Louis Riel and the Metis*, (Pemmican Publications Inc., Winnipeg, 1988).

Friesen, Gerald, *The Canadian Prairies: A History* (U. of Toronto Press, Toronto, 1987).

Golding, Professor Martin P., *Philosophy of Law*, (Prentice Hall Inc., Englewood Cliffs, New Jersey, 1975)

Granatstein, J. L., *Who Killed Canadian History?* (HarperCollins Publishers, Toronto, 1998)

Hale, Sir Matthew, *The History of the Pleas of the Crown*, (E. & R. Nutt, and R. Gosling, 1736.
—— *Pleas of the Crown, a Methodical Summary, 1678* (Professional Books Limited, London).

Hardcastle, Henry, *A Treatise on the Construction and Effect of Statute Law*, (Stevens and Haynes, London, Third ed., 1901).

Hardy, W. G., *From Sea Unto Sea, The Road to Nationhood 1850-1910*, (Doubleday & Co., New York, 1960).

Hill, Douglas, *The Opening of the Canadian West*, (Academic Press Canada, Don Mills, Ontario, 1967).

Holy Bible, Books of Matthew and Luke.

Howard, Joseph, *Strange Empire, Louis Riel and the Metis People*, (James Lewis & Samuel, Toronto, 1952).

Knafla, Louis and Richard Klumpenhouwer, "Lords of the Western Bench", *The Legal Archives Society of Alberta*, 1997.

Maxwell, Sir Peter Benson, *On the Interpretation of Statutes*, (William Maxwell & Son, London, 1875); and 2nd ed. (1883).

McInnis, Edgar, *Canada, a Political and Social History*, (Holt, Rinehart and Winston, New York, 1961).

McLean, Don, *1885, Metis Rebellion or Government Conspiracy?*, (Pemmican Publications Inc., Winnipeg, 1985).
—— *Home from the Hill, A History of the Metis in Western Canada*, (Gabriel Dumont Institute, Regina, 1987).

Milton, John, *Paradise Lost*.

Moore, Christopher, *The Law Society of Upper Canada and Ontario's Lawyers 1797-1997*, (U. of Toronto Press, 1997).

Morton, Desmond intro., *The Queen v Louis Riel*, [Trial Transcript], (U. of Toronto Press, 1974).

Morton, Desmond and Reginald H. Roy, *Telegrams of the North-West Campaign, 1885,* (Champlain Society).

Morton, W. L., *Manitoba, a History,* (U. of Toronto Press, 2nd ed., 1970, Toronto).

National Archives of Canada ("NAC"), "Macdonald Papers" Vol. 62; Vol. 106; Vol. 107; Vol. 108; Vol. 197; "Records Relating to Louis Riel and the North-West Uprising", Vol. 819; "Records of the Department of Justice", Vol. 1421-24.

Newman, Peter C., "Rewriting history: Louis Riel as a hero", *Maclean's Magazine,* April 12, 1999.

Olesky, Ronald L, "Louis Riel and the Crown Letters", *Canadian Lawyer,* February 1998.

Osborn, P. G., *A Concise Law Dictionary,* (Sweet & Maxwell, London, 1964) 5th ed.

Owram, Douglas, *Promise of Eden, the Canadian Expansionist Movement and the Idea of the West 1856-1900,* (U. of Toronto Press, 1980).

Parkin. George R., *Sir John A. Macdonald,* (Morang & Co., Toronto, 1909).

Pope, Joseph, *Correspondence of Sir John Macdonald,* (Oxford University Press, Toronto, 1921).

Prince Albert Daily Herald, March 26, 1935, "Survivors Recount Experiences ...".

Prud'homme, Judge L. A., "La Famille Goulet", in *Memoires de la Société Royale du Canada,* Vol. 29, 3rd series (1935).

Queen, The v. Louis Riel, [Trial Transcript], Desmond Morton intro., (U. of Toronto Press, Toronto, 1974).

Radzinowicz, Sir Leonard, *A History of English Criminal Law,* (Stevens & Sons, London, 1986), Vol. 5.

Regina Leader, 1 October, 1885.

Riel, Louis, *Collected Writings of Louis Riel,* George F. G. Stanley ed., (U. of Alberta Press, Edmonton, 1985), Vol. 3.

"Riel's Mental State, Opinions of Dr. Clark of the Toronto Asylum", *The Toronto Globe,* November 18, 1885.

"Riel Trial, The", *Toronto Globe,* July 11, 1885

Roy, Pierre-Georges, *Les Avocats de Quebec,* (Levis, 1936).

Selden, Master John, *Mare Clausum*, trans. Marchamont Nedham (ed. 1652) bk. 2, Ch.24.

Senate Debates, 1877.

Shakespeare, William, *Hamlet*.
—— *Macbeth*.
—— *Merchant of Venice, The*.

Siggins, Maggie, *Riel, a Life of Revolution*, (HarperCollins Publishers Ltd., Toronto, 1994).

Sprague, D. N., *Canada and the Metis, 1869-1885*, (Sir Wilfrid Laurier Press, Waterloo, 1988).

Stanley, George F., *The Birth of Western Canada*, (U. of Toronto Press, 1960).
—— "Last Word on Louis Riel, The – The Man of Several Faces", *Louis Riel, Selected Readings*, ed. Hartwell Bowsfield (Copp Clark Pitman Ltd., Mississauga, Ont. 1988), p. 42.
—— *Louis Riel*, (McGraw-Hill Ryerson Limited, Toronto, 1985).

Stephen, Sir James Fitzjames, *A History of the Criminal Law of England*, (Macmillan & Co., London, 1883), Vol. II.

"Taché Collection", *St. Boniface Historical Society Archives*.

Taswell-Langmead, Thomas Pitt, "English Constitutional History from the Teutonic Conquest to the Present Time", (Stevens & Haynes, London, 1886).

Thomas, Lewis H., "A Judicial Murder – The Trial of Louis Riel," in Howard Palmer ed., *The Settlement of the West*, (U. of Calgary Press, Calgary, 1977).
—— "Louis Riel", *Dictionary of Canadian Biography*, Vol.XI 1881-1890, (U. of Toronto Press, Toronto, 1982).

Toronto Globe , July 11, 1885 and November 18, 1885.

Toronto Mail, The, Wednesday, August 26, 1885.

Winnipeg Telegram, July 18, 1911, Interview with Hugh John Macdonald.

Winnipeg Free Press, August 2, 1911, Letter from Roger Goulet.

Woodcock, George, *Gabriel Dumont* (Hurtig Publishers, Edmonton, 1975).

Winnipeg Real Estate News, January 16, 1998.

TABLE OF CASES

Calvin's Case (1608), 7 Co. Rep Ia., 77 E.R. 377.

Henderson v. Sherborne, 2 *Meeson & Welsby* 239 (1837).

Joyce v. Director of Public Prosecutions [1946] 1 All E.R. 186 (House of Lords).

King v. Casement, [1917] , *1 King's Bench* 98.

London County Council v. Aylesbury Dairy Co. (1898), 1Q.B. 106.

McNaghten's Case [1843-60] *All England Reports* 229 (House of Lords); 8 E.R.718.

Morgentaler et al versus the Queen, [1988], 44 *Dominion Law Reports*, 4th ed. p.385.

Mulcahy v. The Queen. 1868 *Law Reports, English and Irish Appeals*, p.306.

O'Brien v. The Queen, [1849] 9 *English Reports*,1169.

Rumball v. Schmidt, (1882) 8 Q.B.D., p. 608.

Queen v. Connor, (1885) 2 *Manitoba Law Reports*, 235 (Man. Queen's Bench).

Queen v. Kah-pah-yak-as-to-cum, "One Arrow", CSP 1886, #52, p. 13.

Queen v. Riel, (1885) 2, *Manitoba Law Reports*, p.302.

Queen v. Riel, (1885) 2, *Manitoba Law Reports*, p.321.

Queen v. Riel, [Trial transcript], Morton, Desmond intro., (U. of Toronto Press, 1974).

R .v. Bank, Cro. Jac. 41(2 Hale, 178).

Riel v. The Queen [1885] 10 *Appeal Cases*, 675 (Privy Council).

Reference re Position of Chief Justice of Alberta re Harvey and Scott (1922); 64 SCR, p. 135.

Rumball v. Schmidt (1882), 8 Q.B.D p.608.

Tuck & Sons v. Priestner, [1887] 19 Q.B.D., p. 638.

U.S. v. Dougherty, 473 F. 2d 1113 (1972).

Williams v. Her Majesty the Queen, [1998] 1 SCR p.1128.

INDEX

Aberhart, William, 10

Adams, Pres. John, 149

Addresses to the jury, 148-62

Adhering to King's Enemies, 195

Adjournment of Trial — see Trial, ... adjournment

Aikins, J. A. M., 79; 96-98

Aikins, James C., 97

Alberta, 33; 38

Alienist, 70; 87; 99-100; 137; 139-41; 153

Allan, Sir Hugh, 39

American Revolution, 149

amnesty, 25; 30; 69; 170; 214; 233

Amyot, Col., 65-66; 93

André, Fr. Alexis, 37; 114-15; 117; 127-31; 135; 152; 159-60; 164; 212-14; 230; 239; 254

Appeal of conviction, 207-16

Application to Privy Council, 217-19

Archibald, Adams George, 26; 28-29; 37

Assiniboia, 17; 23-24

Assywin, 41; 108-10; 250

Astley, John W., 95-96; 107; 112; 161

Australia, 182; 186; 190; 199; 241

Bacon, Francis, 148; 198

Banff, AB, 42

Barnabé, Evelina, 31

Barnabé, Fr. Fabien, 30-31

Batoche, 43; 45; 49; 52; 101; 103; 105-08; 111-14; 130; 147; 163; 177; 268; 272

Battleford, Sask., 108; 161

Beauport Asylum, 31; 133-134; 160

benchers, 85-86

Bennett, R. B., 90

Berton, Pierre, 41

Big Bear, Chief, 61; 63; 80; 89; 152

Bill C-417, 11; 272

Bill of Rights, 38; 113; 248

Blake, Edward, 29; 56-57; 60; 171; 236-37; 251-52; 264

Borden, Robert L., 89; 92

Boucher, Marguerite, 15

Boulton, Charles, 24

Bourget, Bishop Ignace, 30; 131

Bowell, Mackenzie. 30

Boyne, Battle of, 37

British North America Act, 35

British subject, 50-51; 59; 67-69; 71-72; 81; 95; 101; 105; 166; 177; 181; 215-16; 260; 265

Brooks, Edwin, 66; 105; 158; 234; 237-38; 251-52

Brooks, Sgt., 109-10

buffalo & buffalo hunt, 16; 35; 37; 40; 100; 118-19; 132

Bumsted, J. M., 13; 242

Burbidge, George W., 60; 79; 82; 86-88; 221-22

burden of proof, 55; 72; 137; 141; 154; 165-66; 212; 246; 279

Burgess, A. M., 71; 100; 208; 238; 248; 253; 261

Cameron, Mr. (MP Huron), 102-03

Campbell, Alexander, 12; 45-48; 60; 79-80; 82; 86; 105; 155; 203-07; 217; 219-26; 228-29; 231-34; 237; 239; 242; 247; 266

Canada, 10-11; 13; 17; 20-23; 25; 27; 32-36; 39; 44; 47-48; 50-51; 52-53; 55-56; 64; 68-69; 73; 75; 83-84; 86; 88-90; 92; 97; 105; 113; 117-19; 126; 140-41; 145-46; 148-49; 151-56; 157; 167; 170-71; 175-76; 178; 180-84; 186-89; 192-94; 199-202; 204; 206; 213-14; 219-20; 226; 233; 235; 240-41; 251; 261; 264-65; 270; 272

Canada East — see also Quebec, 89-90; 92

Canada First Movement, 20

Canada North West Land Company, 45-46; 73; 85

Canada West — see also Ontario, 89; 95; 204-05

Canadian Bar Association, 97

Canadian Charter of Rights & Freedoms, 63-64; 69; 76

Canadian Lawyer, 80; 223; 226

Canadian Pacific Railway, 40-42; 46; 73; 85; 97; 239

Canadian Party, 20

Caron, Adolphe, 44-45; 88; 91; 111; 126; 224; 226; 228; 258-60; 266-67

Caron, Corinne, 88; 91

Carroll, Lewis, 194

Cartier, George Étienne, 29-30; 39; 213; 241

Casement, Sir Rodger, 195

Casgrain, Thomas Chase, 66; 82; 88-89; 91; 123; 129-32; 259-60

certificate of naturalization, 68-72; 101

Champlain, Samuel de, 27

Champ de Mars, 240

charges against Riel, 48-55; 59; 64; 67; 71-72; 81; 87; 95; 101; 105; 138; 166; 175-78; 182-89; 198; 201-02; 211; 215; 254; 260-61; 264-65; 270

Cicero; 89

citizen, 32; 50; 100; 148; 200; 216; 250-51

279

Clark, Dr. Daniel, 127; 137-41; 152-54; 160; 165; 212; 214; 245-46; 258; 269

Clarke, Henry J., 96

Clarke, Lawrence, 57-58; 110

Cleveland, Pres. Grover, 43

Clinton, Pres. Bill, 223

Cochin, Fr. Louis, 62

colonies, 179; 193-94

commission evidence, 103-04; 249; 254; 261; 268

common law, 50; 74; 137; 194-96

conflict of interest, 57; 91; 221; 243; 254; 258-60

Connor case, 77-80; 86; 92; 95-97; 164; 209; 211; 222-223; 225-26; 234; 247; 262; 266

Constitutionality — see jurisdiction of the court

Convention of Forty, 23; 113

Conservative Party, 10; 39-40; 69; 82; 204; 227; 240-41

Cosgrove, Francis, 66; 105; 168; 238; 251-52

Council of Assiniboia, 17; 23-24

court, 21; 25; 44; 47; 54; 59; 61; 63; 67; 70; 72-80; 82-83; 86-101; 103; 105; 113; 116-26; 128; 132-33; 135; 138-39; 141-44; 146; 155; 159; 163-64; 167-70; 175-76; 178; 180; 196-97; 199; 203-07; 210-12; 215; 217-19; 222-23; 225-26; 234; 236; 242-48; 250-52; 254; 256-58; 260-63; 266; 268-70

Court of Queen's Bench (Man.), 67; 77-78; 80; 95-97; 164; 203-07; 211; 215; 217-19; 222-23; 225-26; 228; 242-43; 245; 247; 260; 262; 266; 270

CPR — see Canadian Pacific Railway

Crerar, Thomas, 10

Crown counsel, 59-61; 64; 66; 76-78; 81; 83-91; 96; 100-02; 105; 116; 120-21; 123-24; 131; 134; 140; 142-44; 147-48; 153-54; 156; 159-64; 168; 171; 176-77; 186; 188; 200; 218-19; 234; 238; 246-47; 249; 257; 261; 263; 265; 268

Crown rebuttal witnesses, 141-147

Crown witnesses, 105-116

Crozier, Major Lief, 41; 107-10; 113; 131; 145; 161; 209; 212; 250; 253; 255; 267

Dafoe, John W., 240

Daily Manitoban, 167-68

Davidson, William M., 18; 26-27; 158; 237-38

Davis, Jefferson, 241

Deane, Peel, 66; 105

Deane, R. Burton, 45; 147

death penalty, 24; 48-49; 55; 64; 75; 77; 95; 167; 178; 184-85; 187; 193-94; 199; 202; 240-42; 251; 261

defence committee — see Riel, Louis

defence witnesses, 127-40

demurrer, 54; 59; 77-78; 81; 95; 99

Dennis, Col. J. Stoughton, 20; 23; 36; 57

Dewdney, Lt. Gov. Edgar, 114; 129; 229-31; 236-37

Dickens, Charles, 139

Dickson, Ch. Justice, R. G. B., 250-52; 269

Drummond, Edward, 137

Dublin, Ireland, 190

Dubuc, Joseph, 29; 203; 205; 211

Duck Lake, 41; 43; 49; 51-53; 105-09; 112; 118; 129; 147; 163; 177; 250; 253; 267

Duke of Monmouth, 203

Dumas, Michel, 32; 43; 70; 100-01; 103; 122; 208; 249; 253-54; 261; 268

Dumont, Gabriel, 32; 38; 43; 70; 73; 100-01; 103; 108; 111; 122; 161; 208; 215; 249; 253-54; 261; 268

Dumont, Isadore, 41; 108-10; 250

Durham, Lord, 241

Dwarris, Fortunatus, 197-98

Edward III, 54; 105; 163; 175-77; 195; 200-01; 261

England (the Realm), 175; 179; 180-81; 184; 186; 189-93; 198-99; 201-02; 265; 270

Epitome of Parliamentary Documents, 232

Eratt, Edward, 66; 105

evidence — see Crown rebuttal witnesses; Crown witnesses and defence witnesses

Ewart, John S., 95-98; 207; 210

exile, 19; 25; 30; 36; 50; 69; 170; 214; 233

Exovedate, 108; 113; 116; 127; 131; 145

Exovede, 113; 145

Expansionist Movement, 33-42

Federal (Exchequer) Court, 86

felony, 187-88; 193-95; 198-99; 202

Fenian Act, 55; 64; 87; 188

Fenians, 29; 170; 213

Finlason, W. F., 180

Fish Creek, 43; 49; 52-53; 105-06; 108; 111; 147; 161; 163; 177

Fiset, Romuald, 30; 45; 83; 91-93; 117; 125-26; 150; 243

Fitzpatrick, Charles — see also Short-comings of Riel's Lawyers, 58-59; 66; 70-78; 82-83; 87-88; 90-95; 97; 99-103; 108-

12; 117; 119-26; 130-35; 138-40; 142-44; 148-55; 158-63; 168; 186; 207; 210-11; 217-18; 243-47; 249-50; 253-61; 266-67

Fort Carlton, 58; 110; 161

Fort Garry, 21; 23-24; 26; 36

Fourmond, Fr. Vital, 66; 115; 127; 131-32; 135-36; 152

Franklin, Benjamin, 149

Friesen, Gerald, 13; 16

Gaboury, Marie-Anne, 15

Garnot, Philip, 127; 130-31; 136

Gilroy, John C., 227

Giroday, Philippe Boyer de la, 18

Goulet, Elzear, 26-28; 239

Goulet, Helen Jerome, 239

Goulet, Louis, 96

Government & Parliament of Canada, 9; 11; 22; 32; 35; 37; 39-41; 43; 56; 64; 75-76; 83; 97; 130; 148-49; 157; 176; 194; 209; 212; 218; 231; 233; 248-49

grand jury, 47; 77; 211; 222-23

Grant, Pres. Ulysses S., 31

Great Coalition, 80; 204; 220

Greenshields, James N. — see also Shortcomings of Riel's Lawyers, 58-59; 66; 70; 74-76; 78-79; 82-83; 91; 93-94; 99-102; 107; 112; 122; 125; 143; 145-47; 150; 159; 243-45; 247; 252-55

Hale, Sir Matthew, 180-81; 194; 196

half-breeds, 10; 15-16; 20; 32; 34; 37-38; 100; 106-07; 110; 114; 123-24; 128; 130-31; 146; 148; 156-57; 161; 170; 172; 214; 220-21; 224-25; 231; 233; 236; 248

Hardcastle, Henry, 197

Harington, John, 149

Harvey, Horace, 90

Hebert, Louis, 27

high misdemeanor, 182-83

high-treason — see treason

House of Commons, 56; 65; 69; 88; 92-93; 97; 102-03; 170; 204; 206; 233; 237; 248; 251; 264

Hudson's Bay Company, 15-18; 20; 23; 29; 34; 36; 40; 57; 77; 110; 113; 145; 264

Hughes, Betty, 238

Humpty Dumpty, 194

Imperial Colonial Laws Validity Act, 75

imperialism, 20; 33-34; 40; 51; 53; 59; 75-77; 84; 98; 177; 182-83; 185-87; 189; 201; 235

Indians, 31; 34; 38; 40; 61-62; 81; 89; 106-07; 114; 147-48; 151-52; 161; 170; 172; 214; 233; 238

indictment, 47; 51-52; 73; 99; 166; 168; 177; 198; 211; 223

injustices, 67; 72; 122; 124; 161; 170-71; 175; 189; 199; 202; 216; 225-26; 241; 250; 254; 257; 264-72

insanity plea, 71; 111; 118; 127-29; 137; 151-52; 157-59; 165; 212; 217-18; 221; 234; 243-46; 255; 258; 260; 263; 268-69

Ireland, 15; 29; 37; 180-81; 184; 189-92; 241

Irish famine, 184; 190

Irvine, Acheson G., 57-58; 116

Isbister, James, 32

Islam, 144

Jackson, Thomas E., 107; 112; 161; 165

Jackson, William Henry, 59-60; 66; 86-87; 107; 221; 240

Jarvis, Maj. E. W., 107

Jefferson, Pres. Thomas, 149

Jefferson, Robert, 108

Johnstone, Thomas Cooke — see also Shortcomings of Riel's Lawyers, 54; 78; 81-82; 95-97; 99; 112; 125; 150; 176; 186-87; 209; 244; 247; 261

Judges of Appeal Court, 203-06; 234

judge's role, 250

Judicial and Political Improprieties, 266-67

Jukes, Dr. Augustus, 60; 143-44; 212; 228-32; 237-38; 244; 258

jurisdiction of court — see also Realm, 66; 73; 74-91; 94; 99; 164; 168; 203; 210-12; 217-19; 234; 243; 245-48; 252; 256; 260; 262-63; 265 66

jury, 26; 46-47; 52-53; 55-67; 69; 72-80; 86; 91; 93; 96; 98; 100; 105; 110; 112-13; 116; 130; 134-38; 140-41; 143; 147-72; 176-77; 186: 188; 200; 210-11; 214-15; 217; 220-25; 228-29; 231-32; 234; 236-39; 244-46; 248-53; 255-58; 261; 263; 265-67; 269-71

justice, 45-46; 62; 67; 72; 80; 103; 105; 171; 175; 216; 224-26; 241; 266-67; 272

justice of the peace, 46; 56; 64-65; 67-73; 77; 79-80; 86; 147-48; 155; 163-64; 168; 210; 220; 265; 267

justification, 70; 99-100; 109-10; 128-29; 155; 157-59; 218-19; 243; 248-55; 259; 267; 269; 272

Keenan, Sgt. Harry, 114

Kerr, George, 108, 165
Killam, Albert C., 203; 206; 209-15
King Charles II, 17; 33; 203
King in his Realm, 199-201
King James II, 203
King, W. L. Mackenzie, 141

Lagimodière, Jean Baptiste, 15
Lagimodière, Julie, 15
land division, 20-21; 23; 36; 40; 111; 120
land grant to Metis, 25; 29; 32-33; 36-38; 114; 170; 213-14
Langevin, Hector, 237
Lansdowne, Lord, 233; 235-36; 271-72
Lash, John B., 107; 161
Laurier, Wilfrid, 92; 97; 103; 240
Lavell, Dr. Michael, 228-32; 237-38
Law Reform Commission of Canada, 251
Law Society, 85; 98
lawyers in the trial and appeal, 82-98
leading questions, 133-34; 165
Lee, John, 31
legal opinion re Realm, 178-79
Le Jeune, Henry, 64-65; 77; 147-48; 155; 163; 168
Lemieux, François-Xavier — see also Shortcomings of Riel's Lawyers, 65-66; 70-71; 73; 78; 82-83; 87; 90-95; 97; 99-102; 110; 117-32; 150-51; 155; 158; 207; 210; 243-45; 247; 254-58
Lépine, Ambrose, 30
levy war, 55; 87; 175-77; 183; 185; 187-88; 192-93; 199-202; 270
Liberal Party, 30; 60; 82; 91-92; 236
Limoges, Benjamin, 65
List of Rights, 21-25
Local allegiance, 49-51; 81; 105; 177-78; 265
Longue-Pointe Asylum, 31
Lougheed, Peter, 10
Lourdes, France, 115
Lower Canada — see also Quebec, 15; 89

Macdonald, Hugh John, 27-28; 43
Macdonald, John A., 12; 21-23; 25-26; 29-30; 34-35; 38-43; 45-49; 60; 69; 79-80; 85-86; 91; 94; 97; 126; 171-72; 176; 189; 194; 203-07; 214; 220-41; 247-48; 259; 266-67; 271-72
Mackenzie, Alexander, 30; 32; 39; 69
Mackenzie, William Lyon, 241
Maclean's Magazine, 11; 13; 141

Mactavish, William, 22; 24
Madison, Pres. James, 149
magistrate, 12; 46-47; 56; 63-66; 68-69; 72-73; 75-76; 86; 105; 148; 164; 210; 220; 242; 267
Magna Carta, 58; 74
Mahomet (Muhammad), 144
Mair, Charles, 20; 24-25
Mallet, Edmond, 31
Manitoba, 9-11; 25-26; 28-29; 98; 113-14; 116-17; 146; 153; 156; 169-71; 205-07; 213; 222; 224-25; 222; 224; 233-35; 239-40; 242; 264; 266; 272
Manitoba Act, 25-26; 33; 36-37; 98; 170
Manitoba School Question, 98
Manning, Preston, 10
Maxwell, Peter B., 196-99; 202
McCarthy, Dalton, 85
McDougall, William, 21-24; 34-36
McGee, Thomas D'Arcy, 35
McKay, Joseph ("Gentleman Joe"), 41; 108-10; 250; 253
McKay, Thomas, 109; 161
Maclane case, 200
McMahon case, 200
McNaghten, Daniel, 137
McNaghten Rules, 134; 137-40; 142; 153; 165; 212; 230; 232; 245
medical commission, 12; 171; 227; 232; 271
mens rea, 137
Mercier, Honoré, 91-93; 240-41
mercy,
...denied, 227-41; 271-72
...jury recommendation, 12; 26; 168; 170; 172; 231; 236; 238; 271
Merryfield, Walter, 66; 105
Metis, 9; 11; 15-17; 19-21; 23-26; 28-32; 34; 36-38; 40-44; 47; 57-58; 63; 65; 70; 73; 80; 82; 95; 100; 106-07; 110-15; 118-19; 122; 124; 127; 129-30; 145; 148-499; 151-52; 155-58; 169; 206; 213-14; 226-27; 235; 238-40; 250; 253-54; 259; 266; 271
Middleton, Maj. Gen. Frederick, 43-45; 65; 71; 73; 84; 107; 111-13; 144; 146-47; 153; 156; 209; 212-213; 224; 226; 236; 246
Miller, James A., 204-05
Milton, John, 106
Mitchell, Hillyard, 110
Monet, Marguerite dit Bellehumeur, 31
Montana, 31-32; 38; 70; 100-01; 114; 148; 160; 172; 213; 249; 253-54; 261; 267-68
Montreal, P.Q., 9; 16; 18-20; 30-31; 45; 83; 92; 131; 203; 228; 240

More, Sir Thomas, 48-49
Mormons, 135-36; 141; 144
Mowat, Oliver, 97
Mulcahy case, 178

National Policy, 39-40
natural allegiance, 49-52; 67-68; 72; 105; 265
Naturalization Act, 1870 (UK), 50; 68-69; 71; 200; 216; 260-61; 265
Naturalization Act, 1881 (Can), 51; 68-69; 71; 200; 216; 261; 265
Nault, André, 21; 36
Nault, Napoléon, 70; 100-01; 103; 208; 249; 253-54; 261; 268
Ness, George, 107; 164-65
Newman, Peter, 13
Nolin, Charles, 23; 96; 113-21; 123-24; 136; 154; 157-58; 160-61; 164-65; 268
Nolin, Rosalie, 115
North-West, 22; 33-34; 37-38; 40-41; 56-57; 65; 73; 80; 113; 117-18; 145; 157-58; 160; 172; 213-14; 248-49; 251; 266
North West Company, 16
North West Mounted Police, 41; 45; 47; 57-58; 73; 107-09; 114; 116; 141; 143; 147; 230; 250; 253; 255; 267
North West Territories, 27; 33; 38; 41; 46-47; 49; 51; 53; 56-59; 61; 64; 68-69; 74-77; 86; 89; 113-14; 148-49; 152-53; 156; 164; 167; 178; 186; 193; 201-02; 207; 209-12; 217; 220; 222-25; 229; 235-36; 244; 253; 258-61; 266; 271
North-West Territories Act, 1880, 47; 56; 59; 64-65; 68; 74-77; 123; 125; 135; 203; 210; 216; 218-19; 247; 263; 267
North-West Uprising, 10-11; 21; 38; 40-41; 43-44; 49; 52; 62; 73; 96; 100; 109-10; 233; 236-37; 240; 248; 250; 253
Nor'Wester newspaper, 20

Oblate priests, 37; 127; 129; 131-32
O'Brien, William Smith, 189-91; 241
O'Donoghue, William, 29
One Arrow, Chief, 61-62
Ontario — **see also Upper Canada,** 9; 11; 25; 26-29; 33; 35; 37; 39-41; 49; 74; 82; 85; 89; 95; 97; 102; 187; 205-06; 222-23; 230; 227; 234-35; 237; 240; 271
Orange Order & Orangemen, 24-26; 29-30; 33; 37; 58; 85; 89; 103; 227; 240; 271
Osgoode Hall, 89; 98
Osler, Britton Bath, 47; 52-55; 59-61; 64; 66; 76-77; 79- 80; 82; 84-87; 93-97; 101-02;

105-06; 120; 123; 128-29; 132-36; 138-42; 147; 153; 155; 166; 171; 176-77; 186-88; 200; 219; 222-23; 247; 249; 254-55; 261; 265
Ouellette, Moïse, 32

Pacific Scandal, 30
Painter, Henry J., 66; 105
Papineau, Louis-Joseph, 241
Peel, Sir Robert, 137
Pembina, Man., 17; 22
penal laws, 195-202
perjury, 154
petitions, 32; 38; 110-11; 114; 128; 130; 156; 161; 214; 227; 248-49; 251; 253-54; 259
Piggott, Joseph, 147
Pitblado, Rev. Charles B., 44; 143; 146-47
Pope, Alexander, 151
Pope and the Papacy, 107; 117; 119; 131-32; 136; 156
Poundmaker, Chief, 108; 152; 161
Poyning's Law, 190-92
pre-colonial English Statutes, 189; 193-94
Prince Albert, Sask., 37; 116; 233
Prince Rupert, 17; 33
Privy Council, 52; 90; 217-19; 225; 234; 243; 246; 249; 255; 258; 260; 262-63; 270
prophets, 9-10; 106-07; 112; 118; 124; 138; 144; 156; 171
Provisional Government, 16; 21; 23-25; 27-29; 33; 36; 45; 69; 113; 115; 233; 271

quatuor maria, 180; 188-89; 199; 201-02
Quebec — **see also Lower Canada,** 15; 18; 20; 27; 29; 31; 35; 82; 90-94; 101-02; 116; 125; 159; 187; 223; 227-28; 231; 235; 237; 240-41; 272
Queen's counsel, 82
Queen Victoria, 61; 81; 88; 108; 165; 193; 205

railway, 33-35; 39-40; 93; 239
Realm — **see also Realm definitions,**
...beyond the Seas, 182
...Dominions or other countries, 181-86; 199
...England, 180-81; 186; 265
...excludes Australia, 182
...excludes Canada, 167; 179; 182; 192
...*extra quatuor maria,* 180; 189; 202
...general, 166-67; 175; 178-202
...*intra quatuor maria,* 180-81; 201
...joint legal opinion, 178-79
...levy war in, 175; 177-78; 192
...misleading use, 175; 189
...Nova Scotia excluded, 179

...not pleaded, 186
...summary, 201-02
...United Kingdom, 189
Realm definitions — see also Realm
...Finlason, W. F., 180
...Hale, Sir Matthew, 181
...meaning of, 178-89
...Selden Master John, 180-81
rebellion, 36; 38-39; 44; 70; 100; 109-13; 128-29; 131-32; 144; 146; 148-50; 154-55; 158-59; 162; 164; 228; 231-33; 235-36; 240-42; 249; 254-55; 272
rebuttal witnesses, 113; 141-47
Red River Resistance, 10; 16; 19; 21-27; 36; 49; 59; 169; 271
Red River Settlement, 15-18; 20-21; 23; 25-26; 28; 33-36; 113-14; 170
Reed, Hayter, 57
Regina, Sask., 10; 12; 44-48; 56; 58; 60; 73; 82; 85-88; 95; 99-101; 116; 130; 133; 143-44; 146-47; 151; 153-54; 167; 172; 207; 209; 223-26; 230; 243; 248; 266
Richardson, Hugh, 43; 51-53; 56-63; 67-68; 72; 77; 79; 81; 84; 90; 119-26; 140-41; 147-48; 153-55; 157-58; 163-69; 171-72; 175; 177; 186; 188; 200; 208; 210-11; 215; 219; 223; 234; 237-38; 244-47; 249; 253; 256-57; 261; 264-65; 268-70; 272
Riel, Jean Baptiste, 15
Riel, Jean Louis, 15; 17-19
Riel, Louis — see also Trial
...address to jury, 155-58
...advocate of rights, 38
...affidavit, 70; 99
...against insanity plea, 88; 91; 117-24; 150; 156-58; 243-46
...amnesty, 25; 30; 69; 170; 214; 233
...appeal hearings, 207-19
...arraignment, 73
...ball and chain, 83; 207
...Beauport Asylum, 31; 133-34; 160
...bill of exoneration, 11; 272
...birth & education, 15-19
...bounty on, 171
...burden of proof — see burden of proof
...charges, 48-55; 67; 72; 95; 163; 166; 177-78
...closing statement, 169-71
...compensation request, 117; 129-30; 152; 160; 164; 170; 209; 212-14
...CPR, 41-42
...Crown allegations, 106-07; 160-61
...Crown counsel, 154-55; 161

...custody of, 44-45; 147
...defence committee, 83; 92; 94; 125-26; 150
...defence witnesses, 125-41
...different faces, 9
...dissension with lawyers, 93; 117-24
...elections to Parliament, 9; 30; 93; 170
...emotional breakdown, 30-31
...evidence against, 105-16; 141-47
...execution, 233-37; 239-41
...exile, 30; 32; 50; 70; 170; 214; 233
...Exovedate, 108; 113; 145
...Father of Confederation, 272
...founder of Manitoba, 11; 156; 272
...hero & legend, 13-14
...impecunious, 83; 100; 125-26; 158; 214; 243
...indictment, 51-55
...injustice to — see Injustices
...intelligence, 18; 44; 95-96; 143-46; 160; 237
...invitation to North-West, 32; 160
...jury, 63-66
...justification, 70; 91; 99; 100; 109; 128-29; 155; 157-59; 218-19; 248-49; 254-55; 259; 267; 269; 272
...law clerk, 19
...lawyers, 82-98; 242-63
...Longue-Pointe Asylum, 31
...Manitoba, 11; 156; 170
...material witnesses, 100-01; 103; 208; 249; 253-54; 261; 268
...mercy denied, 227-41
...mission, 9; 30; 145; 156; 213; 244
...Montreal period, 18-19
...Nolin relationship, 113-16
...non-British subject, 51; 67; 71-72; 101; 166; 260
...not-guilty plea, 81; 99
...opera, 10
...poem, 18-19
...political refugee, 30
...postage stamp, 10
...President of Provisional Government, 23-24
...Privy Council, 217-19
..."prophet", 32; 106-07; 118; 124; 130; 138; 156; 171; 208
...Provisional Government, 21-25; 28; 33; 36; 45; 69; 113; 115; 233
...Realm — see Realm
...Red River Resistance, 10; 16; 19-25; 27; 36; 49; 169; 271

...religious beliefs, 111-12; 132; 146; 151; 156; 239
...return to Red River, 20
...school teacher, 32
...Scott, Thomas — see Scott, Thomas (Red River)
...self-defence, 109; 129; 157-58; 250; 255; 267
...sentence, 171-72
...shortcomings of lawyers, 242-63
...state documents, 101; 268
...statues, 10; 156
...surrender, 43-44; 111-12; 122; 150
...technical treason, 236; 272
...trial on merit request, 91; 117-24; 126; 171; 243; 255; 260; 267
...trial procedure; 64
...trial site, 44-48
...unfairness to — see also injustices, 161; 166
...unlawful conviction, 175-202
...U.S. citizenship, 32; 50; 70-72; 101; 122
Riel, Marguerite, 31
Riel, Sara, 31
Ritchot, Fr. Noel J., 25
Robertson, Beverley, 61
Robinson, Christopher, 47; 59; 71; 76-79; 82-84; 94; 96-97; 99; 101-03; 105; 120-21; 124; 131; 143-44; 153; 159-63; 168; 171; 219; 223; 247; 268
Robinson, John Beverley, 83
Roman Catholic Church, 9; 18; 63; 65; 111; 115; 130; 136; 239
Roman Catholics, 16; 112
Ross, Harold, 107
Roy, Dr. François, 31; 127; 133-36; 139; 141; 151-53; 156; 160-61; 212; 245-46; 258; 269
Rupert's Land, 15; 17; 20-22; 33-36; 50; 113; 200; 206
Ryan, Matthew, 242
Rykert, Mr. (MP), 103-04

St. Boniface, Man., 29
St. Boniface Cathedral, 240
St. Laurent, Sask.., 37; 115; 131
St. Paul, Minn., 17; 19; 29; 31
St. Vital, Man., 10; 15; 29
Sanderson, Thomas, 107
Saskatchewan, 10; 15; 21; 23; 25-26; 32-33; 37-38; 128; 214; 221; 235-36; 238; 240; 250
Saskatchewan Uprising — see also North-West Uprising, 33; 96; 169-70; 235
Sayer, Guillaume, 17-18

Schultz, John Christian, 20; 23-25; 29
Scott, David Lynch, 82; 89-90
Scott, Thomas (Red River), 24-29; 36; 45; 49; 69; 113; 227; 233; 237-39; 271
Scott, Thomas (North-West), 59-60; 96; 240
Selden, Master John, 180-82; 188
Selkirk, Lord (Thomas Douglas), 15; 17
Selkirk Settlers, 15-17
sentence, 11; 147; 157; 168-69; 171-72; 190; 229; 236-37; 259
Shakespeare, William, 49; 55; 151; 172, 239
Shortcomings of Riel's Lawyers
...conflict of interest, 258-60
...criticism of, 242-43
...doomed strategy, 243-55
...errors and omissions, 260-63
...insanity plea, 243-46
...jurisdiction challenge, 246-48
...lack of full defence, 243; 255-58; 260-61; 267-69
...mistreatment of Riel, 255-58
...no justification plea, 100; 248-55
...no Realm argument, 270-72
...unauthorized strategy, 269-70
Siggins, Maggie, 129
Sivell, Rhoda, 238
Smith, Donald A., 23; 29; 40-41
Smith, Joseph, 144
Snow, John A., 24
Somers, Harry, 10
spin doctor, 231
Stanley, George F. G., 14; 22; 27; 63; 65-66; 109; 152
Statute British North America Act, 35
Statute 36 George III, Ch.VII, 181-83; 199
Statute 57 George III, Ch.VI, 183-86; 199
Statute 10 Henry VII, Ch.22 (Poyning's Law), 190-91
Statute 35 Henry VIII, Ch.2, 181
Statute Imperial Colonial Laws Validity Act, 75
Statute of treason-felony (Can) — see Treason-Felony Statute, 1868 (Can)
Statute of Treasons 1351, 12; 47-48; 53-55; 64; 73; 87; 95; 105; 163; 166-67; 175-203; 216; 237; 240; 249; 261; 264-65; 267; 270
Statute 11 & 12 Victoria, Ch.XII, 184-87; 199
Statute 31 Victoria, Ch.LXIX, 54; 95; 176; 187-89; 261
Stephen, George, 40-41
Stewart, Alexander D., 51; 53

Stipendary Magistrate — see Magistrate
strict interpretation, 195-202; 265
Sullivan, Michael, 65
Supreme Court Amendment Act, 1949 (Can.), 219
Supreme Court of Canada, 63; 206; 219; 250

Taché, Bishop Alexandre, 18; 25; 29; 62; 79; 91; 126; 151; 242; 245
Taché, Étienne-P., 79; 204; 220
Tallin, G. P. R., 83
Taylor, Thomas W., 80; 203; 205-06; 208-15; 262
Tompkins, Peter, 107-08; 112; 161
Tompkins, William, 107
Toronto, ON, 25; 33; 83-85; 95; 97; 102; 159; 206
traitor, 9; 51; 61; 172; 181-82
transportation, 182; 184-86; 190; 241
treason, 11; 47-50; 54-56; 58-62; 64; 66-67; 73-75; 77-78; 86-87; 89; 95-96; 101; 105; 123; 138; 149; 155; 157; 161; 163; 166; 171-72; 175-79; 182-95; 200-01; 211-12; 218-21; 225-26; 231; 233-37; 240-41; 249; 251; 255; 257; 264-67; 272
treason-felony, 48-49; 54-55; 59-62; 66; 86-87; 89; 95-96; 166; 176-78; 184-85; 221; 237; 240; 249; 251
Treason-felony statute (UK) — see *Statute 11 & 12 Victoria, Ch.XII*
Treason-Felony Statute, 1868 (Can), c.69, 54; 95; 176-78; 184; 187-89; 192-94; 199-02; 251; 261
Trial — see also burden of proof; charges against Riel; insanity plea; jurisdiction of court; jury; and justification
...adjournment, 70-71; 94; 99-104; 121; 126; 154; 161; 244-45; 249-50; 252-53; 255; 268
...Crown's address to jury, 159-62
...Crown rebuttal witnesses, 141-47
...Crown witnesses, 105-27
...defence's address to jury, 148-55
...defence witnesses, 127-41
...errors and omissions, 260-63
...evidence — see Crown rebuttal witnesses; Crown witnesses; and defence witnesses
...full defence (lack of), 248-58; 260-63; 267-69
...justice of the peace, 46; 56; 64; 67; 73; 79; 86
...lawyers, 82-98
...magistrate — see also Richardson, Hugh, 56
...mercy recommendation, 168
...opening address, 105-06
...procedure, 64; 106
...Riel's address to jury, 155-58
...Riel's closing statement, 169-71
...sentence, 171-72
...site, 44-48
...verdict, 167-68
...Winnipeg v. Regina, 45-47
Trudeau, Pierre E., 76

ultramontane, 136; 227
ultramontanism, 136
United Kingdom, 183-89; 191; 193; 199; 241
United States citizenship — see Riel, Louis
United States Court of Appeal, 251
Upper Canada — see also Ontario, 33-34; 74-75; 83-85; 89; 97-98; 200; 203; 205; 240

Valade, Dr. François-Xavier, 228-32; 237-38
Van Horne, William, 41-42
Vankoughnet, L., 71; 100; 208; 248; 253; 261
verdict, 44; 47; 49; 59; 67; 147; 158; 163; 166-69; 171; 228-29; 232; 253; 265
voyageurs, 16

Wallace, James, M., 141-43; 212; 258
Wallbridge, Lewis, 79-80; 86; 155; 203-05; 207-15; 217-18; 220-26; 247; 262; 266-67
Walters, Henry, 107
Washington D.C., 10; 31
Washington, Pres. George, 149
Willoughby, Dr. John H., 107; 110-11; 161
Winnipeg, Man., 10; 15; 27-28; 41; 44-47; 71; 79; 86; 96-98; 101; 107; 146; 156; 167; 203-07; 220-26; 266
Wolseley, Col. Garnet, 25-28; 36-37; 170; 239
Wood, Edmund B., 204

Young, Brigham, 135-36; 139; 141; 144
Young, Capt. George Holmes, 44-45; 113; 142; 143-46; 153; 156; 160; 164; 212-13; 246
Young, Rev. George, 45; 113

Bottom Edge Dirty
Apr 25/06

286